Genetic Algorithms and Applications for Stock Trading Optimization

Vivek Kapoor
Devi Ahilya University, Indore, India

Shubhamoy Dey
Indian Institute of Management, Indore, India

A volume in the Advances in
Computational Intelligence and
Robotics (ACIR) Book Series

Published in the United States of America by
  IGI Global
  Engineering Science Reference (an imprint of IGI Global)
  701 E. Chocolate Avenue
  Hershey PA, USA 17033
  Tel: 717-533-8845
  Fax: 717-533-8661
  E-mail: cust@igi-global.com
  Web site: http://www.igi-global.com

Library of Congress Cataloging-in-Publication Data

Names: Kapoor, Vivek, 1974- author. | Dey, Shubhamoy, 1964- author.
Title: Genetic algorithms and applications for stock trading optimization /
  by Vivek Kapoor and Shubhamoy Dey.
Description: Hershey, PA : Engineering Science Reference, [2021] | Includes
  bibliographical references and index. | Summary: "This book offers an
  overall general review of internal working of Genetic Algorithms (GAs)
  in search and optimization, and their use in to find out attractive
  stock trading strategies"-- Provided by publisher.
Identifiers: LCCN 2021009739 (print) | LCCN 2021009740 (ebook) | ISBN
  9781799841050 (h/c) | ISBN 9781799870777 (s/c) | ISBN 9781799841067
  (eISBN)
Subjects: LCSH: Stocks--Mathematical models. | Genetic algorithms. |
  Genetic programming (Computer science)
Classification: LCC HG4661 .K326 2021 (print) | LCC HG4661 (ebook) | DDC
  332.64/201519625--dc23
LC record available at https://lccn.loc.gov/2021009739
LC ebook record available at https://lccn.loc.gov/2021009740

This book is published in the IGI Global book series Advances in Computational Intelligence and
Robotics (ACIR) (ISSN: 2327-0411; eISSN: 2327-042X)

British Cataloguing in Publication Data
A Cataloguing in Publication record for this book is available from the British Library.

For electronic access to this publication, please contact: eresources@igi-global.com.

Advances in Computational Intelligence and Robotics (ACIR) Book Series

ISSN:2327-0411
EISSN:2327-042X

Editor-in-Chief: Ivan Giannoccaro, University of Salento, Italy

MISSION

While intelligence is traditionally a term applied to humans and human cognition, technology has progressed in such a way to allow for the development of intelligent systems able to simulate many human traits. With this new era of simulated and artificial intelligence, much research is needed in order to continue to advance the field and also to evaluate the ethical and societal concerns of the existence of artificial life and machine learning.

The **Advances in Computational Intelligence and Robotics (ACIR) Book Series** encourages scholarly discourse on all topics pertaining to evolutionary computing, artificial life, computational intelligence, machine learning, and robotics. ACIR presents the latest research being conducted on diverse topics in intelligence technologies with the goal of advancing knowledge and applications in this rapidly evolving field.

COVERAGE

- Pattern Recognition
- Automated Reasoning
- Evolutionary Computing
- Machine Learning
- Fuzzy Systems
- Natural Language Processing
- Computational Intelligence
- Algorithmic Learning
- Heuristics
- Adaptive and Complex Systems

IGI Global is currently accepting manuscripts for publication within this series. To submit a proposal for a volume in this series, please contact our Acquisition Editors at Acquisitions@igi-global.com or visit: http://www.igi-global.com/publish/.

Titles in this Series

701 East Chocolate Avenue, Hershey, PA 17033, USA
Tel: 717-533-8845 x100 • Fax: 717-533-8661
E-Mail: cust@igi-global.com • www.igi-global.com

To our mentors and sources of inspiration

Prof. Dr. S. M. Dasgupta
Prof. Dr. A. P. Khurana

Table of Contents

Section 3
Genetic Algorithms in Finance

Section 4
Genetic Algorithms in Other Areas

Preface

In today's world most solutions are obtained by following cross disciplinary approaches. Soft computing based intelligent systems are powerful in nature and good at finding solutions of various types of NP hard or complex problems. In past few decades soft computing methodologies such as Genetic algorithms (GAs), Neural Networks (NNs) and Fuzzy Logic have made an impact in finding solutions to such problems. These artificial intelligence based processes do not possess any magic wand. Rather, a lot of thought processes, hard work, creativity and knowledge of the systems are needed to get a break through and obtain positive results. There are a significant amount of findings available from the research work done on these techniques in past few decades. It would be too large a task to write about the entire research that has been done in the field of intelligent stock trading systems. Our objective of writing this book is to provide knowledge in "limited width but in-depth" instead of a "broad and large scale manner". Our book will largely focus on the working of Genetic Algorithms (GAs) and how they can be used to find optimized trading rules.

Unlike other books on this topic, we have tried to implement Genetic algorithms in the field of stock trading in a practical manner. We have explained how we can integrate Genetic algorithms with technical analysis in various ways. GAs is the search and optimization procedures which are based on the Darwin theory of natural selection. This book encourages the reader to get a broader picture of GAs and its working and how to apply it in various fields in addition to the stock trading. This book could be used as a text book for better understanding of Genetic Algorithms (GAs). It can also act as a guide to various technical indicators and how they can be combined it with Genetic Algorithms (GAs) to obtain better results.

A large part of the book is devoted to explaining Genetic Algorithms and their working. It is shown that GAs are computation based general purpose optimization algorithms. Practitioners of GAs may be from diverse backgrounds. Many of them may be from non-computing backgrounds. To make it accessible to all these parts of the audience, the tone of the book has been intentionally kept largely ' non-technical'. Every new concept has been introduced and discussed at a relaxed pace in order to provide better understanding to the readers. A basic understanding of mathematics especially algebra and probability is the background expected. Computer programming ability, at an introductory level, in any high level language would help the reader implement and write computer code of the Genetic Algorithms. All the source code in this book has been written in C++.

The stock market is the new battle ground where traders with their knowledge of novel techniques try to make profit. Our book initiates the reader in that direction. From the wide variety and sheer volume of research and publications, it is observed that technical analysis has wide acceptance in the stock-trading community. Due care is taken to provide specialized knowledge of various popular technical indicators in a concise manner. However, a basic introduction about the common and most popular indicators is exhaustively explained and discussed in this book. The way of obtaining accurate results with the optimized use of these indicators is explained in some detail. Light is thrown on how combination of various technical indicators can be used to formulate a trading model, with the help of a case study. The procedure to integrate these models with GAs to find appropriate trading parameters has been explicated. Though the focus is on stock-trading, this book lays the foundation for readers interested in applying Genetic Algorithms in any field.

The Book has been intentionally sub divided into four parts. The chapters are grouped into four major categories. First part deals with the working of soft computing methodologies such as Genetic algorithms (GAs), Neural Networks (NN) and Fuzzy logic etc. with an added weight on the explanation of Genetic Algorithms (GAs) both theoretically and mathematically. Chapters 1 & 2 explains the brief working of some of the principle components of soft computing i.e Genetic algorithms (GAs), Neural Networks (NN) and Fuzzy logic etc.. Chapter 3 gives a brief description about the basic theory of Genetic algorithms (GAs) and explains Genetic algorithms (GAs) by a hand calculation. Chapter 4 explains the mathematical ramification of Genetic algorithms (GAs) and its power to search in n dimensional search spaces. Second part deals with the explanation and implementation of Genetic algorithms (GAs) as a whole. Two full bound chapters is dedicated to explain internal working of Genetic algorithms (GAs). As Genetic algorithms (GAs) appears to be a black box technique explanation about more sophisticated and nature inspired operators is given in detail. In chapter 5 implementation of Genetic algorithms (GAs) using C++ language is being done. Chapter 6 various frequently asked questions (FAQ's) are answered about Genetic algorithms (GAs) to clear its myth. Chapter 7 explains about the interaction between various Genetic algorithms (GAs) operators as a whole. Chapter 8 gives us a brief overview about other biologically inspired advance operators which we may use in future working. Part three of the book gives detail analysis about the stock market technical indicator literature and how they can be used in combination with each other to find profitable trading strategies. With the help of various case studies we try to explain how we can use Genetic algorithms (GAs) to optimize the parameters of this technical indicator based trading rule. Chapter 9 gives a brief description of various traditional techniques along with Genetic algorithms (GAs) and agent based artificial intelligent based system to forecast the market. Chapter 10 explains the theory and practical side of the use of various commonly used both simple and sophisticated technical indicators. Chapter 11 discusses about the optimization process and working of Genetic algorithms (GAs) in financial domain and business modelling. Chapter 12 gives a practical insight how various trading models are proposed and interfaced with Genetic algorithms (GAs) in order to optimize their parameters to get optimal results, with the help of five different case studies. Part 4 of the book gives us an insight to the implementation of Genetic algorithms (GAs) in various other areas. Brief introduction about the working of several nature inspired algorithms is also given. By reading reader may instigate itself to use them in their respective fields. Chapter 13 briefly describe the working and application of Genetic algorithms in other field of science and engineering. Chapter 14 gives a short insight of various other Nature inspired algorithms.

It is shown that use of Genetic algorithms in a systematic manner in the finance domain can give spectacular results. It is also shown that application of Genetic algorithms in practical situations is an art and requires both analytical ability and creativity. We have demonstrated, through the case studies, that with proper use of GAs in business modelling, significant financial gain are achievable.

Much of work present here comes from various research articles and books related to engineering optimization, business modelling and decision support systems. The authors sincerely thank and appreciate all the contributors of those publications. Last but not the least, the authors are grateful to their families including parents, wives and children without whose patience and involvement this work would not have been possible. Thank you.

Section 1
Genetic Algorithms, Neural Networks, and Chaos Theory

Chapter 1
Introduction to Expert Systems, Fuzzy Logic, Neural Networks, and Chaos Theory

ABSTRACT

The power of genetic algorithms (GAs) and related expert systems such as fuzzy logic, neural networks, and chaos theory and other classifier systems is truly infinite in nature. The above stated procedures are sure to happen in the near future, and there is no chance for it not to occur. GAs, fuzzy logic, neural networks, and chaos theory are all biologically-inspired algorithmic procedures, as they all are linked to the world of biology in some way. Market represents the ideas of traders. In the present environment, the market is driven by the ideas generated by the use of these AI-based expert systems and it is causing huge competition in making profits. This chapter is planned to be a detailed introduction of various popular expert systems such as GAs, neural networks, fuzzy logic, and chaos theory and their usages. Researchers in the past have proved that these computational procedures could have far reaching effects in the stock trading system.

1.1 INTRODUCTION

The procedure of trading in stock market is ever changing in nature. Various theories and mathematical models designed by various researchers worldwide compete with each other simultaneously. Generally each theory has two

DOI: 10.4018/978-1-7998-4105-0.ch001

type of logic i.e is one is buyer logic other is a seller logic. Both parties should sensibly or logically justify their actions. In past years when use of computers were of limited in nature, then theories compete with each other at the speed of human mind. The maximum speed was what human mind could generate logic. Today we are living in a different world or in age of technology transformation.

Chaos theory, Neural Networks, fuzzy logic and GAs are the new soft computing techniques by which you can beat the market and make profits in today's competitive scenario. These above listed techniques generate better trading strategies with the help of computer generated logic. This helps us to take decision at a very high speed, beating the human mind i.e with in a fraction of a mille second.

Lot of people in the traditional stock trading community are not in favour of this type algorithmic generated logic for trading (Lederman et.al, 1995). Some says these techniques are not in favour of market and it should be closely regulated. Traditional stock traders also claim that algorithmic trading generates chaos or noisiness in the market and gives computer professional a one-sided upper hand. The issues arising due to these procedures are of great concern. In next paragraph I am discussing and falsifying these concerns rose in detail.

Firstly there is not an iota of proof to prove that computerized algorithmic trading is the reason behind the noisiness or instability in the market. Time to time there are both bearish and bullish runs in the market. There are n numbers of factors which contribute noisiness or chaos in the market. Due to algorithmic trading and introduction of computers, decisions are taken at a faster pace and trading procedures lasts for a few seconds. In contrast introduction of computers squeezes the volatility or noisiness. In order to conclude or falsify the claims ultimately it is the human mind that takes the final decision.

Secondly stock market is a free space. Nobody stops you to make capital by using some novel idea i.e with the help of computers. Stock market is always or in most of the times is in a state of chaos. Here the idea which is fittest in nature gives you the best results. There is no harm to use an algorithm in combination with the processing power and hi tech speed of computer to generate parameters or strategies that cannot be generated alone with the human mind to make decision in the stock market.

Thirdly we are in an era of technological transformation. Those do not adopt newer technologies or procedures will be obsolete in the years to come. It is being observed that older traditional static methods are known to everybody. In today's scenario they are of no use to us. So in order to be in competition, better AI based soft computing approaches are needed to remain and to make profit from the market.

Fourth computer based algorithmic trading is the talk of the town, weather some one likes it or not. A lot of newer generation traders have come to know about it. It is the fact that computers are the futures and they going to stay. Those traders or investors that do not use these techniques in generating decisions will defiantly incurred losses in the near future. They will be doing so on their own risks. We are not saying that all strategies or rules or parameters of the rules are generated by computers, here computers are only used only as a tool. They only used to implement human generated logic with the speed of light. Those people in the stock market who do not encapsulate their logic with computer systems are in a state of loss. Computerized base soft computing procedures are used to generate short term, medium term, and long term strategies. Our book takes into account short term strategies that are generated by these algorithms. In past many people has criticized these short term strategies i.e generate indicator for trading on daily basis. If we increase the time duration to make decision, then it is a different ball game altogether.

1.2 STOCK TRADING SYSTEM AND BIOLOGY

Stock market is a chaotic place. Strategies used to generate profit must be of dynamic in nature. They are ever changing in nature. Some of the strategies which generates profit in past are not commonly in practice as they had become outdated and are no longer viable (Meredith et.al, 2002). The fittest of the strategy survives for a longer duration of time. They effectively generate result with the help of some input parameters and try to tap chaos in the market. In this sub portion we will discuss the resemblances in the field of biology and business. These resemblances are by chance and not due to any intention. It is seen by various researchers in past that much business or stock trading environment mimics the principles of biology i.e survival of fittest or some patterns are presents in both stock trading systems and nature.

Chaos theory, neural network and GAs (Focardi et.al, 1997) are in some way or the other represents some form of systems that exists in nature in form of biology. Chaos theory generally tries to tap noisy or disorderly pattern that are always abundance in nature. Neural network is similar to the working of neurons in the brain i.e transforming random input signal into meaningful output signals. Genetic algorithms are based on Darwin theory of survival of fittest.

In GAs we represent the problem in form of chromosomes. These chromosomes are represented by their fitness function. Generation after generation newer chromosomes is generated with better fitness values. Those chromosomes with higher fitness score are generally selected for mating and their genes are passed over to next generations.

In chaos theory we generally define mathematical expressions that generate complex or noisy patterns which are similarly presented in the nature. Some equations are simple in nature but after some iteration they generate complex patterns. Chaos theory is an attempt to explain the nature, but neural networks and GAs are designed after nature. Neural network is a replica How brains functions? Genetic Algorithms are a replica of evolutionary process present in the nature. Above process utilizes learning from the nature to solve complex problems.

All these above (Chaos theory, Neural networks, Fuzzy logic, GAs) algorithms are under the arena of soft computing. One thing that is common in them is the use of computer programming language in implementing them. We cannot implement them manually. Researchers are attracted towards these algorithms and lot of researchers is being done on them in past years. Implementing of these algorithms requires a large processing power and huge memory, which can only be provided by the use of computers. In running Chaos theory, neural networks, Fuzzy logic and GAs requires a large number of repetitive tasks until a desired solution is reached. In chaos theory, the final mathematical equation that represents the noisy patterns is generated by successive iterations (nearly 100 No,s) In neural network random numbers are encapsulated with input variables and thus prediction is done. This process is repeatedly over a large number of iteration until our error is minimized significantly. While solutions in case of GAs initially random population of chromosomes i.e solutions are generated. Chromosomes with higher fitness score are reputedly selected by a randomized selection operator. They are mated and transformed over to generate newer chromosomes and represents population for next generation. This process is repeated successively until desired solution is reached or population gets exhausted or converges to a particular value. To implement all these techniques we need extensive use of processing power of computer. With an exponential increase in the processing power of computers in past years, a lot of people are doing research in the field of Chaos theory, neural networks, Fuzzy logic, GAs. We are also using computers in other fields also i.e for communication, data processing etc.

Researchers has shown that Chaos theory, Neural networks, Fuzzy logic, GAs (Goldberg, 2002) are newer soft computing techniques that are giving better results as compared to traditional techniques. Implementing these techniques is just like entering an explored valley, as whole process can change the thinking process and view about the world.

1.3 EFFICIENT MARKET HYPOTHESIS ON THE BASIS OF NATURE INSPIRED ALGORITHMS

Stock market represents the investor view. Market absorbs every new type of information, external or internal and reacts according to it. Thus in a way we say market is efficient (Focardi et.al, 1997). It takes a lot more effort to beat the market. Though we can make money out of the market and beat it. For this we should be better equipped with the latest information about the market and newer mathematical models to predict the bearish and bullish run of the market. Hence stock market is a lucrative space to make money out of it. It also consists of a undesirable feature of risk and uncertainty in it.

In past a lot of researchers had discussed the concept of market efficiency with varying claims. Some claims that these newer soft computing methods are of no values. It is impossible to beat the market as market is inherently efficient. Some says that any newer mathematical model has an intrinsic value and it adds value to your investment. This debate just goes on. There are three forms of market efficiency reported 1. Weak form, 2. Semi strong form, 3. Strong form. We are going to explain them step by step:

1. Weak form of market efficiency: Here market represents all past prices and trading volume history.
2. Semi strong form of market efficiency: Here prices in market represent all publically available information.
3. Strong form of market efficiency: Here prices represent all private and inside information. Here even inside traders cannot make profit from it.

Our biological based soft computing methods later explained in this book are here to bet weak form of market efficiency. I am giving certain descriptions or arguments which tell that biological based computer algorithms can beat weak form of market efficiency:

1.   It is assumes that knowledge of these algorithms is not acquired by all. It is not easy to understand these above stated algorithms and techniques to apply them in financial domain. Thus it is believed that use of these algorithms can beat weak form of efficient market hypothesis and we can make high level profits by using them.

2.   Ability of human mind to identify complex pattern is often limited. But with the use of huge processing power provided by computers and use of this nature inspired algorithms. It has proven to be boon in the field of financial engineering. They help us to find complex pattern of a very high degree in the market data, which a human mind cannot identify it.

3.   Technical patterns also help us to find common patterns in the market data. Technical analysis works on the assumption that market works on a crowd mentality. Hence patterns representing these herd mentality is better understood by using a combination of technical analysis and biologically inspired algorithms.

Literature from the financial world has shown that an interest of traders in nature inspired algorithms is increasing day by day, as they were able to make profits from it. Thus these above state algorithms replicate the natural living systems in order to solve the problems that cannot be solve with the help of human mind alone. Algorithms are the set of instructions or procedures that instructs computers to find much better solutions as compared with the solutions obtained from the traditional techniques. Computers had got huge processing power, while these algorithms are of heuristic (Hit and Trial) nature. They locate useful pattern in a noisy environment and help us to make important decisions in the financial markets. Below we are explaining a brief description of these above stated algorithms:

1.3.1 Chaos Theory

There was always intuition among researchers to apply chaos theory in stock market. Past researches have shown that they were not wrong on their part. Stock market always represents chaos. Chaos theory is self-explanatory in nature and can be used for prediction (Lederman et.al, 1995). Past researches has proved that to forecast any system by using traditional techniques is not easy. Since chaos theory cantered on chaos and is a dynamic process. Chaos theory science has grown up exponentially and it is only due to the increasing processing power of computers. Since procedure of calculation in chaos theory is of repetitive in nature. High processing power of computers together with large memory is ideal environment to implement and run chaos theory for prediction of any system.

1.3.2 Fuzzy Logic

This soft computing is based on "Theory of Fuzzy sets", which is new to soft computing environment. Fuzzy logic imply man made rules based on logical reasoning, that a trader faces it while trading in the market (Lederman et.al, 1995). An example for fuzzy logic for traders is "IF the price is slightly above moving average and in past it was much above the moving average, then we will consider that it will not cross moving average line downwards.

1.3.3 Neural Networks

Neural network is also one of the nature inspired algorithm and soft computing technique which replicates the working of neurons in the brain. Development in the area of neural networks depends upon the understanding of working of brain. Neural network is a parallel processing, self-adaptive algorithms used to solve hard problems (Lederman et.al, 1995). In past, in the initial stages of research, large expectations of exaggerated results had led to a disappointment. But the research accelerated at a uniform pace and today's researchers from all over the world has significant interest in this algorithm. Neural network is being applied due to its ability to solve complex and NP hard problems in various fields of industry. Organizations are coming up with various commercial software's designed on Neural Network to solve a particular problem in finance or in investment applications.

1.3.4 Genetic Algorithms

We had seen from the previous related literature that GAs is becoming popular day by day (Goldberg, 2002). It is a form of artificial intelligence technique that mimics nature. It is based on the Darwin theory of survival of the fittest. It is a artificial intelligence technique that represents artificial life. Genetic algorithms in its steps consist of biological evolution (i.e crossover, mutation, selection etc.). GAs are particularly an optimization technique which is used to optimized a parameter set of a mathematical model, rules set or virtually any type of optimization. In stock trading system GAs can be used parameters of a pre define trading rule or rules it. Here initial set of rules or parameters are generated randomly. These set of rules or parameters are mated i.e through a process of crossover and mutation to form a newer set of rules and parameters. Now those set of rules or parameters which are better fit (fitness is defined by fitness function) are selected for next generation of crossover and mutation to get newer better results. This process is repeated until desires solution is obtained or solution gets stuck up. GAs can be implemented, individually to solve a particular problem or can be implemented with other knowledge based systems such as neural networks, Fuzzy logic etc. GAs is heuristic based system which replicates the system of survival of the fittest.

To put an end to this discussion in terms of artificial intelligence, there is a clear distinction between each of these techniques; these techniques have some slack or light similarities also. These all techniques are explained in detail in the next chapter.

1.4 CONCLUSION AND ORGANIZATION OF THE BOOK

Our book is divided into four parts. First part discusses about the various soft computing algorithms. Chaos theory, Neural Networks, Fuzzy logic and GAs are the examples of it. These all algorithms are described in detail and comparison between them is also made. Second part explains the external working of GAs detail. It explains how design changes or operator parameter changes in GAs will have an impact on the solution quality. Third part explains how GAs can be applied to optimize trading strategies for stock market. This whole process is described in detail. Finally the forth part, we will discuss how GAs are applied for other applications. We will also discuss the prominent work done by other researchers in the area of GA. In last we will also discuss some next generation nature inspired algorithms.

First four chapters of this book explain Chaos theory, Neural Networks, Fuzzy logic and GAs. Since this book is all about GA working. GAs is explained in detail in the coming chapters as compared to other nature inspired soft computing techniques. In comparison to GA explanation, other techniques are explained in a very general way, and not in detail. Major historical development in other techniques and development in them is also explained. Research is moving in a very fast pace in all these NI algorithms, but we had made an attempt to include basic and current state of art work in all these areas in our book. Frequently asked question related to GAs are answered in this book. Genetic Algorithms are represented as GAs popularly in the past literature and in the research community.

Part two of this book explains the internal mechanics of GAs and its operators. It also give us some insight about the advance operators of GA. Chapter 5 and 6 explains GAs in simple executable steps. Some experiments done about the internal working of GA are explained in this chapter. After discussing the internal working of GA, we turn our attention towards advance GAs operators used in search and optimization in chapter 8.

Part three of this book helps us to apply GA to find various attractive stock trading strategies. Chapter 10 gives insight to various technical indicators used to forecast and to tell when to invest and when to divest from the market. This chapter also explains the methodology of the popular technical indicators often used in the investment literature. Here the explanation is of very general in nature. Chapter 12 explains how GAs can be applied to find attractive parameters for various technical indicators to get better rewards. It help us to find how GAs is employed to find optimal trading rule parameter, but it is only a starting point.

This book closes with part four portion which speculate about some other application of GAs and other explanation of newer nature inspired algorithms, which has come into the picture.

The whole content of this book is process oriented. Rather than result oriented. The method here shows that how GA can be applied to search attractive trading strategies parameters of a single indicator based system or multiple indicator based system also. Because our book is all about GA, hence explanation of GAs is by far the largest. But the readers or researchers interested in other nature inspired algorithms will see plenty of literature about in our book. My best wishes to the readers to move into the exciting world of GAs and its application in stock trading systems. Those who will be left behind will bite the dust. This is my perception about this book.

REFERENCES

Focardi, S., & Jonas, C. (1997). *Modeling the Market- New Theories and Techniques, Frank J.* Fabozzi Associates.

Goldberg (2002). *Genetic Algorithms in Search, Optimization and Machine Learning*. Pearson Education.

Lederman, J., & Klein, R. A. (1995). *Virtual Trading- How any trader with a PC can use the power of Neural Nets and Expert Systems to boast Trading Profits*. Probus Publishing Company.

Meredith, J., Shafer, S., & Turban, E. (2002). *Quantitative*. Business Modeling. South Western Thomson Learning.

Chapter 2
Introduction to Biologically Inspired Algorithms

ABSTRACT

In order to find more sophisticated ways to remain in competition in the stock market, investors and analysts are finding procedures based on nature-inspired artificial intelligence-based algorithms. It is seen that interest of researchers has grown in these technologies in the past years. These newer techniques have changed the investment arena of the stock market. A lot of thought process, hard work, creativeness, and knowledge about these algorithms are required to implement them in the stock investment area. In the past, few people have had the privilege to implement and obtain better results by using these algorithms. But with the access to affordable computing systems and experts with the knowledge of these computing systems, we can take advantage of making profit from the market. This chapter explains the detail working of these AI techniques such as chaos theory, neural networks, fuzzy logic, and genetic algorithms in detail.

2.1 INTRODUCTION

The wording "Artificial Intelligence" was first used by John Mc Carthy. Research in this field has already started in 1940's. Acceleration in research in this area comes in 1970's and 1980's when these techniques were applied in stock trading system. As invention in the area of computational power came radically, these technologies become easier to implement and were

DOI: 10.4018/978-1-7998-4105-0.ch002

less time consuming. It took really long time by the trading and investment community to accept that AI can be applied to stock trading environment. There were practical reasons for it. First traders found altogether new field which AI represents and it was difficult for them to understand its nutty gritty. Second there was no radically software available to get the results. Third in the initial phase there was absence of hardware and processing power to implement AI based techniques as they were computationally intensive in nature (Lederman et.al, 1995).

To start with the years of main frame computers, there were languages such as BASIC, FORTRAN, Pascal and COBOL to implement. Researchers used to write code of the logic generated by them in these languages. After the invention of personal computers, similar programs or codes were run on new and powerful processing machines. This trend continues and later advance software tools to implement trading systems come into picture. These tools were based on various programming languages and have better data handling and graphic capabilities. These tools help us to write codes to implement and test mathematical formulas of any technical indicator together with the use of simple IF.....Then rules. These rules were tested on past historic data to test their viability. For example with the help of these tools one can write code and implement rule. (e.g. If present price crosses the n day moving average line in the upward direction then buy signal is generated, if it crosses in downward direction then sell signal is generated). This is a knowledge based system on which AI technique can be applied (Focardi et.al, 1997).

With the increase in the processing power of computers and workstations, many more complex rules can be implemented and tested. Thus these rules based systems are replaced by the knowledge based systems, which uses combination of both rule based and artificial engineering. Here advance programming languages such as PROLOG and LISP comes into picture (Meredith et.al, 2002). As various AI based soft computing algorithms such as GAs, Neural Networks, Fuzzy logic and Chaos theory comes into picture interests of the trading community increases (Baur, 1994). Researchers in their results have found that these techniques were profitable and locate profitable pattern in the noisy stock data just like a able stock trader. Thus as the years passed by, various innovative commercial software comes into existence and they grab hearts and minds of the stock traders. Thus in this way a large number of stock traders began to use these commercially available software's. Hence in this way artificial engineering and knowledge based systems gets a strong foothold in the non-so technical stock trading community. Now a dys more and more stock traders are using it and making profit through it.

In comparison to technical trading systems these artificial intelligence based knowledge systems works on rules and proper logic. It helps the technically sound user to implement expert system based on the logic and is flexible and robust in nature. This system helps the trader to take judgment and lowers the degree of uncertainty which is the inherent feature of the stock market.

2.2 WHY ARTIFICIAL INTELLIGENCE IN STOCK TRADING IS THE TALK OF THE TOWN?

In this section we will discuss why trading community is attracted towards AI. Attraction towards AI grew after the computer implementation of already developed and tested trading system. With the help of processing power of computers development time and processing time of newer trading systems is reduced. Thus much more powerful, innovative and profitable trading system comes into picture and tested in a very short duration of time.

With knowledge of programming languages these trading rules are implemented in computers. Thus knowledge of a successful trader can be accessed long after the trader he or she has left the market. This helps to back test a trading system on a large quantity of historic or past data in a very short duration of time. More processing power help us to implement and test n numbers of trading rules in a very less span of time. Thus interest of traders in stock market grew in AI based techniques. With the invention of more and more advanced programming languages AI based systems can be implemented with a greater flexibility. Thus developers here replicate the behaviour of successful traders and their ability to found profitable patterns in the noisy data. Our brain can identify these patterns, but with a great difficulty. With the use of computers more complex patterns can be recognized. Hence GAs, Neural Networks, Fuzzy logic and Chaos theory are appealing to the trading community as they represents the knowledge which was inherited by successful traders after a vast experience. These all systems are self-adaptive in nature i.e they adapt in accordance to the market conditions.

Thus the results given by researchers has revolutionized the decision making process in the stock market. This algorithmic trading has added a new myth in the stock trading world. Due to abundance of literature, easiness and straight forwardness about these techniques has resulted in explosion of various new ideas in this field. Thus these systems act as a magical genie which generates profitable strategies which are beyond comparable in the wildest imaginations. Myth is that these algorithms are generally a black box technique, which does not require much of the system knowledge information. These algorithms are mystical, as they add a feature of randomness in their working. They all promise potentially profitable strategies or rules. Here the process of system development requires a large part of work to be done on the trader part itself. In the coming section we will take a deeper look at these technologies through a futuristic window.

2.3 KNOWLEDGE BASED SYSTEMS

Knowledge based systems (also known as expert systems) is a logical rule based reasoning that mimic if.........else type of logical thinking (Deurgio, 1998). The rule can be of crisp logic or true false in nature also. In addition to the financial systems knowledge based systems are being used to develop a game, play chess, used in medical diagnosis, prove certain mathematical theorems etc. Though there is a very little work published about the implementation of knowledge based systems in stock trading area, but some implementation in finding asset allocation, rating of bonds, mutual fund trading etc can be found. There are reports that these proven systems are used among private or individual traders.

2.3.1 The Components of Knowledge Base Systems

There are three components of knowledge based systems which are explained in detail below: 1. Inference Engine 2. Rule Based 3. Data base.

1. Inference Engine: This is the main core of the system. The inference engine processes the rules and finds the exact results for the problem. Inference engine consists of set of rules or facts, which generate results or achieve a particular goal. Result here is a new conclusion generated from the previous facts or a new set of rules generated from the previous rules.

    For example: Rule # 1: All programmers are tall.
    Rule # 2: All men are programmers.
    Conclusion: All men are tall.

Inference engines are knowledge based shells; various advanced logic oriented programming languages such as PROLOG and CRISP are used to implement inference engines.

2. Rule Based: It consists of set of logical statements or IF...... Then rules of the problem that is being addressed. These set of rules are generated by the person expert in that particular field with a huge experience. In case of stock trading rule set is generated by a stock trader having successful experience. For example rule set for trading system will look like as given below:

    IF (Moving average of shorter duration) > (Moving average of longer duration)
    THEN Buy
    Confidence level 0.80
    OTHER WISWE Sell

3. Data Base: It consist of past or historic data of the problem that is being addressed by the knowledge based expert system. Our rule set and reasoning function will be applied on that particular data to find solution of the problem. From this he can make an inference that whether he can apply that rule set for future data or not to generate profit.

2.3.2 How to Construct the Knowledge Base

Initial rule sets are the basis of knowledge based systems. These rule sets are constructed by a field expert having a vast amount of knowledge in that field. Inference engine is constructed by using popular logic based programming language such as PROLOG, LISP etc. Programmer cast the rule by using one of the programming languages in which he is comfortable. Services of one or more than one expert having knowledge of that domain is desirable to construct knowledge based system and see how well the inference of knowledge based system performs and right decision can be made from it. The above rule set formed is not of self evolving in nature as seen in other techniques. But in order to have these inference engine relevant rules has to be changed manually from time to time, as market condition changes. Well defined rules will lead to better and accurate result.

The performance of knowledge based systems depends upon the consciousness, clear cut mind set, subject knowledge level and experience of domain experts. We would avoid experts the experts who generate rules by mere thinking or by instincts. There should be synergy between the rules formed, proper implementation of it will lead to better and accurate results. Thus results obtained will match with the results generated by traders, when he is doing trading by himself. Continuous testing and changes in rule set will fine tune the system according to the market conditions. That is why knowledge based system is run on the historic or past data. If it generates better results according to our expectations then it is used for future use. Otherwise we should modify the rule set and newer rules should be inserted and older rules should be deleted to improve its performance.

2.3.3 Problem With Knowledge Based System

There are several reasons that knowledge based systems has not gain popularity as compared to other soft computing based systems. Since formulation of rule set in knowledge based systems depends upon the expert we had roped in. Thus there is really lack of experts in the area of stock trading system that can generate profitable rules. Second knowledge based system is not flexible in nature i.e changes in them has to done manually from time to time and are not of self-evolving in nature. Knowledge based systems are brittle in nature and in their working too. You really need intervention of some expert to change the rule set and to make it relevant in the changing market condition.

If set of rules formulation depends upon the particular patterns to make inference, then you should implement a hybrid system which will use another algorithm to formulate the pattern in the past data. Other drawback is that if a rule set is formed by the expert with a proven track record generates huge losses, and then you had to start fresh as a whole. Knowledge based systems are not of adaptive in nature. You really need human intervention to make these knowledge based system relevant to the changing market conditions. Thus rules in the knowledge based system should be updated from time to time. Otherwise knowledge based system will go in vain and will be obsolete very soon.

2.4 CHAOS THEORY

Anyone who deals with the stock market must have seen various types of vibrations and confusing trends in the market. Thus market represents chaos as it is an inherent feature of it. Chaos theory as name suggest is self explanatory in nature. In chaos theory often an equation of n degree is introduced to represent the system of all states (Baur, 1994). Working of chaos theory depends upon the feedback of result obtained from the previous equation into the next one. In Chaos theory we play with the variables of the equation. Chaos theory star with some initial condition and is purely a trial and error activity, which results in an effective prediction of system behaviour. Chaos theory can be applied to any system that exhibits turbulent behaviour. Due to this reason researchers are applying Chaos theory in the field of stock trading as it also exhibits a turbulent and non linear behaviour. In a bullish market risk is low and returns are higher. After bullish run market enters into a chaotic phase where risk dominates the rewards. Chaos theory equation helps us to find the time movements when to invest in the market and when to do farewell to the market. It helps us to study relationship between various parameters of markets and help us to identify repetitive patterns that occur in the market. Chaos theory is complex in nature which covers a variety of issues. From stock trading stand point, following points are important:

1. Past researches has shown that with the help of Chaos theory forecasting in turbulent phase of market is possible with a high degree of accuracy.
2. After a period of stability, some degree of turbulence entered in the market. This is a indication that one should take quick decision during that period.
3. Chaos theory provide improved analysis behaviour as it takes into consideration of various other financial relationships.

2.5 FUZZY LOGIC

Fuzzy Logic system is just like a traditional "Crisp Logic", which is used to draw rules, inferences that come to some conclusions (Rajasekaran et.al, 2007). Fuzzy Logic is successful and popular because it expresses the statement with a certain degree of indistinctness. These statements are not fully in black and white, but they contain grey shades in them. Expression of Fuzzy Logic statements include the terms "Slightly above", "very much below". These statements cannot be totally true or totally false, but true or false to a greater or lesser degree. It is often very difficult to represents such grey shades of reasoning in traditional knowledge based systems as discussed previously. Fuzzy Logic is popular among the traders as it formulates such type of grey shades in the rules in a natural way.

2.5.1 History

Fuzzy logic is first generated from the theory of fuzzy sets by mathematician named Lotfi Zadoh. It is somewhat similar to the traditional knowledge based systems as studied earlier. Here also you have to take services of an expert to form rules and to implement it with the use of technology. Various components of Fuzzy logic system is similar to the traditional knowledge based system such as inference engine, data base and rule set. The only difference between knowledge based system and Fuzzy logic based system is that here rules represents certain degree of greyness i.e they are made up of crisp logic and they contain certain degree of uncertainty in it. Due to this reason system developers are attracted towards it and are spending more time and energy in implementing fuzziness in the rule.

2.5.2 Method to Get Fuzziness in Our Rules

Here in order to incorporate fuzziness in our rule "greater than" and "less than" phrase will be replaced by "slightly high" and "slightly less". For example in a traditional based system we consider a rule "If ratio of closing price of stock and its Moving average os greater than 0.5 value of the technical indicator than buy". Here if the ratio comes out to be 0.6 then according to the rule we should buy. There are various other numbers between 0 and 1 scale for example 0, 0.1, 0.2, 0.3,.........0.7, 0.8, 0.9, 1.0. Here in fuzzy system we have two new terms such as "slightly high" and "slightly Low". Hence value between 0.3 to 0.5 is considered to slightly above while value between 0.5 to 0.7 is considered to be slightly above. Thus in this way a new crisp set or fuzzy set of slightly above and slightly below values are created. Here we had to specify the degree of truth which each number is the member. Thus in this way we had grey shades in our expression. Thus with the values between 0 and 1 we can define membership function. The whole process of assignment is called fuzzy frication. Thus in this way vagueness in the expression is defined and represented.

Consider the Figure 1.

Closing price to the moving average Vs Degree of membership X axis represents ratio of closing price to the moving average and y axis represents

Figure 1.

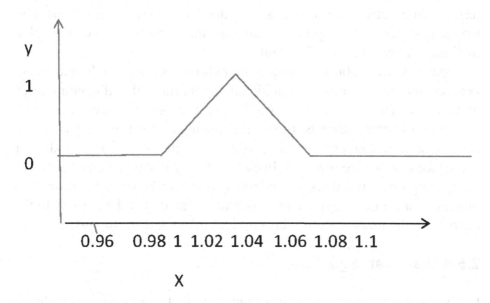

Degree of membership i.e price slightly above moving average. It is seen that when degree of membership is 1 then ratio of closing price to moving average is 1.02. When ration of price to moving average is 1.04 or 1.01 then it can be considered slightly above to a certain degree or partially true. Here we do not restrict our membership function to true or false but we also had a membership function between 0 and 1. Thus this is known as crisp logic.

Thus by proper formulizing of various rules representing grey shades one could built a fuzzy engine as it is done in knowledge based systems. Thus from now working will be same as that of knowledge based system. We will test the system and asses it on the basis of its performance. It means the matching of the results obtained by the fuzzy system with the result obtained by the expert. If there is a great degree of degradation in the performance then we will have to look and change the rules and membership function.

2.5.3 Advantages

Main advantages of Fuzzy logic are that it attempts to precisely represent the degree of judgment of a trader and its thinking about the market more accurately. Traders does not take decisions in the market by defining sharp boundaries, but the often take decision which involves certain degree of probability and range of values. Thus knowledge of a trader cannot be formulated exactly in traditional knowledge based system, as it is done in the fuzzy system. Fuzzy system consists of smaller rules set as compared to traditional knowledge based system.

Fuzzy system is robust as compare to traditional knowledge based system in all conditions "If rules in a traditional system states that if opening price of a stock is above 0.5 greater than moving average of n days, then buy." But what if opening price is 0.48 of the moving average of n days, then in case of traditional knowledge based system, it will not give a buy indicator and hence loss will be incurred. In case of Fuzzy system rule is defined as "if opening price of a stock is moderately above or below 0.5 greater than moving average of n days". Thus moderately values will be defined in the crisp set of the fuzzy system. This provides robustness to the system.

2.5.4 Disadvantages

Fuzzy system consists of same disadvantage as that in traditional knowledge based system. Here the efficiency and efficacy of the system depends upon one factor i.e who has written the rules and how expert he is in stock trading system". It depends upon his knowledge and his experience. Fuzzy system is not self-adopting in nature i.e they does not learn on their own. They need manual intervention on writing and rewriting the rules and change membership function values according to the market conditions and prove their robustness.

2.6 NEURAL NETWORK

Neural network is a class of nature inspired soft computing process. This technique replicates the working of neurons in the human brain (Rajasekaran et.al, 2007). Neural network does a parallel processing of data at a single period of time. They are self-adapting in nature. Research in Neural network stated in 1930's and 1940's. Initially main researchers in the field were Allen Turing, Warren Mc Cullough, Water Pitss, Donal Hebb and many more. Work and results from neural network get their legitimacy in 1980's. Lot papers on the topic neural network were published. Various conferences on neural network were organized nationally and internationally. Practically there has been a successful attempt to apply in almost every field. Neural network based commercial software are also coming up.

2.6.1 Working of Neural Networks

Neural network mimics the function of human brain. Now we will discuss the working of human brain. In brain there are various nerve cells known as neurons. Human brain consists of various types and sizes of neuron which have various nerves called dendrites hanging or connected to other neurons. Signals are carried between various neurons through these dendrites. Nerve signals are of binary in nature. Neurons calculate each of the incoming signals. If the signal sum crosses the onset value, then the signal is passed to the other neuron or discarded.

Human brain consists of complex structure of neurons connected to each other in n number of ways. Due to this human brain act like a multi-processor and performs various human related tasks in a single period of time or act like a parallel processing system. We replicate this process of human brain in our neural network system. Neural network can be implemented in a hardware where electronic circuit replicate the working of neurons or it can be implemented by using a programming language in a software mode.

In our neural network terminology neuron is referred as term node. Here input signals are taken and output signals are generated. Various weights are assigned to input signals and they are sum up to produce the output. A simple modus operandi of simple neural network is shown in Figure 2.

Figure 2. A Simple Neural Network Architecture

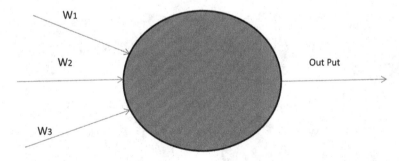

Now we discuss the steps that occur in between input and output. i.e in the nodes. Initially weights are assigned to the input signals in a random fashion. Neural networks are self-adaptive in nature, so the values of these weights will alter in successive iterations. There are altogether number of methods which can be used to adjust weights assigned to the input layers. Generally weights are multiplied and summation is done.

Neural Network is a layered structure. Neural Network architecture can be of different sizes. It can have two input variables to a few hundred variables. It can have from to two to three layers to a dozen of layers. There can be n combination between input variable and number of layers in neural network. It depends upon the problem to be solved and computational complexity a machine can handle. Past researches had found that three to four numbers of layers are sufficient to solve any given problem. Addition of more layers does not have much impact on the solution quality, but it increases the time to generate the results by few seconds depending upon the problem. Number of input variables, neurons and layers vary upon the problem which we are solving.

Let us say our neural network model has two layer of nodes as shown in Figure 3.

Figure 3. A Two Layered Neural Network Model.

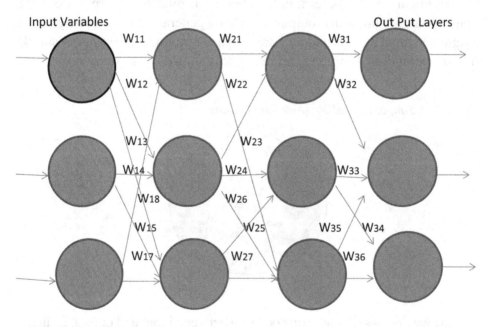

Inputs are given to the input layers which are passed to the second layer. The output of the input layer is passed to the second layer and from it to the third layer and finally to the output layer. From this user gets output from the network. The intermediate layers between input and output are known as hidden layer. These layers neither receive direct inputs and they neither give direct output to the outer world. They are not directly connected to the outside world.

As shown in the above figure all the nodes in the neural network are connected to each other directly or indirectly. The connection can be made to each other in a variety of fashion. There can be many input signals but it can have only one output signal. This output signal from a node can be transmitted or forwarded to the other node in the next layer. This type of neural network is known as feed forward network. When an output signal is transmitted backward, then it is known as feedback network. Increase in number of nodes will lead to the increase in number of possible ways in which connection can be made.

Hidden layers are not connected to the outside world, but they contain knowledge value in them, hence they are important. There is no thumb rule to find the number of hidden layer in the neural network architecture and in what ways they can be connected to each other. These layers remove noisiness or error from the information or data as it moves from layer to layer in the hidden network.

Now we will discuss what happens in the node. The learning takes place at the node. The weights of the node are adjusted, and due to the self-adaptive nature of neural network, thus desired output is generated. One of the methods for weight correction is known as back propagation. In this difference in value between actual output and required output is measured or calculated. Thus using these values weight of the output layer is adjusted. This entire process is repeated n number of times. There are two types of learning process supervised and unsupervised. In unsupervised learning the weights of the system adjust by themselves i.e system teaches to itself. In case of supervised learning process weights are steadily adjusted to produce required output. Thus adjustments of weights are done repeatedly in many training cycles. Due to this error between actual data and desired data is minimized. When error is squeezed up to an acceptable level then training cycle is said to be complete. The final weights in this case are used to find output for next set of input data.

Advantages of using Neural Network are that they can integrate large amount of information to get the desired output. Neural Network architecture is such that it learns from past experience and is self-adaptive. It does not depend upon the expertize to be given by the expert traders in case of knowledge based systems and Fuzzy Logic. Neural Network when properly used has got ability to pinpoint profitable patterns that exists in the market data. Making profitable strategies from neural network is not an easy task. Neural Network is a trial and error activity which requires a high degree of sophistication. It requires hard work and dedication. As we had studied Efficient market Hypothesis (EMH) earlier which states that one cannot beat the market. It is not totally true but partially true. There are numerous tiny profitable patterns hidden in the noisiness of the stock data which would be exploited and capitalized to make profit. This all requires a lot of hard work and proper implementation of Neural Network. Past researches have shown that to beat EMH partially is not impossible with the help of Neural Network.

2.7 GENETIC ALGORITHMS

Genetic Algorithms popularly known as GA's is not purely an artificial intelligence (AI) technique, but it is a heuristic based technique which is based on Darwin theory of natural selection i.e survival of the fittest (Goldberg, 2002). Actual genetic algorithm is a computer program that represents artificial life. GA in all is a procedure represented in various steps and is a truly an optimization procedure. In nature new breed of organism evolve and who are best that survive. Thus in case of GA it is based on the theory of survival of the fittest. Both in nature and GA there is factor of randomness, recombination and selection by the means of survival of the fittest and is an adaptive process. Thus GA is total replica of nature's survival of the fittest. These three features of randomization, recombination and selection makes GA an optimization process that helps in finding better solutions to a given problem whose best solution is not known. GA's are used as a solution provider to a number of NP hard problems. They are used to optimize parameter values of a mathematical model or an equation, rules of trading, neural network weights or to evolve hybrid systems etc. It is achieved by the process of breeding, recombination and selection of more suitable solutions after generation and so on. GA has a wide potential and can be applied in a variety of potential areas.

2.7.1 History

Genetic Algorithms was first developed as it first come into picture by mathematician and psychologist known as John Holland in the year 1975. It is an optimization algorithm. Research in GA's is gaining momentum in

1990's. During this period a lot of commercial and user friendly software's based on GA comes into existence. For example Evolver, LOGIVOLVE etc. Various other software's that used combination of GA and Neural network to generate profitable strategies which is known by the term "neurogentics" are also in the market. Here we use GA to optimize weights of neural networks in back propagation method.

Santa Fe institute developed a computer-generated stock market. Here traders were actually a computer programs which do trading of some virtual stocks that were distributed between them. In this project GA is discussed in detail. Some articles also discussed that how GA can be used to evolve new trading rules in stock market. Initially rules were generated using LISP rules and GA was used to optimize these rule sets. Past researches give us an indication that interests of stock traders in GA is increasing day by day. GA's are general purpose algorithms till not graphical user interface of GA comes into existence. Various computer programming languages provides flexibility by which they could implement GA to solve a particular problem. In fact neural network is the past and GA's are the present. Here later in our book we will discuss how GA's can be used to optimize a trading system either in the form of a rule set or parameter set of a rule. In the coming section we will see how GA could be used to optimize a stock trading system briefly. Detail description will be done in the latter half of this book.

2.7.2 How Do Genetic Algorithms Work?

Basic concept is already discussed by various researchers such as Goldberg, Koza, Davis etc. To start with a GA, a thoughtful process is needed. First solutions of the problem must be mapped to genes or chromosomes i.e encoding. Encoding solution of the problem can be done in number of ways. i.e binary encoding, order based encoding, real values floating point number encodings, linked list tree type structure, variable size encoding etc. We can use any type of this encoding to our satisfaction, those suites to a particular problem. These codes can represents a set of rule, parameter of rules, weights of neural network architecture etc. In the next step we have to define fitness function, which will define ranking of a particular solution the population. Here element in the population will define the fitness score. More the fitness score more is the probability of the solution or genes or chromosomes to get selected for mating or breeding with other solution or genes or chromosomes through a selection process. Selection process should be biased, so that more fit solution must be selected. Newer solution is to be generated and replaced by older solution. Thus in this way one generation is completed. Thus several generations are allowed to evolve until desired solution is obtained or population in genetic algorithms gets exhausted. Thus above mentioned procedure is a basic genetic algorithm. The detail GA consists of five steps Selection method, breeding or mating, fitness function calculation, replacement. Detail working is explained in the following described steps:

1. Generate a random population with the help of random function given in the programming language. Each member of the population represents a gene or chromosome or a solution. Don't worry at the initial quality of solutions obtained. At the end of GA you would see many fascinating solutions that you will not believe in.
2. With the help of selection operator which is actually biased in selecting solutions with a high fitness score for mating. Crossover and mutation operators are applied to it step by step. There are also a set of many other advance genetic operators also. But crossover and mutation operators are the basic one. Crossover does recombination of the existing solution and is exploitative in nature, while mutation allows new variation in the population and is explorative in nature. Population number is kept constant after every set of mating.
3. Replace the current population with the new population.
4. Check the fitness score of the individual member of the new population. If desired solution is not obtained then repeat step 2 to 4 until desired results are obtained or stagnation in population is reported or number of generations in GA kept is completed.

Here idea of crossover is that mating of superior solutions will result better solutions, as selection operator is biased to select better solution with a high fitness score. Thus comparative bad or inferior solutions will be left out generation after generations as there is a little possibility of it to be selected. Due to mutation operator stagnation in the population is avoided, to a large extent. Otherwise population will reach dead end after few generations. Due to mutation newer search spaces are continuously added in the population. Thus in this way better solutions are obtained generation after generation and optimization of a particular system is performed.

2.7.3 How Genetic Algorithm Is Applied in Stock Trading System- An Example

We can apply Genetic Algorithm to a moving average rule (Bauer, 1994). Suppose there are two moving averages, if shorter moving average line is above the longer moving average line then buy signal I generated. If longer moving average line is above the shorter moving average line then sell signal is generated. Genetic algorithms can be used to optimize the time period of both shorter and longer moving averages. Now consider a technical indicator moving average convergence divergence (MACD). It consists of four moving averages. Genetic algorithms can be applied to optimize the lengths or time periods of these four moving averages. First three moving averages are used to calculate moving average convergence/divergence oscillator and a signal line; fourth moving average is compared with the current price. A buy signal is generated if MACD oscillator is above the signal line and price is above the fourth moving average line. A sell signal is generated in the opposite case i.e MACD oscillator is below the signal line and price is also below the fourth moving average line.

To apply Genetic algorithms we had to optimize the length of time periods of the four moving averages. All the lengths of the moving averages are integer's values. Thus a chromosome represents a series of integer values. A random population, representing these sequence of four integers are generated, where each chromosome being unique. Before generating this random population range of these integers are being defined. We will also have to define the fitness function that will define the behaviour of each of the chromosome i.e these integers' values or parameters of moving averages profit or loss is generated, and fitness score is assigned to it. After this selection operator is applied on to the population. It will select chromosomes which will have better fitness values or score for mating. After this new population is generated and will be replaced by the older population. Now we will see that newer population have better chromosomes representing moving averages that will have higher fitness function or profit. Thus generation after generation we will be able to find better set of parameter values that give higher profits.

Below we will explain the mating process of Genetic algorithms in case of MACD indicator in a brief. Mating process consists of mainly two operators' i.e crossover or mutation. Suppose there are two chromosomes parent A and parent B representing series of four integer's i.e Moving averages.

Parent A : A1.A2.A3.A4
Parent B : B1.B2.B3.B4

Crossover Process

Parent A : A1.A2. | A3.A4   *Parent A : 17.22. | 53.7*
Parent B : B1.B2. | B3.B4   *Parent B : 27.20. | 11.3*

Offspring A : A1.A2.B3.B4   *Offspring A : 17.22.11.3*
Offspring B : B1.B2.A3.A4   *Offspring B : 27.20.53.7*

Mutation Process: Here one or more integers will be mutated in the chromosomes i.e their value will be altered by new values. Suppose we have following offspring.

Offspring A : 17.22.11.3
Offspring B : 27.20.53.7 $\rightarrow To\,be\,replaced$

After mutation of the two member integer in the offspring A and B, will be replaced by some other integer.

Offspring A : 17.29.11.3
Offspring B : 27.20.53.2 $\rightarrow To\,be\,replaced$

The basic theory about crossover is that if the moving averages of parents are good and profit generating if used. Then by the process of recombination it will generate better offspring which will generate higher profits. There is also a possibility that it may not work. But good feature of two systems recombined in a simpler way will generate a better system or parameter sets. Hence cross over is useful. The particular position we take from each parent is determined randomly and it varies each time mating is done or crossover process occurs.

Basic engineering of mutation is that it introduces diversity in the population, thus preventing chromosomes from being stagnant. Due to mutation newer patterns or integers will appear in the population which leads to search newer spaces and better solutions will be reported. There may be many patterns which when recombined with the existing patterns or integers will give a great solution. Hence introduction of these patterns in the chromosomes of the population is done by the process of mutation. Thus random recombination of the existing chromosomes (Crossover) and introduction of random fragments in the chromosomes (Mutation) encapsulated by the selection operator navigate altogether a random procedure in the right direction.

There are many other advance genetic operators which we will discuss later in this book, which can be used in combination with crossover, mutation and selection operator to generate optimal solution. There is no fixed schema which tells us that all these operators can be used in such a fixed pattern. The different combination of the use of these operators in GA varies from problem to problem. Past researches has shown that standard use of together crossover

Figure 4. A Simple Genetic Algorithm.

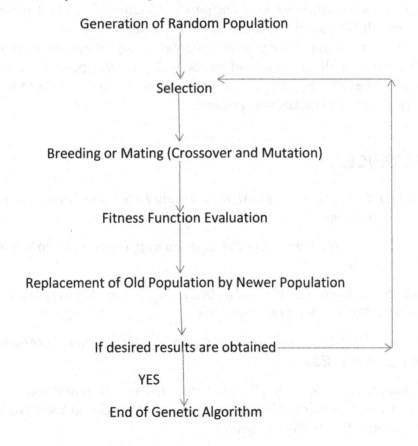

(recombination) and mutation (introduction of random structures) are able to solve the problem with a better efficiency. This proves the robustness of Genetic Algorithms in all cases.

2.8 CONCLUSION

Competition in the market is increasing day by day. It is becoming difficult to make profit from the market with the use of traditional approaches. Since stock market is a zero sum game which means that for every profit you earn, someone will be on a loss on the opposite side. Thus formulation of strategies is important. As seen in this chapter with the popular use of Artificial Intelligence to formulate strategies, someone who does not pay attention to artificial intelligence in stock trading will be on the looser side. This is even indicated in the past researches. Thus it is now necessary to remain updated with artificial intelligence technologies if one wishes to make profit in the market. As these techniques is gaining popularity day by day, use of artificial intelligence help to keep you ahead in stock trading.

You would be assured that you can better face competition and win profits with the study of all the chapter of our book. Here every page of the book you read and every program you do the experiment will make your trading strategy sharper and makes you a winner.

REFERENCES

Bauer, R. J. Jr. (1994). *Genetic Algorithms and Investment Strategies*. John Wiley and Sons, Inc.

Delugio, S. A. (1998). *Forecasting Principles and applications*. Irwin McGraw Hill Publications.

Focardi, S., & Jonas, C. (1997). *Modeling the Market- New Theories and Techniques. Frank J*. Fabozzi Associates.

Goldberg. (2002). *Genetic Algorithms in Search, Optimization and Machine Learning*. Pearson Education.

Lederman, J., & Klein, R. A. (1995). *Virtual Trading- How any trader with a PC can use the power of Neural Nets and Expert Systems to boast Trading Profits*. Probus Publishing Company.

Meredith, J., Shafer, S., & Turban, E. (2002). *Quantative Business Modeling.* South Western Thomson Learning.

Rajasekaran & Vijaylakshmi Pai (2007). *Neural Networks, Fuzzy Logic, and Genetic algorithms, Synthesis and Applications.* Prentice-Hall of India Private Limited.

Chapter 3
Introduction to Genetic Algorithms in Search and Optimization

ABSTRACT

This chapter is all about introducing genetic algorithms in the search process, which are based on the theory of natural selection, genetics, and survival of fittest. By detailed understanding of the algorithm, one would be able to apply it in your respective field for optimization. At the end of this chapter, the reader will have acquired basic theory and working of these algorithms. Since genetic algorithms are used in diverse fields, the tone and language of this chapter is kept simple and casual for better understanding. Genetic algorithms in this chapter are applied through a hand calculation example. Genetic algorithms are basically mathematical calculations based on Darwin's theory of survival of fittest. This chapter gives a detailed understanding of the theory and working of genetic algorithms based on hand calculation examples. Comparison of genetic algorithms with other search procedures is also done.

3.1 GENETIC ALGORITHMS- AN INTRODUCTION

Genetic Algorithms is a search and optimization algorithm based on the Darwin theory of survival of fittest (Goldberg, 2002). Here various strings are selected according to their fitness function, they are then recombined with

DOI: 10.4018/978-1-7998-4105-0.ch003

each other and some random string patterns are also introduced in it to form new strings. This is a innovative search procedure which searches various vantage points parallel through this recombination and randomization process. These vantage or superior solutions cannot be finding alone with the help of human mind. Here the solution of the problem is represented or mapped into bit of strings or by alpha numeric characters etc. After every generation new set of superior solutions are created by recombination of various other fittest old solutions. While recombination and introduction of bit strings is a fully random process. But due to the introduction of selection operator, it is not a simple random walk. These two procedures in genetic algorithms search various points in the solution space parallely and found new search points with a superior performance which cannot be found manually.

Initially genetic algorithms and its procedure are founded by John Holland (1975) and his students at university of Michigan. This algorithm mimics natural adaptive process mathematically and is implemented with the help of a computer program. This has leads to the advancement in artificial intelligence based search procedures.

Researchers have found genetic algorithms to be effective, robust in all environments. Genetic Algorithms provides a delicate balance between its productiveness and effectiveness (to produce desired effect) which is essential to remain in competition in various adverse environments. Robustness i.e to produce desired results should be an inherent property for artificial intelligence systems. Property of robustness in a artificial intelligence system reduces the cost of design. If a particular system is adaptive in nature then result given by it will be for longer duration. Hence the algorithm designers should take a note that this system can only excel if it contain properties such as robustness, competence and springiness. These all features along with the feature of addictiveness and to find new solutions are found in nature. Genetic Algorithm mimics these entire features from the nature which is rare in other soft computing technique found so far. Thus the popular notion is that no one can beat the nature as nature is robust, self-adaptive and self-repairing. Past researches in genetic algorithms has shown that it provides robust and fascinating results when applied to complex problems. Past published research has shown that GA is effectively used to solve problem in the field of business, economics, engineering and scientific applications. Reason for the popularity of genetic algorithms is that the steps involved to implement genetic algorithms are simple and it do parallel search in various points at a given point of time. There is no restrictive assumption in genetic algorithms as there are in various other soft computing algorithms. In this chapter we will learn explore and experience the exploitative and explorative features of genetic algorithms in detail.

3.2 VARIOUS OTHER POPULAR CONVENTIONAL, OPTIMIZATION AND SEARCH TECHNIQUES

It is very important to know the working and blackness in various other conventional optimization procedures which leads to the development of sophisticated and advance techniques such as genetic algorithms (Deb, 2002). In past there were three popular type of search procedures: (a) Calculus Based (b) Enumerative Based (c) Random.

Out of these three test procedures calculus based is the most popular. Here the peak of function and its parameter is found by setting slope of the function equal to zero or definition of peak is exploration of those points where slope is zero or null in all ways. Thus this may lead us to find or get trap in local optima and think that it is a global best solution. This is the main lacuna in calculus based test procedures as they lack in the effectiveness to find a best solution. Local optima found in this case may be a better solution

Figure 1. Showing local and Global Optima

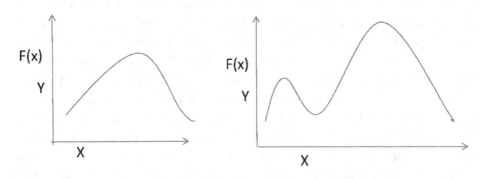

when compared with the neighbourhood points in the search space. Figure 1 shows a complete picture of local and global optima.

In these procedures if we get trapped in the lower optima then we will miss the global solution or the peak. Hence there are no features in calculus based system to get out of these local peaks and find the global peak. Further improvement of result can only be done by starting fresh or by a random restart. These two functions above in the figure are one peak or two peak

Figure 2. Function showing noisiness.

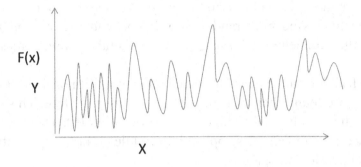

functions. But the real world's problem consists of numerous discontinuities, multi peak and noisy search spaces as shown in Figure 2.

Hence to find global maxima and global minima by using calculus based search procedures is risky. Thus calculus based search procedure solves problems in a limited or simple domain. Hence for this nature we do not recommend calculus based search procedure to anyone. To find global optima in noisy and discontinuous function then calculus based search procedures are not fully robust in nature for all types of difficult problems.

Second type of search procedures are enumerated search procedures that can be used to find solutions for different problems. In this case the search procedure will start with looking at an objective function value at every given point in an finite or infinite search space, one at a time. This type of procedure is simple in nature as there is less computational complexity involve in it. Drawback is that it can be effectively used where numbers of possible combinations are less. In case of larger search spaces, searching various points one at a time is time consuming and is not practically possible. Enumerative search procedure is a curse to use it in a large, noisy and discontinuous search spaces. Thus it is not suitable to use it for complex real world problems.

Third type of search procedure is random search procedure or algorithm. Random search procedure tries to rectify the lacuna or squat arrivals of both calculus base and enumerative search schemes. Yet past researches had found that results obtained by random search procedures in various problems are not very encouraging and efficient. Genetic Algorithms is not fully random search procedure but a randomize search technique. Genetic Algorithms use random tool to search various points in parallel at a given point of time in a highly noisy and multidimensional search space. Use of random function as a guide in search space seems to be very strange, but real world problems consists of many such cases. Simulated annealing is one such type of random search technique which helps us to find minima or maxima points in a search space. One thing is clear that random search procedure uses random function to exploit the parameter search space and is not totally a directionless search technique.

As we had done an exhaustive search on comparison of these traditional techniques, we found then that they are not robust in nature. This does not mean that these traditional techniques must be discarded. These techniques can be used in many simpler applications, while complex application may need many hybrid applications.

If we compare all the three schemes we discussed earlier i.e specialized, enumerative and robust scheme for various problems. We found that past researches have shown that robust schemes perform well for complex problems. Enumerative schemes perform well for simpler or particular set of problems. Even the hybrid system created by joining two or more optimization techniques gives good result as compared to enumerative or random walk technique. Later part of this book will show that how genetic algorithms are robust when applied in any way and fill the gap created by these schemes.

3.3 WHY WE NEED OPTIMIZATION?

Before we study genetic algorithms in detail, we will first define what is optimization? If optimization definition is clear then we will find out what we want to optimize i.e it can be a function, parameters of a function, rule set etc. Last but not the least what are we going to gain by this process of optimization and when we will get optimized parameters.

Optimization means perfection i.e the best solution or best parameters found so far. One of the degrees of best or worst value is defined that we went down to the methods or procedure to obtain it in a whole. Optimization can be done to do improvement in approach or improvement in optimal point find until now i.e improvement in a process or improvement in the optimal point itself. In comparing various other optimization procedures we judge them from quality of solutions that had found not by the procedure or by their internal process.

For example consider a case of stock trader (Bauer, 1994). How do we find that the decision taken by him is good or bad? It depends upon the amount of profit he has earned or not. If all the traders in the community are earning profit then he will be judged by the ranking he achieves in the trading community or by the amount of profit he has earned. What was his overall efficiency? In real world, optimization is just like to obtain better results from the previous ones or relative better solutions than find until so far. Thus importance of optimization is that, we do a little bit of improvement in satisfying level of performance. Higher degree of optimization means attaining perfection in a whole. In next section we will see how Genetic Algorithms is better with other traditional techniques. We will also study that how GA will help us to achieve higher degree of optimization i.e perfection.

3.4 DIFFERENCE BETWEEN GENETIC ALGORITHMS AND OTHER CONVENTIONAL METHODS

Genetic Algorithms are of new class of artificial intelligence based soft computing technique. Past researches have shown that GA has proved to be robust in various adverse environments as compared to the traditional or conventional techniques. GA differs from conventional techniques in following ways:

1. In GA parameter set or rule set are coded or mapped into binary strings or alpha numeric characters. Thus GA optimized these coded or mapped strings not the actual parameters or rule set.
2. In GA we have a well-defined fitness function. The quality of string is judged by the fitness score of that string not by other supplementary knowledge of the system.
3. In a given search space the GA procedure search parallel in various number of points, not a single point.
4. GA use probabilistic or is a random walk algorithm. It does not find fixed or distinct rules.

Here in GA, parameter set which is to be optimized should be mapped to a finite length binary or alpha numeric string. For example we want to optimize a function F(x) where F(x) = x, the value of x can be in between 0 and 31. In case of a conventional method we start with a fixed value and start searching new values until higher values is reached. But in case of GA we have to code the value of x to finite string length. Here in our problem we code it to a binary string length of 5 bits i.e 00000 is the lowest value 0 and 11111 is largest value 31. Thus every combination of 0's and 1's gives us some values. For example string 01011 gives us values $2^0 + 2^1 + 2^3 = 1 + 2 + 8 = 11$. The neutral of our problem is to get maximum value of F(x). In case of conventional techniques we will nonstop deal with the x value. We will start with a value and using the conventional technique transition rule, we will get one value one after other. But in case of GA we will use coding of the possible solution into a binary string. Due to the fact parameter of value or value of x is represented by a finite bit binary string. In our problem parameter value is represented in a 5 bit binary string. Thus GA can exploit the string in 2^5 ways in comparison to the parameter value itself as it is done in conventional technique. Thus there is a number of limitations in other conventional methods i.e lack of continuity, uni modality, lack of search space etc.

In case of other traditional optimization methods, we start from a single point and by using the conversion rule prescribed; we jump from point to point until desired result is obtained. This conventional technique is not proper and robust as there is a possibility to get locked into false peak in a many peak or multimodal function. By gap GA work on many points i.e a population of strings parallel. Due to this feature, possibility to get locked in a false peak is very less as compared to other conventional techniques. Thus GA starts with a population of strings and generates better fitness strings generations after generations. This random population of strings are generated by flipping a coin i.e Head = 1, Tail = 0. For example if the population of size n is four. The initial random population generated is

```
01011
11001
00101
11000
```

After the creation of random population, successive populations are created using various operates given in GA. Thus we see GA works at a time on various points instead of one starting point as in case of conventional technique. This feature of GA adds a flavour of robustness in it.

One more difference between a conventional and GA based search procedures is that conventional techniques needed auxiliary or system information in order to climb a peak. While GA search are blind. GA only needed the fitness function information or values of the various strings generated generation after generation in order to be an effective search and optimization technique. This feature of GA makes it the most accepted method for every problem as compare to other search techniques. GA refuses to use the auxiliary information related to the problem, due to this it is a broad based scheme and different from other schemes. Thus until now we came to know that GA are blind search techniques and are robust in all circumstances.

Traditional techniques uses deterministic rules while GA uses probity based operators and random walk to find an optimal solution. Use of these two features help GA's to search new spaces towards that region where there is a possibility of improvement. It helps us to find many vantage points in a multi peak function.

After reading this section we had come across four points which are of major differences between traditional and GA based search procedures:

1. Use of binary coding to represents various points in a search space.
2. Search from an initial population generated, not from a single point.
3. GA's are total blind search techniques. They do not need system information to move forward.
4. Probabilistic operators together with random walk help GA's to search newer search spaces in a multi-dimensional search spaces.

These above features make GA a robust search technique and give an upper hand as compared with other conventional search procedures. In next section we introduce a simple Genetic Algorithm for its better understanding.

3.5 A SIMPLE GENETIC ALGORITHM- INTRODUCTION

Genetic Algorithms are a combination of evolution and computation (Rajesekaran et.al, 2007). Charles Darwin first gave the theory of evolution and survival of the fittest in 1830's. Charles Babbage develops a computing machine based on analytics in 1833. After so many years these two theories come together in Genetic Algorithms. GA's mimics the artificial life in form of computer programs. GA's procedures are based on genetics and survival of fittest. GA's effectively search from a pool of solutions to find some more attractive solutions for various problems whose best solutions are not known so far or NP hard problems.

The search procedure in GA is based on Darwin theory of survival of fittest. The population is worked by various operators until superior solutions rule the population. The GA procedure consists of various steps which can be combined and implemented in various permutations and combinations. The main purpose of this chapter is to give you a broad over view of GA and its manual implementation.

3.5.1 Biology Behind Genetic Algorithms

Study of genetics is all about past physical features of our fore fathers. In genetic science we do research about the working of genes and how their features are transmitted from one generation to other.

All the living being is made up of cells which contain in them the past inherited features. These cells are in form of a grouping and these structures are known as chromosomes. Thus the hereditary information is coded within genes and chromosomes and infinite number of combination can come up from this information. This genetic system of each organism is called a genotype. Probability of our survival, development and our working efficiency is determined by this genotype. This genotype is the coded structure while the decoded structure is known as phenotype. Thus genes are the coded structure. Two persons may have almost same genes, while some minor changes in genotype will make substantial changes in phenotype. Human beings generally consist of 46 pair of chromosomes out of which 23 come from mother side and 23 comes from father side. In biology each chromosomes member moves in a pair and exchange their genes. This process is known as crossover. Thus in a pair of 23 genes only one gene either from father side or mother side is dominant in each parameter, which is transmitted to the future generation. Thus crossover does not produce new genes, but new pair of genes or genetic material. Thus there can be nearly 19 trillion different combinations of male and female genes. Thus all individuals in this world are unique.

Thus there is copying of genetic material from one generation to other. In the process of copying certain amount of alterations or imperfections are added to it, which is known as mutation. Possibility of mutation is very less, but it generally adds much needed genetic diversity in the population of genes. Short term effect due to mutation is very less, but in a long run it leads to noteworthy changes in maintaining genetic population diversity.

Thus Darwin theory of survival of fittest depends upon adaptation and natural selection process. Due to the natural selection process newer off springs are produced. Offspring with superior genetic material adapt to the situation and survive, while inferior off springs which are insufficient, which does not comes up to the expectations are discarded from the nature, does not takes part in the next generation selection process.

Crossover and mutation process produces vary combination of genes which are inherited from the fore fathers. Thus new individuals are formed. Individuals with more favourable gene combination result in a highly fit persons. Here there is a higher possibility that its character tics being passed to next generation. While inferior ones die or discarded from the selection process. Thus genetic algorithms are based upon the concept of evolution and adaptation, which are the main pillars of Darwin theory of survival of the fittest. Post Darwin period, a lot of advance research is done on it. But GA's are based on elementary findings of Darwin theory.

3.5.2 Genetic Algorithms Step by Step

A genetic algorithm as concept was developed by mathematician and philosopher John Holland of University of Michigan. He publishes many of his research on adaptive systems during 1960's. His book "Adaption in Natural and artificial Systems" published in 1975 is said to be bible of Genetic Algorithms. Many Ph. D students were guided by him on topic of Genetic Algorithms.

Earlier in the previous section we had studied the concept of biology and genes, which forms the background and basis of various steps and procedure of genetic algorithms. Later in this section we will describe GA as a whole. Genetic algorithms give attractive solutions or near to optimal solutions or solutions better than obtained from other procedures for NP hard problems. GA is an optimization algorithm for problems which has large search spaces. In many complex problems or in large spaces the word optimization has no meaning. It is a very vague concept. Some solution obtained by GA may not be optimal in the near future. So we can say instead of optimal solution, GA found many attractive solutions for the problems on which it is applied.

The starting point of GA is how to represent a problem. Popularly binary strings are used to represent the solutions of the problem. Let us say our problem $F(x) = x$ where $x \leq 31$. For this problem the maximum value or optimized value of x is 31, by using simple mathematics. But by solving this problem with the help of GA we have to represent the solution in form of binary strings. To explain the problem representation procedure of GA we will review some binary arithmetic concept.

Binary arithmetic is of base2 natures and is totally different from conventional arithmetic of base10. Base2 arithmetic is simpler because it contains only two digits i.e 0 or 1. While base10 arithmetic consists of digits from 0 to 9. Computer as a machine understands the language of binary arithmetic. For example the decimal value 264 is represented as $2 \times 100 + 6 \times 10 + 4$. Here three positions correspond to 10^2, 10^1, and 10^0. Similarly 101 in binary arithmetic is represented as $2^2 \times 1 + 2^1 \times 0 + 2^0 \times 1$. i.e $4 + 0 + 1 = 5$. Here three positions are represented by 4, 2, 1 instead of 100, 10 and 1 in decimal system. Thus to represent number 63 we need six position of binary number i.e 111111 as compare to two position in decimal equivalent. Hence 100001 is coded as: $2^0 \times 1 + 2^1 \times 0 + 2^2 \times 0 + 2^3 \times 0 + 2^4 \times 0 + 2^5 \times 1 = 1 + 0 + 0 + 0 + 0 + 32$ i.e 33.

Now coming back to our problem 10010 could be one of the solutions of the problem which is represented as $2^0 \times 0 + 2^1 \times 1 + 2^2 \times 0 + 2^3 \times 0 + 2^4 \times 1 = 0 + 2 + 0 + 0 + 16 = 18$. To represent our problem in a binary state we need five binary positions. Hence least value is 00000 and maximum value is 11111. Thus any of five binary bit string, it represents a chromosome. O's and 1's represents genes. Since chromosomes reveals the physical characteristics of a living organism. Hence binary bit string is represented as one of the solution of the problem. The solution can be superior or inferior which depends upon the binary value given.

After the understanding of binary arithmetic and representation of problem as a binary string we will now explain the GA actual steps or procedure.

Step 1: First initial population size has to be decided. For example we had set population size to five. We will use random function to generate bits of 5 bit strings of the solution. We will flip the coin to see if bit generated is 0 or 1. For example if our five individual strings are: 10000, 00110, 00001, 10001, 11000. After converting these binary strings into decimal equivalent we get 16, 6, 1, 17 and 24. Every time we run this part of program in computer we will get different binary strings as these strings are produced using random number generator. The problem which we had taken is very simple one. Real world problems are of complex in nature. Here five bit representation of string will have at most 2^5 potential solutions. But in real world complex problems will have trillions of solutions. Hence to represent these problem bit string length must be of range 40 to 50. Population size be of 100 to 150 individuals.

Step 2: In order to represent the population performance we need fitness function formula. This fitness score of an individual of the population will decide which individual in the population will be selected for mating to generate individuals for next generation.

GA's are designed in such a way that fitness values of individuals or average

Table 1. Genetic Algorithm initial random generated population.

Sr. No.	Binary String	Decimal Equivalent	f1/∑f1	Fitness Score Expected Count f1/ f9Avg.)	Actual Count for Selection
1	10000	16	0.25	1.25	1
2	00110	6	0.0937	0.4687	1
3	00001	1	0.0156	0.0781	0
4	10001	17	0.2656	1.3281	1
5	11000	24	0.375	1.875	2

SUM 64
Average 12.8
Max. 24

fitness values of the population increases generation after generations. In case of our problem, see Table 1.

Thus the decimal equivalents closer to 31 will have higher fitness value and decimal equivalent closer to 0 will have lower fitness value according to our problem.

Step 3: Here the better performing individual or individual having high fitness score from the population will be selected for mating to produce individuals for next generation. It is not the case that poor performing individuals will not be selected for mating, but they will have lesser chance to get selected and produce individuals for next generation or to pass their binary genes to the population of next generation. There are number of selection schemes which we will discuss in part 2 of the book.

In our above example fifth string has highest fitness and fitness score is 1.875. While 2nd string has lowest fitness score of 0.0781. This calculation of fitness score is actually sampling sequence, which will be done for all individuals of population in every generation. Thus next generation individuals will again be judged by their fitness score and sampling sequence will be applied to them as well.

Step 4: Here next generation individuals are generated from present population pool by using various operators. There are a variety of traditional and advance level operators, which we will study later in this book. Two of the most powerful operators inspired by biology are crossover and mutation. In case of crossover operator selection process will choose two random strings from the parent pool depending upon their fitness score. In our case suppose 2nd and 5th string i.e 00110 and 11000 are chosen. After this we will randomly choose a point in between the string to cut it into two parts. Now the two strings look like 00—110 and 11—000. Now weather crossover will be performed or not will be defined by the probability decided by us. If we decide probability of crossover to be 0.75 then we will generate a random number between 1 and 100, if its value comes between 1 and 75 then we will perform crossover and we will exchange the head and tails of the two strings selected. Here head of first string will be combined with the tail of second string and vice versa. Our strings now become 00000 and 11110 which corresponds to the value 0 and $2 + 4 + 8 + 16$ i.e 30. Thus it is to be seen crossover resulted in to creating fit individual near to the optimal solution.

Thus it is seen that crossover is a total random process. Here we select two strings that are selected randomly. The point where crossover is to be performed i.e where to cut two strings is also generated randomly. The decision to perform crossover or not will be decided by a random number generator. Thus randomness is the main character tics of crossover and overall of genetic algorithms. Here random operative seems to be useful since it takes search in many unexplored spaces or directions which are beneficial. Mathematical formulation of crossover is bit thorny. It will be discussed in detail in next chapter. Thus explaining crossover in a simple, we cut the search space in a simple and efficient way to obtained newer search spaces. As shown that higher fitness was obtained and it guides you in right direction or region.

Mutation is just another powerful operator included in genetic algorithms. It is also biologically inspired. In case of mutation each and every bit is selected, if mutation is to be performed then if there is a 0 then it is to be altered to 1 and vice versa. Generally mutation probability is kept very low i.e 0.01% i.e only 10 bit in 1000 bit. Mutation helps us to add much needed genetic diversity to our population. It takes the search procedure into slightly different direction. Researchers have found that high mutation rates take the search procedure just like a random walk.

Thus it is seen that by using these two operators we transform the population towards higher fitness values generations after generations. If a particular bit pattern is needed or is optimal, then with the help of selection operators, the individuals having that bit pattern are selected repeatedly for crossover and mutation to produce individuals for next generations. Since selection of a individual depends upon the fitness score of the individual. Hence crossover gives some guarantee that a particular bit pattern will be passed on to the population of next generation. Thus with the help of selection operator we are also taking consideration of the fitness score of individuals of previous generations.

Step 5: After completing this whole procedure return to the step 2 and repeat step 2 to step 4 procedure until population converges or optimal values are generated. Since selection procedure is taking place based upon the fitness score of individual string. Due to it good string drives out bad string and bad string drives out ugly string and so on. Thus bad string is replaced by good string and good string is replaced by best string as generations passes by. Crossover also stuff the optimal string pattern into various individuals strings thus driving out bad string pattern. This process is repeated again and again till optimal string is obtained or homogeneity in the population is reached. If all string in the population is of same pattern, then crossover will not be useful. Then only mutation can add much needed genetic diversity to the population. If all strings in the population are homogeneous and optimal then mutation will act as a spoiler. Here application of mutation operator will destroy the situation and will not improve it. Mathematical model to represent crossover and mutation operators are explained in the next chapter.

Crossover produces newer quality of strings. It may produce both superior and inferior results thus diverting the research. Crossover can disrupt newer patterns that are required. Thus in order to avoid this situation genetic algorithm must be fine-tuned. The fine tuning of GA is explained in chapter 2 of this book. By fine tuning of GA population can be converge quickly, but this will result in poorer quality of solutions. There is a competition between speed and quality of solution obtained. If one is achieved then compromise on the other has to be made.

Larger population sizes will lead to a large number of fitness function evaluations and large amount of processing power and time. But this will lead to better and attractive solutions. Then if selection process is greedy in nature, then they will quickly drive out the inferior solution and population will quickly converge. In this process other unexplored search areas will be left out and solution quality will be compromised.

3.5.3 Genetic Algorithm: A Working Solution by Hand

Let us apply genetic algorithm problem to this optimization problem given below:

This problem is of maximizing the value of F(x) whereas F(x) = x. where value of x is $0 \leq x \leq 31$.

Here we will first do mapping the decimal values of x to some finite binary length string. Here we will code the value of x to a binary length string of length five bits. Here each bit could be of value 0 or 1. First we will make a brief review of decimal and binary arithmetic. In case of decimal arithmetic it is to the base 10 (0 to 9), while binary arithmetic is to the base 2 (0, 1). For example value of 327 in decimal will be represented as $3 \times 100 + 2 \times 10 + 7 \times 1$.

While in binary arithmetic it is of base 2 i.e. 0 or 1. Thus a 5 bit number 11001will be represented as $2^0 \times 1 + 2^1 \times 0 + 2^2 \times 0 + 2^3 \times 1 + 2^4 \times 1, 1 + 0 + 0 + 8 + 16 = 25$.

Table 2. Population generated after first generation.

String No.	Binary String Randomly Generated	Decimal Equivalent	f1/∑f1	Fitness Score Expected Count f1/ f9Avg.)	Actual Count for Selection	% of Total
1	10000	16	0.25	1.25	1	25
2	00110	6	0,0937	0.4687	1	9.3
3	00001	1	0.0156	0.0781	0	1.5
4	10001	17	0,2656	1.3281	1	26.5
5	11000	24	0.375	1.875	2	37.5

Sum 64
Average 12.8
Maximum 24

To start with we generate initial populations randomly. If population size is of 5 number and every individual is a 5 bit number. Then we will toss or flip a coin 5 × 4 i.e 20 times or we can generate population randomly by putting values of 0 or 1 in every bit position depending upon the tossed result. Thus by using these binary bits of finite length GA can deal effectively with a variety of problems and explore various complex search spaces. Consider Table 2.

After generation of initial population randomly in genetic algorithm, we start with reproduction in our next step. Here we select individuals from the population randomly, but on the basis of fitness function. It means that population with higher fitness value has higher chances to be get selected

Figure 3. Simple Reproduction of allotted strings using Roulette Wheel according to their fitness function.

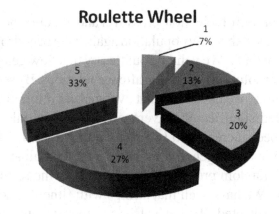

for mating and to pass their genes into next generation. Here roulette wheel selection technique as shown in fig. below is the most popular.

After the selection of strings with roulette wheel selection technique, we perform crossover and mutation operations on them. In crossover strings are selected randomly and mated by using randomly selected sites within the string. Seeing the above given table two strings 10000 and 00110 are selected for crossover, the crossover site is 1, which will yield two new strings 10110 and 00000. The results of the other string that are crossed are seen in Table 3.

The last operator mutation is done bit by bit basis with a very low frequency. If probability of mutation is 0.01, with 25 bit we expect 25 × 0.01 / 100 = 2,5 bits will undergo mutation in every generation. Our by hand simulation procedure shows that an 2 bit mutation occurs i.e changes from 0 to 1 had taken place.

Table 3. Crossover and Mutation operation performed.

Mating Pool (Crossover Site Shown)	Crossover Site (Randomly Selected)	New Population	F(x) Value
1 1 0000 (16)	1	10110	22
0 1 0110 (6)	1	00000	0
00001 (1)		Mutation 10001	17
100 1 01 (17)	3	10000	16
110 1 00 (24)	3	Mutation 11101	29

SUM 84
AVERAGE 16.8
MAXIMUM 29

After one generation of selection, crossover and mutation new population is generated. We will test this new population against the backdrop of results. As shown in the above table. We validate our theory that how genetic algorithms will generate better solution generation after generations. By seeing the results from the above table, we have seen that average and minimum performance has been improved significantly. Average fitness of initial population was 12.8 which have been increased to 16.8. Maximum fitness has been improved from 24 to 29 in a single generation. Due to the combination of selection operator with the random process, improvements in the results are not fake or just by chance. We have seen that strings with fitness function above the average value are selected. We have also seen that strings with schema 11_ _ _ or 1_ _ _ are generally of the fitness values above the normal value. In the next chapter we will make a better understanding of this schema concept or about similarity concept.

Thus by simulating genetic algorithms with hand has given confidence that some interesting or quality solution can be generated for large and complex problems. In order to have better understanding of genetic algorithm, we need to know that what should be processed so that it leads us to achieve optimal result. For this we will have to examine the raw string that has been processed by using different operators such as crossover and mutation. Research in this field has given us the theory of "Similarity Template" which in turn has given "Building Block Hypothesis". These two things are discussed in next chapter in detail.

3.5.4 Learning About Similarities Between Genetic Algorithms and Biology

It has been clearly seen in the previous section that mystery about the operations in GA is cleared by study of building blocks. The theory about building blocks and its mathematical concepts are clearly explained in next chapter. Since GA is a combination of natural biology system and computer science terms. Until now we have seen the working of strings in GA. We talked about crossover, string position and mutation in GA. In this section we will see how these terms are replica of terms used in biology. Here term "String" used in genetic algorithm is a replica of term "Chromosome" in biological system. In case of nature chromosome gives the genetic system of the organism. The genetic system is called "Genotype". Similarly in genetic algorithm analogous to this term "genotype" we called it by the term "Structure".

In biological system organism formed by combination of chromosome or genetic system is called phenotype. While in case of GA decoded string is known as parameter set, or solution alternative. Coding procedures of the string in genetic algorithms is generally numeric in nature. In natural system we say chromosomes consist of genes, which takes some values called alleles. Thus gene position is identified by gene function and it is given by locus. While in case of GA chromosomes are represented as strings. String consists of values. These values depend upon the binary bit positions in the string. The comparison between natural and genetic algorithm is given in Table 4.

Table 4. Comparison between Genetic Algorithm and Natural Genetics Terminologies.

Nature	Genetic Algorithm
Chromosome	String
Gene	Feature
Allele	Feature Value
Locus	String Position
Genotype	Structure
Phenotype	Parameter Set or Decoded Solution

3.5.4 Genetic Algorithm Program

Genetic Algorithm is advantages to implement because we need to change a small position of code we move from one problem to another. Most of the functions in GA software are of general in nature. Thus GA software is flexible and reusable. In nature GA works on string population, but since string length, population sizes vary from problem to problem. Reusable GA software should have taken consideration into changes in these parameters before starting to work. After that selection, crossover and mutation operators should also allow the differences in string length and population size.

GA is the black box technique, they works on the bit strings without having knowledge of the system parameters, which they are optimizing. They don't work or attack on the problem itself. The only part of the problem that interfaces with GA is the fitness function. Fitness function requires decoding of the string and putting the values in the problem defined formula, which gives the fitness score of that individual string. Thus the fitness score calculation function in the GA software or procedure is of non-generic in nature. Fitness function formula is problem dependent and it varies from problem to problem.

To implement Genetic Algorithm to solve a particular problem, you only need to implement problem in form of a bit string. You must have same mapping formula for calculation of fitness score. GA's are somewhat blind search techniques that do not require the problem information to march forward. GA works only with the strings and rest of GA procedures must include operators such as selection, crossover, mutation etc. takes care of finding the optimal solution. GA's are rather simple to use. Now a day as the popularity of GA's are increasing coders are coming out with the GA software packages which are simple to run.

3.6 TEN THINGS ABOUT GENETIC ALGORITHMS

1. The work on GA is not of recent in nature. GA was discovered in 1975 and lot of researchers has put their energy in brain to make GA success. Many international conferences such as GECCO are only dedicated to works on GA only.
2. A lot of work has been done in verifying the internal working of GA and GA applied in various fields of engineering. A very little work is

done on GA applied in the stock trading system, which we are going to cover in this book.

3. Here problems must be translated or represented into binary strings. This requires a lot of thought process and broad understanding of problem itself.

4. The problem representation in form of binary string (sequence of 0's and 1's) requires a form of creativity and a high degree of imagination. Past researches have shown that GA has already been applied to almost all types of problems.

5. GA's are started by randomly generating population of individuals representing possible solutions. Thus a small amount of knowledge about the problem is needed to start with GA.

6. There must be a proper procedure which represents the problem solution in form of a binary string. A fitness function formula must be there which is use to give the string its fitness score.

7. Selection operator are designed in such a way that string with a comparative high fitness score will be selected for mating or transferring their bit pattern into next generation population.

8. Genetic Algorithms operators such as crossover and mutation helps in searching various unexplored areas for complex problems. Cross operator is exploitative in nature, while mutation operator is explorative in nature.

9. The basic steps from 6 to 8 described above are done repetitively till the population losses its genetic diversity or the fittest solution is obtained.

10. GA's are fast, flexible and easy to implement for large search spaces where number of possible solutions are of infinite in number and best possible solution is not known. GA help in finding many vantage point in a limited number of function evaluations. In case of finding stock trading strategies GA's speed and power helps in generating better parameters or rules as found previously.

3.7 CONCLUSION

Careful study of this chapter leads us to the proper understanding of GA's, their internal working and their power to find optimal solutions.GA mimics the natural biological process which are robust, efficient and officious as living being adapts to variety of environmental conditions. By taking out the feature of the natural system and replicating it in GA artificial life, we try to make the algorithm more robust and effective. Past researches have shown that GA proves its worth when applied to complex problems.

In this chapter we have tried to explain the working of various GA operators such as selection, crossover and mutation etc. GA works on strings as they are coded to represent parameters set or some rule. Selection, crossover and mutation are applied in a series to create new population which represents newer solutions. The above mention operators are of simple in working, which works in values, random number generation, copying of string, string exchange at a random point etc. Despite having less complexity in it, results obtained by applying these operators are operators are superior to the results obtained from conventional search techniques. We had done simulation of GA by hand for one generation and seen its power. Following are the differences that GA have with other conventional optimization techniques:

1. Works on the coding rather than problem parameters itself.
2. Search parallel from a population at various points not at a single point.
3. GA is a blind search or black box search technique.
4. Operators are of stochastic and heuristic in nature not having deterministic or discrete features in it.

If a problem function consists of a large number of local peaks, it is difficult to fool GA as it works on coding or binary strings and on population, not a single point. Due to this we do not stuck to a false peak as GA search many points parallel.

GA's are only dependent on fitness function formula not on whole of the problem information. Thus problems where information are not available, other techniques failed to work on it. Due to this feature GA can be applied to any type of problem which is well defined or not. Thus the simple GA we had studied in this chapter is recommended to be use in diversified fields. In next of the coming chapters we will see the mathematical foundations of GA and its implementation of GA in a programming language and application of GA in a practical problem of a stock trading system.

REFERENCES

Bauer, R. J. Jr. (1994). *Genetic Algorithms and Investment Strategies*. John Wiley and Sons, Inc.

Deb. (2000). Optimization for Engineering Design: Algorithm and Examples. Prentice Hall of India Private Limited.

Goldberg, D. E. (2002). *Genetic Algorithms in Search*. Optimization and Machine Learning Pearson Education.

Rajasekaran & Vijaylakshmi Pai. (2007). *Neural Networks, Fuzzy Logic, and Genetic algorithms, Synthesis and Applications*. Prentice-Hall of India Private Limited.

Chapter 4

Genetic Algorithms (GAs) and Their Mathematical Foundations

ABSTRACT

In this chapter, the authors back GA procedures using old mathematical facts. More rigorous working of mathematical facts about GAs are raised in this chapter. In fact, there are a large number of similarities in the population of strings. The authors see how GA exploits these similarities to generate good solutions. So, in this whole procedure they show which schema or pattern will grow and which pattern will die or be lost as generation passes by due to the effect of selection, crossover, and mutation operator. The study of this building block hypothesis, leads to better understanding of GA. It will also help us to reach optimal solutions in much less time.

4.1 GENETIC ALGORITHMS REVISITED

GA's are a budding search and optimization procedures. Past researches have shown that it is useful for complex engineering optimization problems. GA's mimics nature in a large way and represents a artificial life. GA's are soft computing based search and optimization procedure based on Darwin theory of natural selection. John Holland of university of Michigan was first to publish his work in 1975. After this a large number of his students and other researchers contributed towards the advancement of work on GA's.

DOI: 10.4018/978-1-7998-4105-0.ch004

To this date there are only few books (Goldberg 1989) are available and few conference proceeding or conferences related only to GA are available to the researchers.

4.2 WORKING PRINCIPLES OF GENETIC ALGORITHMS

Let us consider a constraint optimization problem (Hupt et. Al, 2004). It is a maximization problem.

Maximize $F(X_i)$;

$(X_i)^L \leq X_i \leq (X_i)^U$, i=1,2,3……….,N

Suppose $F_1 (X_1, X_2)$ is a function with two variables

Here variables are coded into some string configurations. The length of string depends upon the solution accuracy we want. Larger the length, larger the accuracy. For example 8 bit strings is used to represent the two variable function then (00000000, 00000000) and (11111111, 11111111) will represent the lower and upper limit points $(X_1^{(L)}, X_2^{(L)})$ $(X_1^{(L)}, X_2^{(L)})$

Mapping rule for this 16 bit string to symbolize a point in n dimensional search space is

$$Xi = X_i^{(L)} + (X_i^{(L)} - X_i^{(L)})/ (2^{li} – 1) \times \text{decoded value of string } S_i \qquad (1)$$

Here Xi is coded in a substring Si of length li. Formula for decoded value of binary substring Si is given by $\sum_{i=0}^{i-1} 2^i S^i$ where $S_i \in (0, 1)$.

String S is represented as $(S_{i-1}, S_{1-2}, …………….S_2, S_1, S_0)$. For example 8 bit binary string (10000001) has decoded value as $[1 \times 2^0 + 0 \times 2^1 + 1 \times 2^2 + 0 \times 2^3 + 0 \times 2^4 + 0 \times 2^5 + 0 \times 2^6 + 0 \times 2^7 + 1 \times 2^8]$ ie $[1 + 0 + 0 + 0 + 0 + 0 + 0 + 256]$. If X_i is represented by 8 bit then 2^8 i.e 256 substrings are available, as each bit can take position 0 or 1. Here accuracy is obtained with 8 bit string is approximately 1/256 of search space. If the string bit is increased by 1 bit, then accuracy increases by 1/521 of the search space. Thus length of the binary bit of the substring represents the desired accuracy we want. After coding of variables by this procedure, points X_1 and X_2 are found by using the above equation 4.1. Thus the function values are calculated by substituting the values of X_1 and X_2 in the objective function F(X) equation.

Fitness Function: Above example is a maximization problem, since GA based on theory of survival of the fittest. If there is a minimization problem then it is to be transformed into a maximization problem by some means or a suitable equation. For maximization problem fitness function is considered as same objective function i.e F (X) [Fitness Function]= f (x) [Objective Function].

For minimization problem fitness function should be transformed into maximization value. Thus fitness function formula is

F(X) = 1/ (1+ f(x))

This equation does not alter the location of the string. Here by this equation we convert minimization problem into maximization delinquent. Here fitness function of the string is known as string fitness.

After defining the coding procedure, fitness function GA procedure starts with the generation of population of random individual strings. Fitness function of each string is calculated. After this selection, crossover, mutation operators are applied to generate new population of individual strings. This process continues until termination conditions are met with. There are n termination criteria. For example optimal or desired solution is obtained or string population is exhausted or no genetic diversity is left in the population or total i.e maximum number of generations is performed in the GA.

4.2.1 GA Operators

Selection is the first operator which comes into the picture (Deb, 2002). Main objective of this operator is to select strings with higher fitness function for mating. It is also known as reproduction operator. There are number of other selection operators in GA. Basic feature of this operator is that they select strings with above fitness function from the population multiple times. Thus string with higher fitness function has higher probability to be selected for mating purpose as compare with string with lower fitness function. Thus the probability of ith string to be selected in GA population is

$$Pi = Fi / \sum_{i=0}^{n} Fi$$

n = Population Size.

One of the most popular operators used for selection of strings in GA literature is known as roulette wheel selection. This scheme is similar to roulette wheel with its circumference is marked for each string proportionate to the fitness of each string. Roulette wheel is spun and each time there is a change, that pointer stops at the circumference which has higher fitness function. The average fitness function of strings in the population is given by the formula:

$$F\left(Avg.\right) = \sum_{n-1}^{n} Fi / n$$

In reproduction operators good strings are repeatedly selected multiple times for mating. Here no new strings are formed. Now arises the crossover operator. Here new strings are formed by exchange of binary bits of two strings with each other. Here two strings are selected randomly and random point is chosen in between the strings and binary bits are exchanged to form a new string. A random crossing site is chosen by exchanging the information on the right side. A simple crossover is shown as below:

```
00 000      00 111
11 111      11 000
```

Two strings chosen for crossover are known as parent strings, while the resulting strings obtained are known as child strings. Crossover is based on basic assumption that parent string with desirable pattern or higher fitness function score will produce child string with much better fitness score. Since if the crossing site is generated randomly, it may happen that if crossing site falls in between the pattern. Then there is a possibility that children string produce may not have high fitness value. This case is not of too much worry because selection operator will discard the child string which has less fitness function in the coming generations. Thus good child string will have higher probability to survive in the coming generations and child strings with less fitness score will have lower chances to be selected for mating and pass their pattern in next generation child strings. Thus overall effect of crossover in combination with selection operator is beneficial. Thus it preserves string with better pattern or schema over generation after generations.

A crossover operator results in a new string. Mutation operator also does the same thing, but it is done in a different manner, as it is applied thinly. Generally mutation operator is applied with small probability. It is applied bit by bit i.e it changes 1 to 0 or 0 to 1. Here the coin is flipped with a probability P_m, if the outcome is true then the value of binary bit is changed, otherwise not. Mutation operator is used to create diversity in the binary bit pattern of the population. If mutation operator is applied with a high probability the GA optimization algorithm will look like a noisy and random walk. As it will destroy the binary bit pattern created by crossover operator.

Thus all the above operators' i. e selection, crossover and mutation are simple and designed to give better solutions. Crossover operator produces better strings by recombination of good sub strings. Mutation operator changes binary bit value of the string to add diversity and to create a better string. There is no guarantee that resulting string generated after the use of these two operators will be a better string as compared to the strings from previous generations. In this case bad strings will be eliminated by the use of selection operator. Thus in this way GA functions and move forward.

4.3 SEARCHING FOR IMPORTANT SIMILARITIES

Now moving deeper towards the understanding of genetic algorithms (Goldberg, 2002), a question comes in our mind that we are only concern over the fitness score of the string to move forward. Apart from fitness values, what other information will help us to obtain a better solution and improve its working. Consider a random generated population of 5 strings as shown below:

```
Strings  Fitness Values
01011         11
11001         25
00101         05
11000         24
```

By seeing these four independent strings one question comes to in our mind that what other additional information we can get from these strings by scanning it from left to right and from top to bottom. First thing that comes to our mind what are the similarities among these strings. Finding similarities between the bit pattern and its associated fitness values that will lead us to better understanding of genetic algorithms in search and optimization procedures. Here we have seen that string started with value 1 on right side has always above fitness score. Hence in our function F (x) = x solution is coded into a five bit binary string. First we see various similarity templates in the string, second we correlate these similarities templates with fitness score of the string. Thus if our study about the above two feature is complete then it will guide us for optimization for particular function precisely with lesser number of function evaluations. This study of template is known as similarity template or schemata.

Thus from the previous section we are clear that we are interested in strings or their fitness score alone, but we are interested in the particular templates or schemata along with their fitness function. We see that if there is similarity between the schemata present in the various strings and their fitness score.

A schema or schemata is generally a similarity pattern which is the subset of string as a whole. In a binary string there are two bit patterns 0 or 1. We introduces a third position * i.e don't care symbol. With this extension we have three possibilities (0, 1, *). Schemata are a pattern matching procedure. Here in every position 1 binary will have to match with 1, 0 with 0, * with *. No No consideration of strings with length 5 bits. Thus if schema *0010 matches two strings (10010, 00010). Here one more schema *000* matches with the 4 strings (00000, 10001, 10000, 00001). Thus schema 0*011 matches with any string with 0 in the 1st and 3rd position and 1 in fourth and fifth position respectively. Thus idea of schema helps us to find similarity among various strings in the population.

Thus with these position (1, 0, *) in a string of length 5 bit we have 3^5 i.e 243 different similarity templates. If we can have K number of alphabets or elements in the position, then for a string of length l we will have $(K + 1)^l$ schemata. Thus by adding * I.e don't care symbol we are making things more difficult. Consider (0, 1), then we had only 2^5 alternative strings. In case of (0, 1, *) we have 3^5 (243) strings or schemata. Considering these strings fitness score and their similarities in the population. Then we had a lot of information that we can exploit to make genetic algorithm search more effective.

Consider a single string of length5 bits: 00000. This string is a member of of 25 schemata because in every bit position you should have value 1 or * (don't care symbol. If a string consists of 2^l schema then for a population of n, number of schema will vary between 2^l and $n \times 2^l$. Thus by getting more information about similarity templates, we will be able to make genetic algorithm search more effective.

If there are between 2^l and $n \times 2^l$ schema in a population, than important question is that how many schemas are processed in an useful or proper manner by the use of selection, crossover and mutation operator in GA. Thus the question is how the use of these operators will result in growth and decay of these schemas generation after generations.

Now we will discuss the effect of working of various operators such as selection, crossover and mutation on growth and decay of these schemas. The effect of selection operator is that it leads to the growth of schema. Since modus operandi of the selection operator is to select string with higher score multiple times. Selection operator does not produce new strings at all. Considering crossover operator it may or may not cut the schema. It depends upon the crossover point which is generated randomly. Consider two schema 0***0 and ***11. There is a possibility that first schema is likely to be decayed as compared to the second schema. Now coming to the mutation operator it rarely disrupts any schema, as it is used sparingly. Thus from the above study we make a conclusion that highly fit and short length schema will propagate generation after generation with a greater frequency. Thus exponential growth of this schema with these properties is known as building blocks. In our next section we will examine how many useful schemas are transferred into next generations? Answered to this question is n^3 for n number of function evaluations. This type of parallelism we exploit in genetic algorithms.

4.4 MATHEMATICS BEHIND GENETIC ALGORITHMS

The working of GA's is straight and simple in nature (Rajesekaran, 2007). In it randomly generated population of n strings are generated, copying and partial swapping of strings is done, mutation is done occasionally. These all procedures is done to produce better strings that the previous one. GA's directly influence these strings, but direct processing of these strings results in an absolute processing of the schema as shown in the previous chapter. We will discuss how the use of selection, crossover and mutation operators results in the growth and decay of the schema more rigorously in this section.

Suppose strings are constructed by using alphabet values V = (0, 1). Suppose the binary strings are represented by lower case letters. If a eight bit string A = 00011011 is represented symbolically as A = $a_1a_2a_3a_4a_5a_6a_7a_8$. Each a_i represents a binary value, which we sometimes called genes. Each a_i can take a value 0 or 1. In this particular string a_1, a_2, a_3 has value 0, a_4, a_5 has value 1, a_6 has value 0 a_7, a_8 has value 1. Thus another string A* can have another ordering such as $A^1 = a_7a_8a_2a_5a_6a_1a_3a_4$

Thus the above is is on off technique in which the string representation and mapping can be done.

Genetic algorithm consists of population of strings, hence A_j, j = 1, 2, 3, ...n where j represent the number of string in the population, A(t) where t mean the number of generation. A_j (t) means j number of strings on the tth generation.

Besides this to represent a schema we need the notion how schema is represented. Let us consider that schema H is made by using three alphabets V+ = (0, 1, *), where * is a don't care symbol which can be either 0 or 1. For example schema H = 0**011**. Hence string A = 01101101 is representation of the schema H = 0**011**. Hence string A = 01101101 is representation of the schema H, because string alleles in 1st, 4th, 5th and 6th position matches the schema values.

Previous chapter has shown that there is 3^l schema or similarity templates present for a string of length l. If number of alphabets are K, then number of schemas are $(K+1)^l$. Thus if population of GA is made is made up of n strings then maximum it can have $n*2^l$ schemas. In order to get acquainted with the working of genetic algorithms, we must know the amount of information that GA's are processing. This can be done if we know the total number of schema's which are present and are processed.

All schemas are different, for example schema 11**0*01 is different from schema *0******, some schema consider the whole string such as 0******1, while other schemas are of short span such as 0*1*****. Thus two notions come into picture, one is schema order and other is defining length. Schema H order is denoted by symbol o(H), it is obtained by total number of fixed binary string position in the template. For example order of schema0*110*1* is 5, while order of schema 1*****1 is 2. The defining length of schema is represented by symbol δ(H). It is actually the distance between the first and last bit position. For example 1******0 the value of δ(H) is 7. For schema *1**100* value of δ(H) is 6. If first and last binary fixed position are same such as 1***** then δ(H) is 0. Thus with the help of these definition such as schemas, schema order, defining length etc. we can access the effect of selection, crossover and mutation on the building blocks or popular schema present in the population. In our next section we wil analyze the individual or combined effect of genetic algorithm operator such as selection, crossover and mutation on the schemas present in the population of strings.

Now we will discuss the effect of selection operator on the number of schemas present in the population. Suppose at a given time t there are m number of schema H within the population A(t). Thus m = m(H,T) selection operator copies or select string according to their fitness. Hence the probability of string to be get selected is $Pi = f_i/\sum f_i$. After selecting n string we have m(H, t+1) i.e one generation has passed by. Thus schema H in the population for generation t+1 is given by formula $m(H, t+1) = m(H, t) * n * f(H)/\sum f_i$. Where f(H) is the average fitness of strings containing schema in it in generation t. If average fitness of whole population is $f^* = \sum f_i/n$ then $m(H, t+1) = m(h, t) * f(H)/f'$

This can be explained in a way such that schema present in the string which have higher fitness score i.e above average fitness score in the population will grow. So schema present in the strings which has lower fitness score as compare with the average fitness of the population will decay. This happens with every schema parallel present in the population. Thus selection operator will select multiple copies of schema whose string has better fitness score and schema in the string having lower fitness score are selected in decreasing number. Thus above average schema's increases or grow, while below average schema's decreases or decay. Thus mathematical form of growth and decay of schema has been represented by this simple equation:

$$m(H, t + 1) = m(H, t) * (f' + c\,f')/f' = m(H, t)*(1 + c)$$

Where c is a constant.

Thus the effect of selection operator is clear; it increases and decreases the trials of above average and below average schema. Thus many parallel schema works in a population of n strings.

Selection operator does not promote or add new string. This is done by the use of crossover operator. Here old strings are copied without making any changes in them. Crossover on the other hand is randomized exchange of strings. It creates newer strings by disrupting the strings at a random generated point. It may or may not disrupt the schema or similarity template. For example consider a string of length $l = 8$.

```
A  = 10110110
H₁ = *0*****0
H₂ = ******10
```

Two schemas H1 and H2 are represented in string A. Now we will see the effect of crossover on these schemas.

```
A  = 10110110
H₁ = *0** ***0
H₂ = **** **10
```

Suppose the random point at which crossover is to be made comes out to be 4, There is a possibility that schema with higher defining length to be disrupted than schema with lower defining length as shown in our example. Thus there is a possibility that schema H_1 to survive compare to H_2. Higher the defining length, higher is the possibility that crossover point is to fall between extreme positions. Thus schema H_1 is decayed with a probability $P = \delta(H_1)/l - 1$. Thus lesser is the defining length more is the probability of it to get survived. Thus formula for survival probability of a schema H with defining length $\delta(H)$ is given by:

$$P_s \geq (1-P_c) \, \delta(H)/(l-1)$$

where P_c = Crossover probability

Thus by combining the effect of selection and crossover operators following expressions is formed:

$$m(H, t+1) \geq m(H, t) * f(H)/f' * [1 - Pc*\delta(H)/(l-1)]$$

Thus schema which has fitness score above population average and short defining length grows. While schemas with lower fitness score as compare to population average and long defining length are going decay.

Last operator used is mutation. If mutation probability is P_m. Mutation is random alteration of bits. Thus probability of schema to survive is $(1 - P_m)$. Thus lower order schema will have larger chances to survive as compared with higher order schema. Thus probability of surviving mutation is $(1 - P_m * O(H))$. Thus the expression representing the combined effect of selection, crossover and mutation operators are:

$$m(H, t+1) \geq m(H, t) * f(H)/f' * [1 - Pc*\delta(H)/(l-1) - P_m * O(H)]$$

Thus summary is that short, low order and above average schema are likely to increase exponentially in the trials to come. Thus it is known as schemata theorem or fundamental theorem of Genetic Algorithm. Calculation representing this theorem is not complex. Thus highly fit schema, combined with short low order schema are selected, recombined and re experimented to form more fit strings or with a higher fitness function. With the above study we have reduced the complexity of our problem. Thus instead of trying every possible combination we were able to build string from these best fractional clarification. Thus this schemata theorem can be used for generalization of results for various functions. But for other deceptive function where best points is surrounded by the worst or finding an optimal solution is to find is just like finding a needle in haystack, this schemata theorem fails. As building blocks are of misleading in nature. Thus to find near optimal solution will take large amount of time.

4.5 CONCLUSION

In this chapter we have done a robust understanding of genetic algorithms working and its performance by its working analysis of concept of schema or similarity templates. The theorem depicts the solution that schema or similarity template which have high fitness score, small essential length, low order have better chance to survive and possibility to pass there bit pattern to the next generation. Thus there is also a possibility that these higher building blocks schema will repeatedly be selected for mating, there will be least possibility that crossover will disturb their bit pattern due to their short defining length. Thus mutation is rare in nature, due to this there is a very less possibility of its effect on these schemas.

Thus we have seen that the use of these three simple operators GA reduces the complexity of the problem to be solved. Thus this high fitness, shorter length, less order schema represents various partial solutions to these problems, which are also known as building blocks. Thus many GA work parallel in many directions at a single point of time. Many new search spaces are explored by recombination of these many similarly templates present in the population. Thus this whole assumption in GA is known as building block hypothesis.

Past researches have shown that function whose solutions re misleading or deceptive in nature, GA have hard time in finding solutions to these problems in such isolated optima type of solutions. But GA in this case of misleading function can be misled to a certain extent. This proves the robustness of GA and it is encouraging. Due to this feature GA's are gaining popularity. Thus mathematical analysis of GA has led to better understanding of its working. In the later sections of this book working GA program in C++ language is written and implemented.

REFERENCES

Deb, K. (2000). *Optimization for Engineering Design: Algorithm and Examples*. Prentice Hall of India Private Limited.

Goldberg, D. E. (2002). *Genetic Algorithms in Search, Optimization and Machine Learning*. Pearson Education.

Haupt, R. L., & Haupt, S. A. (2004). *Practical Genetic Algorithms*. John Wiley and Sons, Inc.

Rajasekaran & Vijaylakshmi Pai. (2007). *Neural Networks, Fuzzy Logic, and Genetic algorithms, Synthesis and Applications*. Prentice- Hall of India Private Limited.

Section 2

Genetic Algorithms Theory and its Working

Chapter 5
Genetic Algorithm (GA) Methodology and Its Internal Working

ABSTRACT

Many practitioners are shy with implementing GAs. Due to this, a lot of researchers avoid using GAs as problem-solving techniques. It is desirable that an implementer of GA must be familiar in working with high-level computer languages. Implementation of GA involves complex coding and intricate computations which are of a repetitive nature. GAs if not implemented with caution will result in vague or bad solutions. This chapter overcomes the obstacles by implementing and defining various data structures required for implementing a simple GA. They will write various functions of GA code in C ++ programming language. In this chapter, initial string population generation, selection, crossover, and mutation operator used to optimize a simple function (one variable function) coded as unsigned binary integer is implemented using C ++ programming language. Mapping of fitness issue is also discussed in application of GAs.

5.1 A WORKING GENETIC ALGORITHM (GA) STEP BY STEP

In this section we will implement simple GA to demonstrate the basic steps or operators of a Genetic Algorithm (Hupt et. Al, 2004). In coming chapters

DOI: 10.4018/978-1-7998-4105-0.ch005

we will deeply look into the fact that how variations in GA's operators can be made to get best possible solution of a hard problem. Other advanced and sophisticated operators will also be discussed there.

In past it is seen that working of GA can be easily understood by applying it to a problem with large search space (Goldberg, 2002). Here we will understand about working of GA by applying it to a simple problem with a large search space.

A Genetic Algorithm Solution: Here the above topic refers to the implementation of a GA, not the solution given by GA. As there are number of variations about GA that can be implemented, solution quality obtained by GA for a given problem is discussed in later chapters of this book. The following steps will discuss about the fundamental characteristics of GA.

1. **Problem representation technique in GA:** The first pot whole or difficulty we have cross in implementing GA is to represent a problem (Deb, 2002). It requires a lot of thought process. GA works with strings which represents chromosomes (Genotype). These strings are potential solutions to the problem. The popular depictions of GA strings are of binary in nature. For example (01101011001). However other representation techniques are also used for ex. Alpha numeric (ep3e752a7p). These all string represents a perspective solution to a problem.

Initially population of strings is generated. These strings represent solution to a problem. These strings are gradually transformed into another string, generation after generation by imitating various biologically based operators. Here two strings will mate or recombine in some way to form two new strings. These newly formed strings may have solution quality better than previous strings. If their solution quality is better than they may influence the population. The most popular and straight forward way to represent a problem is binary encoding mechanism. For example binary number 011011 represents $(0*2^5 + 1*2^4 + 1*2^3 + 0*2^2 + 1*2^1 + 1*2^0)$ i.e value is 27. If we use 6 bits strings then maximum value is 11 11 11 i.e $(1*2^5 + 1*2^4 + 1*2^3 + 1*2^2 + 1*2^1 + 1*2^0 = 63)$ and minimum value is $(0*2^5 + 0*2^4 + 0*2^3 + 0*2^2 + 0*2^1 + 0*2^0 = 0)$. Formula to find a decimal equivalent of a binary string is raise 2 to the power of the string length minus 1. It represents $2^6 - 1 = 63$ for 6 bit string. For 5 bit string maximum number is $2^5 - 1 = 31$. If we use 6 bit string then our optimal solution value lies between 0 and 63, and if we use 5 bit string then our solution or optimal value lies between 0 and 32.

2. **Initialize the population:** There is no hard and fast rule to determine a population size. It can vary for problem to problem i.e from 20 to 200. It is seen that after certain number of iterations population tries to converge or concentrate or intersect around a particular search space or to a point. It means that most of the strings have similar binary configurations. Researchers have done various experiments by implementing GA with different population sizes and try to depict the effect on solution quality. Effect of changes in population size on solution quality is discussed in later chapters. Huge population size represents substantial diversity, which also requires more computation power also. Generally in our example problem we start with a population size of 50. It is a moderate number which simplifies our problem. As one get decided on the population size i.e 50's in number, introductory or first population size is randomly produced. This random initial generation of population is done by righting a code in a programming language of our convenience in computer. If string size is 10 and population size is 50, then there must be either 0 or 1 in 500 number bit positions. The value of 0's and 1's bit position is done actually by generating a random Boolean bit 0 or 1, by a coin toss. There must be approximate 250 bits with 1's and 250 bits with 0's as their values. Results are shown in the table below:

Sr. No.	String	F(x)
1.	0011101010	234
2.	0001010101	75
3.	1000000001	513
4.	1010000010	640
5.	1111111111	1023
6.	0000010011	19
.	.	.
.	.	.
.	.	.
.	.	.
50.	00 00 00 001	1

Initial population of strings generated in Genetic Algorithm.

3. **Calculate Fitness Function:** Now as we have generated initial population, we need to check their solution quality. Hence fitness function of each string is calculated. Fitness function calculation depends upon problem to problem. It can be simple and straight forward and can be time consuming.

In case to optimize parameter of a stock trading rule or to optimize a trading rule itself, fitness function calculation is time consuming and complicated. Fitness function of problem we had addressed later in this chapter is simple, but it has a very large search space i.e of the order of 2^{30}.

4. **Perform Selection:** Here in GA, various members of population compete with each other to get selected for mating, so that their off springs would gradually involve over subsequent generations. GA's are based on Darwin theory of survival of fittest. It means that only those strings have choice to survive which has above average fitness function. Thus GA's selection operators are designed in such a way that all odds are in favor of strings with above average fitness. Poor performer's string will eliminate in the successive generations. This process is in fact done by selection operator.

We start with simple selection operator. Here we will generate ranking of each string, which means that string with highest fitness function will have rank 1 and string with lowest fitness function will have rank 50th in a population with a size of 50. In next step average fitness function of the population is calculated. After that string which had below average fitness function are marked and replace with strings having above average fitness function randomly. Thus in this way average fitness function of the population is increased. We are now ready to perform crossover and mutation operations over the strings in the new population.

Another popular type of selection technique is roulette wheel selection. In this type of selection process string having higher fitness is having higher chances of probability to be get selected for mating and to pass their genes to next generation, then with the strings having lower fitness function or below average fitness function. Thus in this way better strings are entered into mating pool for next genetic operator to be applied. In some cases it is seen that if we are lucky, then in initial random generation of population a one or two strings are generated that have exceptionally high fitness function. So according to our previous selection schemes as discussed above, there will be a larger chance for this one or two strings with exceptional high fitness function to be get selected and replace strings with lower fitness function. This may result into converging of population of strings prematurely. So in this way after 10 t0 15 generations most of the below average fitness strings will be replaced by these close to optimal strings. Thus these strings will dominate the population.

It is widely seen from past work that greedy selection process results in an premature convergence of population. So in this way many optimal solutions and other vantage points which could be searched could be left behind or lost in the previous successive generations. Main drawback of greedy selection technique is that it decreases the genetic diversity in the population very quickly. Hence the chances to find an optimal or close to optimal solution are reduced. So result is that solution quality is decreased and many potential string combinations will be sacrificed in such a way. Thus GA will not have sufficient diversity left in its population of strings to explore the vast search space. This is popularly known as premature or advance convergence problem.

5.   **Perform Crossovers:** It is a very powerful operator presented in nature and adapted by GA. It is of exploitative in nature. Crossover operator helps us in searching various potential solutions. In this process two strings are selected for mating according to their fitness function by selection operator. This result in formation of two strings that may or may not have better fitness function then the parent strings selected. Crossover operator is completed in four steps.

1st step: Two above average strings are randomly chosen from the population with the help of selection operator.

2nd Step: Crossover probability is already assigned in the beginning of GA. If it is assigned 75% then random number is generated between 0 and 100, and if its value comes in between 0 and 75, then crossover is performed otherwise not.

3rd Step: If answer to perform crossover is yes then if string is 10 bit long then a random number is generated between 0 and maximum length of the string i.e between 0 and 10 if maximum string length is 10. If random value generated comes to be 7, then this point will be the crossover point of the two strings.

4th Step: Here we cut each string at the crossover point. First string generated will have bit position 1 to 6 from 1st parent string and bit position 7 to 10 from the 2nd parent string. While 2nd child string will have bit position 1 to 6 from 2nd parent string and bit position 7 to 10 from first parent string. In result there is a exchange of two tail pieces of the parent string. Actual working of crossover is shown below:

1 1 1 1 1 1 1 │1 1 1⎴ 1 1 1 1 1 1 1 0 0 0
0 0 0 0 0 0 0 │0 0 0 → 0 0 0 0 0 0 0 1 1 1

Past researches have shown that higher crossover probability rate is very effective to find optimal solution. But there is no actual value for crossover probability which will be uniform for all the problems, which are going to be solved by using GA's. Again I repeat that crossover is a real powerful tool which results in effective and efficient searching of the search space. It is difficult to picture the actual working of crossover. But I think this example will work for your convenience. It is seen that crossover gains much of the strength through selection operator. Due to the selection operator all the odds are in favour for strings having above average fitness. For example for a particular problem, the pattern 11011 in bit position 5 to 10 leads to a better solution and pattern 0101 from bit position 1 to 4 also leads to a better solution. If a string X has pattern 11011 in its bit position 5 to 10 and string Y has a bit pattern 0101 from position 1 to 4. If selection operator selects these two strings and crossover takes place then there is a larger possibility to have bit pattern 1101100101 through 1 to 10 (Bit numbers are taken from left to right). Thus child string will have fitness more than its two parent string as it has inherited better character tics of the two.

6. 6. **Perform Mutation:** Mutation operator is explorative in nature. It adds the much needed genetic diversity in the population. Procedure of mutation is that it generally converts 0 to 1 and vice versa. It is done bit by bit. Past researches have shown that mutation operator probability is generally very kept very low. If its probability is kept very high then it will disrupt the high order building blocks generated by selection and crossover operators. Here in mutation operator every bit is examined and if the probability permits then we flip 0 to 1 or 1 to 0 in that particular bit position. Below is the demonstration of mutation process:

0 0 0 1 1 0 1 0 1 0

↓

0 0 0 1 1 1 1 0 1 0

If mutation probability is 0.01 then it means roughly 10 out of 1000 bits examined will be mutated. Advance GA implementation allows us to vary mutation rate after every generation.

7. **Check Convergence:** Convergence is generally judged by studying the concept of bais, which means the degree of uniformity in the population. If in a population size of 100 and string length 30. If 75 strings has bit position 9 as 1 i.e 75 strings has 1's and 25 strings has 0's in bit position 9. Then biasing value for that bit pattern is 75. From this study we can easily explain string biasing. So convergence rate depends upon biasing value. If selection operator is of greedy in nature then population will converge at a faster rate. Hence rate of convergence will slow down as generation passes by. Population bias of 95% is said to be fully converge. It is seen that mutation disrupt the string patterns, higher mutation rate will not allow string to converge completely or to a high degree. In the final step after calculating convergence or biasness, we can stop GA or return to step 3 until desired result or convergence is reached. High degree of convergence of biasness means loss of genetic diversity in the population. There may be alternative termination criteria i.e if maximum number of generation in which GA has to run is completed. If convergence rate is very slow then we will have to adjust selection operator, crossover and mutation probability to get it to a acceptable level. If convergence rate is high or there is a premature convergence then we may not get optimal solution. Thus compromise or balance has to be made between quick answer and non optimal solution or high quality optimal solution and be patient.

5.2 SUMMARY OF VARIOUS STEPS OF GA

1. A basic or simple Genetic Algorithm (SGA) is of straight forward in nature (Rajasekaran et.al, 2007). Here all steps of GA can be implemented in various high level programming languages.
2. All the steps of GA's are of similar in nature for all problems. But the only step that is problem specific is fitness function calculation. Selection, crossover and mutation are same for each and every problem. They are applied blindly on the strings. Thus only link between GA and problem is the fitness function calculation. So GA in majority is a black box technique, which is of advantageous in nature. Hence it is clear that

all steps in GA are similar but fitness function calculation varies from problem to problem.

3. GA finds both optimal solution and near to optimal solution. For stock market problem where best solution is not known, the solution obtained by GA is easily acceptable. Here GA finds many vantage solutions and converges on to a practically good solution.

4. GA is well designed for various function optimization. Here one parameter or multiple parameter of function can be optimized to obtain a better value.

5.3 IMPLEMENTATION OF GA IN HIGHER LEVEL LANGUAGE SUCH AS C++

5.3.1 Data Declaration

Genetic Algorithm (GA) works on or process various population strings . Thus basic data structure of GA is string population. String population can be represented in number of ways. We will choose a similar way to represent it. A single string of population will be array of binary string numbers or individuals. Here each string represents a chromosome of each individual i.e the genotype. The decoded string represents parameters or parameters set. Each string has a fitness value i.e objective function assigned to it. A random generated population of strings is shown below:

0011 0101 1010 0100 0011 1111 0011 01value = 0.70289 Parent1 = 0
    Parent2 = 0 Cross Site0
0110 1001 0011 1011 1011 1110 0110 11value = 0.851432 Parent1 = 0
    Parent2 = 0 Cross Site0
1010 0000 1101 1111 1101 1000 0010 01value = 0.564208 Parent1 = 0
    Parent2 = 0 Cross Site0
1111 1100 0001 1010 0011 1000 0011 10value = 0.43923 Parent1 = 0
    Parent2 = 0 Cross Site0
0011 0100 0010 1100 1000 0111 1111 01value = 0.74812 Parent1 = 0
    Parent2 = 0 Cross Site0
1100 1000 1110 1010 0100 0100 1100 10value = 0.298971 Parent1 = 0
    Parent2 = 0 Cross Site0

1011 1001 0011 0110 0011 1000 0010 01value = 0.564235 Parent1 = 0
Parent2 = 0 Cross Site0

1101 1011 1010 0100 1110 1011 1001 10value = 0.403757Parent1 = 0Parent2
= 0Cross Site0

1101 0011 0010 1010 0100 1010 0100 11value = 0.786275Parent1 = 0Parent2
= 0Cross Site0

1011 1101 0100 0001 0000 1101 1001 00value = 0.151398Parent1 = 0Parent2
= 0Cross Site0

1110 0011 1100 1100 0010 1100 1011 00value = 0.206311Parent1 = 0Parent2
= 0Cross Site0

0111 1000 0010 0110 1111 1111 1011 10value = 0.468713Parent1 = 0Parent2
= 0Cross Site0

0011 0111 0010 0100 0011 1101 0111 11value = 0.980233Parent1 = 0Parent2
= 0Cross Site0

0100 1010 0101 1101 0001 1110 0110 10value = 0.351119Parent1 = 0Parent2
= 0Cross Site0

1111 1110 1101 1100 0010 1111 0110 00value = 0.108657Parent1 = 0Parent2
= 0Cross Site0

0000 1111 0011 1111 0110 0110 0101 00value = 0.162536Parent1 = 0Parent2
= 0Cross Site0

1101 1100 0101 1000 0100 1111 0111 11value = 0.983527Parent1 = 0Parent2
= 0Cross Site0

0110 1011 0001 1110 0111 1101 0001 00value = 0.136625Parent1 = 0Parent2
= 0Cross Site0

0010 0110 0011 0011 0101 0000 1111 11value = 0.985034Parent1 = 0Parent2
= 0Cross Site0

1000 1010 0111 1111 0110 0101 0001 11value = 0.885192Parent1 = 0Parent2
= 0Cross Site0

0110 0000 1000 1011 1010 1000 0110 11value = 0.845082Parent1 = 0Parent2
= 0Cross Site0

1011 1100 1101 0100 1110 1011 0100 00value = 0.044383Parent1 = 0Parent2
= 0Cross Site0

0010 0010 0110 0111 1011 0100 1011 01value = 0.705926Parent1 = 0Parent2
= 0Cross Site0

1011 0101 0100 0110 1100 0100 0101 10value = 0.40841Parent1 = 0Parent2
= 0Cross Site0

0000 1001 1000 0110 0111 0011 1011 11value = 0.965721Parent1 = 0Parent2
= 0Cross Site0

1000 0001 1000 0111 0001 1110 0000 00value = 0.007378Parent1 = 0Parent2 = 0Cross Site0

1111 0110 0111 1010 0010 0001 0000 00value = 0.008079Parent1 = 0Parent2 = 0Cross Site0

0100 0000 1101 0000 1000 0010 0001 11value = 0.87897Parent1 = 0Parent2 = 0Cross Site0

1111 0010 1100 1100 1100 0011 0000 10value = 0.261914Parent1 = 0Parent2 = 0Cross Site0

0110 0110 0001 0100 1000 1000 0110 01value = 0.594797Parent1 = 0Parent2 = 0Cross Site0

1111 0100 1001 1110 1010 0100 0000 11value = 0.752287Parent1 = 0Parent2 = 0Cross Site0

0000 0001 1111 0011 1110 0000 0111 11value = 0.969227Parent1 = 0Parent2 = 0Cross Site0

0111 0110 0111 0010 0001 1011 1101 00value = 0.185077Parent1 = 0Parent2 = 0Cross Site0

1010 0011 1000 1110 0110 1011 1001 01value = 0.653714Parent1 = 0Parent2 = 0Cross Site0

0001 1111 0010 1010 0011 0010 0011 10value = 0.442159Parent1 = 0Parent2 = 0Cross Site0

1100 1001 1000 0101 1010 0100 1101 00value = 0.174172Parent1 = 0Parent2 = 0Cross Site0

1010 1011 0001 0100 0000 1011 1011 11value = 0.96583Parent1 = 0Parent2 = 0Cross Site0

0100 1010 1100 1110 0000 0101 0110 11value = 0.853543Parent1 = 0Parent2 = 0Cross Site0

0011 1000 1110 1111 0100 0011 1111 10value = 0.496275Parent1 = 0Parent2 = 0Cross Site0

1010 0011 1010 1111 0101 0000 0100 01value = 0.531919Parent1 = 0Parent2 = 0Cross Site0

1100 1110 1100 1100 0010 1100 1111 00value = 0.237561Parent1 = 0Parent2 = 0Cross Site0

0100 0110 1110 1001 1110 1000 0101 11value = 0.90769Parent1 = 0Parent2 = 0Cross Site0

1000 1111 1011 0111 1011 0101 1001 00value = 0.151241Parent1 = 0Parent2 = 0Cross Site0

0001 0110 0100 0010 0011 1100 1111 00value = 0.238053Parent1 = 0Parent2 = 0Cross Site0

0101 1110 1010 0000 1011 0000 0011 11value = 0.938295Parent1 = 0Parent2 = 0Cross Site0

0001 1010 0000 0110 1000 0010 1010 00value = 0.082115Parent1 = 0Parent2 = 0Cross Site0

average fitness 0.518099 min. value 0.007378 max. value 0.987394 generation = 0

The C++ code given below is self confessed population structure corresponding to the model.

```
struct population
{
int a[30];
float value;
int p1;
int p2;
int crosss;
} oldp[50],newp[50];    → Maximum Population Size
```

5.3.2 Data Type Declaration in C++ Language for GA

Here maximum population size is kept to 50 and strength length is 30. These two parameters could be change from problem to problem. But in our problem upper bound of string length and population size is 30 and 50. Various other declarations are also made in the structure of population. Here population is an array of individuals i.e oldp[50] and newp[50]. Here individual's values is a array of binary values of 0's and 1's. These individuals are called chromosomes and their fitness values are placed in variable named as value. The data type given to value is float. This fitness value is the decoded value of the string. This string is itself an array of numbers with data type declared as int. The values of array will be 0 or 1. Here in our simple genetic algorithm after the random generation of population of strings, basic operators as discussed above are, such as crossover, mutation are applied to the entire population of the strings, not to a single string itself. This is shown below:

```
oldp[50]                    newp[50]
1.                             1.
2.                                  2.
3.                             3.
4.                                  4.
5.Reproduction, Crossover and Mutation    5.
```

```
 .                                          .
 .                                          .
 .                                          .
 .                                          .
47.                                        47.
48.                                        48.
49.                                        49.
50.                                        50.
Generation 1
```

Passing of one population set to another in one generation.

To get this process run in a smoother way, we have declared two population set oldp[50] and newp[50]. These two population set are of non overlapping in nature. Their declarations are shown earlier in the structure declared. The structure of population is declared as global variable in our C++ program. The advantage of having global variable is that in C++ it can be accessed in any of the function declared in the main() program. Thus with these two set of population oldp[50] and newp[50]. Genetic operators such as crossover and mutation are applied to oldp[50] entirely to get newp[50]. There are other effective procedure to store oldp[50] and newp[50] such as pointers. But in order to make things simple we have chosen data types to store these variables in the structure. We could also maintain a single population size, but it will create more confusion that which individual string replaces whom. Here we kept population size constant in each generation. But in advance GA population size may change from generation to generation. Hence to start with and to keep things simple initially we have chosen two sets of non overlapping population with constant size. In the later chapter of our book we will discuss the change in population size have effect on solution quality in detail.

With the structure of population declared, there is a need to implement three operators such as selection, crossover and mutation to be implemented for a successful GA run. But to implement these three operators we need to declare and explain some more data types. Some of these data types are of integer and some are of float types. Initially we had declared maximum population size to 50 and maximum string length to 30. Other important global variables are crossover probability (PC = Cross), mutation probability (Pm = m), sum fitness. The variable sum fitness is given data type float; it is the sum of fitness o the whole population. This variable is extensively used in roulette wheel selection technique. There are few other variables declared in the main program function, which we will be discussing while describing that function.

5.3.4 Implementing Selection, Crossover and Mutation

In this section we will get the explanation about the implementation of these three popular GA operators. We had discussed about the theory and working of these operators in detail in the previous section of this book. So to start with the coding that is same in all these three operators are random number generation.

```
Random: random(101); returns a real pseudo random number
between 0 and 100.
```

```
Random(30); returns a real pseudo random number between 0 and
30.
```

Here this random number generated is stored to a variable declared as integer and is then used further. A more comprehensive explanation about the random number generation is discussed in programming language book of C++.

In our problem we had chosen roulette wheel as main selection operator. The function we had declared is selection() in our main() program. Here in roulette wheel weighted slots are given according to the string fitness values. Our function int selection() returns a integer value or number of the string selected. We had also declared variable as partsum as float data type. Another variable rando gives us the point where the pointer of the wheel is touched down after a random run in our computation procedure. Here sum of the fitness of the population is declared as sumfitness variable with data type as float. This variable sumfitness is declared as global variable in our program, which means that it can be accessed in any function. Sumfitness is already calculated in statistics() function declared in the main program globally. In our procedure sumfitness is multiplied by normalized random number generated r1 and we get a value named rando. After this while loop is implemented with true condition that partsum is greater or equal to the value rando and pointer value i should be less then maximum population size value i.e 50. Hence number of times while loop is executed, the pointer is incremented by 1. After this while loop is terminated, the function return the landed value of the pointer or population index value i.

```
int selection()
{int i; float r1,r, partsum, rando;
partsum = 0; i = 0;
r = random(100);
r1 = (float)r/100;
rando = r1*sumfitness;
while(partsum< = rando && i<50)
 {
partsum = partsum+oldp[i].value;i = i+1;
}
return(i-1);}
```

Roulette Wheel Selection Operator Implementation

The code shown above is a straight forward way to implement selection operator. This operator can be implemented in a more efficient way also. Apart from roulette wheel selection technique there are other selection techniques also which can be used. We are going to discuss these techniques in detail in the coming chapters. This roulette wheel selection implementation code gives us a simplest and effective way to select a parent string for next generation.

After the selection operator comes the crossover operator. Implemented code of crossover operator is given below. Here first two parents' parent 1 and parent 2 are selected by the use of selection operator. Detail procedure of working of crossover operator is discussed in the previous section of the book. By application of this crossover operator two offspring or child strings child 1 and child 2 are generated. The probability of crossover operator and mutation operator is set in the beginning of the main program. Our implementation of crossover operator is similar to the working of crossover operator discussed in the previous chapters.

```
void generation()//Crossover & Mutation
{ //static int f = 0;
int g;
g = random(101);
if(g<cross)    //Crossover
{
for(i = 0;i<50;i = i+2)
{
int crss = random(30);
```

```
// cout<<"crossover site is"<<crss;
// cout<<endl;
int p = selection(); // Selection operator calling
int q = selection(); // Selection operator calling
newp[i].p1 = p; // Parent 1 of offspring 1
newp[i].p2 = q; // Parent 2 of offspring 1
newp[i].crosss = crss; // Crossover site
newp[i+1].p1 = p; // Parent 1 of offspring 2
newp[i+1].p2 = q; // Parent 1 of offspring 2
newp[i+1].crosss = crss;
for(j = 0;j<crss;j++)
newp[i].a[j] = oldp[p].a[j];
for(j = crss;j<30;j++)
newp[i].a[j] = oldp[q].a[j];
 for(j = 0;j<crss;j++)
newp[i+1].a[j] = oldp[q].a[j];
for(j = crss;j<30;j++)
newp[i+1].a[j] = oldp[p].a[j]; }
for(i = 0;i<50;i++)    //Mutation Process started
{
for(j = 0;j<30;j++)
{ int g1;
 g1 = random(1000);
 if(g1<m)
 { if(newp[i].a[j] = = 0)
 newp[i].a[j] = 1;
 else
 newp[i].a[j] = 0;}
      }
} }
 else
{ for(i = 0;i<50;i++)
newp[i] = oldp[i];
for(i = 0;i<50;i++)
{
for(j = 0;j<30;j++)
{ int g1;
 g1 = random(1000);
 if(g1<m)
 { if(newp[i].a[j] = = 0)
 newp[i].a[j] = 1;
 else
 newp[i].a[j] = 0;}
 }
}
    } }
```

Crossover Operator Implementation

Initially we generate a random number between 0 and 100. If its value comes to be less than the value of the crossover number we had decided in the beginning of the program, then crossover will take place otherwise mutation will be performed. If crossover takes place then we will generate a random number between 0 and maximum string length says 30 in case of our example. This random number generated will give us the crossover site. Finally exchange of strings will take place in crossover. Exchange of strings will take place between parent 1 and child 1, parent 2 and child 2, so on. After the successful completion of crossover operator mutation operator will be implemented.

Mutation process is shown in the code. Here we use two nested for loop. First loop represents the maximum population in use and second loop represents string length size. Since mutation probability is kept very low i.e of the order of 1% or 0.01. Which means roughly every 10 bits will be mutated in a total of 1000 bits checked? Here every bit is selected and condition is checked using if else statement. If it comes true then the bit value changes from 0 to 1 and vice versa. Thus in our example random number is generated for 50 * 30 i.e 1500 times. This consumes a lot of time and computation resource. There can be another way, if we already select the bit positions and number of bits which are to be mutated. This type of sophisticated implementation of mutation operator is avoided in order to keep things simple.

Together with the use of selection, crossover and mutation operator we will create a new population newp[50], from old population oldp[50]. After the creation of new population its strings are copied into old population by a simple code using for loop.

```
for(i = 0;i<50;i++)
oldp[i] = newp[i];
```

Thus again on this oldp[50] selection, crossover and mutation are applied and next generation population i.e newp[50] is generated which is again copied into old population oldp[50] and so on, until termination criteria is met with or maximum number of generations are over. So we discussed and implemented these three main genetic algorithm operators. They are mystifying in nature. We have understood their theory and implemented their coding in C++ language.

5.3.4 Calculate Objective Function

We have seen that we pick two strings i.e mate 1 and mate 2 for crossover by using selection() function. We apply crossover and mutation operator in the generation() function. After this we decode the string into their actual parameter values and calculate the objective function. So after the successful implementation of selection, crossover and mutation operators, we will now turn our attention towards problem specific functions. The routines of selection, crossover and mutation are almost same for every problem. For every problem there will be different set of parameters. Thus in orders to calculate objective function of a particular string, first we have to decode the string to find parameter or set of parameters that string represent. After the value of parameter or parameter set is obtained, we then proceed to calculate objective function value associated with the parameter or parameter set, which indirectly represents the string. Depending upon the problem we will have different decoding procedures and objective function calculations. To start with a particular decoding procedure and objective function calculation of the example we have implemented in this book. In our example our binary string is decoded starting from a lower order bit position 0 from left to right by summation of current power of two when bit position is 1 i.e Pow(2,i). This accumulated value is used to find the objective function of thart particular string. The objective function calculation in our simple genetic algorithm is simple calculation of converting binary string into decimal equivalent. Here our objective function is:

$$F(x) = (x \, / \, \text{Coefficient})$$

Since maximum length of our string is 30 bit. Hence coefficient is 2^{30} − 1 i.e 1073741823, which means the maximum value of the string. Thus $F(x)$ for that string with 1's until 30th bit position will be 1 and for minimum value be 0 for string having 0's until 30th bit position. A simple and straight forward code for parameter calculation and objective function calculation is given below:

```
float objfun(int a[]) //Calculate Objective Function
{long int value = 0; int i; float value1;
for(i = 0;i<30;i++)
{ if (a[i] = = 1)
value = value + pow(2,i);}
value1 = (float) value/1073741823;
```

```
return value1;}
Objective Function Implementation
```

5.3.5 Now Start With the Main Program

In our previous sections we had got glimpse about the various data structures used in the GA implementation. In previous section we had implemented selection, crossover, mutation operator function decoded as strings, find objective function or fitness function of the string. Now we have to go for main program and call these functions one by one to get GA program implemented as a whole. Our main program starts by asking genetic crossover and mutation probabilities from the GA user. Initial population will have parent 1 and parent 2 zero as their value. Since initial population is generated randomly. Code for initial population generated function is given below:

```
void initialize()//Generate Initial Population
{ int x,i,j;
time_t t;
srand((unsigned) time(&t));
for(i = 0;i<50;i++)
{ for(j = 0;j<30;j++)
{ x = rand() % 100;
if (x < 51)
oldp[i].a[j] = 0;
else
oldp[i].a[j] = 1;}}
              }
```

Main Program

Here coin is flipped and equal weight age is given for assignment of 0 or 1 to the population string as it is of binary in nature. In our code implemented we generate a random number from 0 to 100. Here random number is generated for every bit. If the value of random number is below 51 then 0 is assigned to that particular bit position otherwise 1 is assigned. This procedure is repeated for every bit position. For this nested For loop is used. 1st For loop represented maximum population size and second For loop represented maximum string length.

84

After generation of main population we go to writereport(); function. This unction print whole string population, their objective function values, parent 1, parent 2 and their crossover site. Initially parent 1, parent 2 and crossover site has been assigned value 0. After that statistics(); function is called which calculates average, maximum and minimum fitness function or objective function values. Code for statistics function is given below:

```
void statistics() //Calculate & print max., min. & avg.
objective function values of a generation
{
 sumfitness = 0;
float avgfitness;
int i;
for(i = 0;i<50;i++)
sumfitness = oldp[i].value + sumfitness;
 avgfitness = sumfitness/50;
 cout<< "          "<< avgfitness;
 float min;
 min = oldp[0].value;
 for(i = 0;i<50;i++)
 { if(oldp[i].value< min)
 min = oldp[i].value;
 }
 // cout<<"min. value"<< min;
 float max;
 max = oldp[0].value;
 for(i = 0;i<50;i++)
 { if(oldp[i].value>max)
 max = oldp[i].value;
 }
 cout<<"       "<<max;
 }
```

Thus statistical routine calculated by us is the minimal acceptable routine. Many other intresting population statistics such as standard deviation or dispersion of the population for a particular generation so far can be strored for future use. So all other advance statistical parameters will be use for detail scrutiny of the GA run to test its robustness. After this writerepot(); function is called to list the string population. Below is the code for writereport(); function:

```
void writereport() //Print Whole Population & their objective
function values & parents p1 & p2, cross over site
{ cout<<"Initial population generated is"<<endl;
for(int i = 0;i<50;i++)
```

```
{ for(int j = 0;j<30;j++)
cout<<oldp[i].a[j];
//cout<<endl;
 oldp[i].value = objfun(oldp[i].a);
 cout<<"value = "<<oldp[i].value;
 cout<<"Parent1 = "<<oldp[i].p1;
 cout<<"Parent2 = "<<oldp[i].p2;
 cout<<"Cross Site"<<oldp[i].crosss;
 cout<<endl;
 }       }
```

Thus listing of the population strings and their objective function values can also be done in various other tabular and graphic form of writing the code in writereport(); function depending upon the problem. This is the simplest form of report we had printed on the screen. This writereport(); function help us to make comparison of results of various generations. This helps us to see the robustness of GA results for a variety of operators used. Thus helps in finding the best individual. To come to an end we had written codes of all the operators and statistical function to check the GA results. Now we will enclose all these function declared and call them in our main function step by step. Below is the code of the main(); function program, in which all the functions are called in a sequential manner.

```
void main()
{ clrscr();
cout<<"Enter mutation probability"<<endl;
cin>>m;
cout<<m<<endl;
//s = m*50*8;
cout<<"Enter crossover probability in percentage"<<endl;
cin>>cross;
for(i = 0;i<50;i++)
{ oldp[i].p1 = 0;
 oldp[i].p2 = 0;
 oldp[i].crosss = 0;}
initialize();//Generate Initial Population
writereport();//Print Whole Population & their objective
function values & parents p1 & p2, cross over site
getch();
statistics();//Calculate & print max., min. & avg. objective
function values of a generation
for(int z = 0;z<50;z++)
{
generation();//Crossover & Mutation
for(i = 0;i<50;i++)
```

```
oldp[i] = newp[i];
//writereport();
calcobjfun();//Calculate Objective Function
statistics();//Calculate & print max., min. & avg. objective
function values of a generation
cout<<"      "<<z<<endl;
getch();
 }
getch();
}
Main Program of Simple Genetic Algorithm
```

5.4 WORKING OF GENETIC ALGORITHM AS A WHOLE TO SOLVE THE PROBLEM

As seen in our previous chapters we have walked slowly and steadily with heavy steps and cover a difficult surface of Genetic Algorithm GA code inch by inch. Now we get a better feel about the GA. We came to know about pros and cons, ins and outs of the Genetic programming ways. We can bell the cat known as GA by implementing it in a variety of ways. There are a large number of codes available over internet i.e in a public view in which GA has been implemented in a variety of ways. There are many codes for a variety of other problems where their parameters are to be optimized. Here until now we have covered implementation of basic operators such as crossover, mutation and selection in code implementation. There are a number of various others advance and sophisticated operators in GA, which helps us to find many peaks in our problem. These advance operators or features will be discussed in the later chapters of the book. At this point I will not be tempted by these fancy features or operators of GA. Now in next section we are going to discuss the results obtained by running our simple Genetic Algorithm program or code we had implemented.

We already explained the test problem which we had over took. Here the string length is 30 bit s and it decipher into a integer. The fitness function is a normal function, $F(x) = x/c$. Where the value of 'c' is used to normalize the value of $F(x)$. Initially in our earlier chapters we have chosen different fitness function i.e $F(x) = x^2$. There we had solved the problem by using simple GA applied by hand. There the string length was short i.e $l = 5$. Thus the search space for it was $2^5 = 32$ points. Practically it could be solved quickly by using any traditional search methods or just by random walk or by brute force technique. But at the starting point our aim was to get an insight about the working of GA. Working with clarity, so we had chosen a limited search space. As we had settled with it, we go for a much difficult and heavier problem with a huge search space. We increased the string from $l = 5$ to $l = 30$. Thus the search space is increased from 32 to 2^{30} i.e $1.07 * 10^{10}$ points. Hence with more than 1 billion points brute force attack is not a viable and quick option. Thus with the increase of search space we had made problem more tougher and appropriate to be solve with the help of GA.

With a large search space in GA we start with the generation of random population of strings. It is believed that a random population initially generated will not have strings that represent good solutions. To start with the running of simple Genetic Algorithm (SGA) code, we are going to decide at what GA operators settings we are going to run the program. Previous researchers has shown that high crossover probability (range 0.75 to 0.95) in combination with low mutation probability (0.01) and moderate population size (50) gives us the desired results. With this we run our SGA program with crossover probability 0.90, mutation probably value 0.01 and population size of 50 for a 50 number of generations. We run our SGA program for 50 generations. Performance graph is shown in Figure 1.

Figure 1. Maximum Performance of GA for various Crossover and Mutation probabilities for function f1.

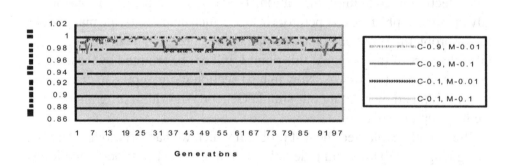

Initial population generated is gen = 0 and population generated after 1st generation is gen = 1, and after that is gen = 3 and so on which is shown below:

$$Population\ size = 50.$$
$$String\ or\ chromosome\ length = 30.$$
$$Total\ number\ of\ Generations = 50$$
$$Crossover\ Probability = 0.9$$
$$Mutation\ Probability = 0.01.$$

$\left. \right\}$ *Various SGA Parameters*

As our results shows that our population begins with a initial average fitness value 1611.13, maximum fitness value is 3452.42. We expect 30 * (1- (Max fitness value)$^{0.1}$) number of strings with fitness value greater than maximum fitness value. By seeing our population we are not so lucky at the beginning. Though average fitness value of population is not too large. We should not feel depressed. As we run GA for few generations our average fitness function and maximum fitness function of strings improves. Our performance increases exponentially as compared to the initial results obtained, which is shown in the graph. So as the generations passes by there is a continuous improvement in average and maximum fitness function of the population. After the run for few generations our results get converge to a particular higher point. In final point difference between average fitness function and maximum fitness function narrows down. Though we do not get the best point, but we are close to the best point in the search space. In some problem population converges prematurely without reaching the top point in the solution. So to avoid such a situation, many variations in design parameters of operators in GA is to be done to achieve better solution. We will discuss this situation in detail in the coming chapters of the book. Avoiding premature convergence will lead us to find many vantage points in the search space. This increases the efficiency of GA and their ability to find better solutions in a variety of NP hard problems.

It was seen that other traditional search techniques converges to a local optima quickly. As there is no means to bring them out of local space. This results in sacrificing the algorithm ability to find a global optima solution. To overcome such situation GA is used. Hence in a hybrid system we use both GA in combination with traditional technique. If in a problem there are many local peaks, start with GA to find these local peaks, as GA ability to fond various vantage points parallel. On these many vantage points are obtained, a traditional technique is applied on these local optima points to get global optima or improve in the result. In this way by applying this hybrid optima technique both efficiency and efficacy is increased. So problem of premature

Table 1. SGA run for generation 1 and generation 2.

Generation 1	Generation 2
0110 0110 0010 0101 0000 value = 1945.796631 Parent1 = 42 Parent2 = 19 Cross Site5	1000 0110 0000 0011 0001 value = 600.81665 Parent1 = 15 Parent2 = 20 Cross Site15
1010 0010 0001 0100 0000 value = 2462.170654 Parent1 = 42 Parent2 = 19 Cross Site5	1100 1010 0010 0110 1100 value = 1574.2854 Parent1 = 15 Parent2 = 20 Cross Site15
1000 0001 1111 1001 1000 value = 1497.41394 Parent1 = 9 Parent2 = 49 Cross Site10	1000 0110 0010 0100 0000 value = 2115.104736 Parent1 = 15 Parent2 = 44 Cross Site8
0101 0100 1101 1110 0101 value = 55.159428 Parent1 = 9 Parent2 = 49 Cross Site10	0001 1001 0000 0010 1100 value = 1005.999146 Parent1 = 15 Parent2 = 44 Cross Site8
0011 0111 1111 1101 1000 value = 2782.719238 Parent1 = 16 Parent2 = 14 Cross Site9	1010 0010 0001 0100 0000 value = 2462.170654 Parent1 = 3 Parent2 = 18 Cross Site17
0110 0111 0110 0001 0001 value = 46.426941 Parent1 = 16 Parent2 = 14 Cross Site9	1011 1111 1100 1110 0000 value = 3434.122559 Parent1 = 3 Parent2 = 18 Cross Site17
1100 0010 0001 0100 0000 value = 2489.162354 Parent1 = 4 Parent2 = 42 Cross Site3	1001 1101 0001 0100 0000 value = 1294.497192 Parent1 = 24 Parent2 = 17 Cross Site5
0110 1010 0010 0101 0000 value = 2130.313838 Parent1 = 4 Parent2 = 42 Cross Site3	0000 1000 0000 0001 0000 value = 3176.683105 Parent1 = 24 Parent2 = 17 Cross Site5
1100 1010 0001 0100 0000 value = 2280.616699 Parent1 = 34 Parent2 = 42 Cross Site5	0001 1000 0010 0100 0000 value = 3142.484863 Parent1 = 44 Parent2 = 10 Cross Site17
0110 0010 0001 0100 0000 value = 2448.775146 Parent1 = 34 Parent2 = 42 Cross Site5	1100 1010 0001 0100 0000 value = 2280.616699 Parent1 = 44 Parent2 = 10 Cross Site17
1100 0111 0111 1101 1100 value = 344.773956 Parent1 = 24 Parent2 = 15 Cross Site4	1001 1000 0000 0000 1110 value = 1503.666504 Parent1 = 24 Parent2 = 13 Cross Site14
0110 1011 1101 0100 1110 value = 1292.128296 Parent1 = 24 Parent2 = 15 Cross Site4	0110 1011 1101 0101 0000 value = 2725.78125 Parent1 = 24 Parent2 = 13 Cross Site14
1011 0111 0001 1010 0100 value = 662.473633 Parent1 = 0 Parent2 = 46 Cross Site3	1000 0110 0000 0010 1100 value = 1867.874756 Parent1 = 15 Parent2 = 10 Cross Site17
1000 0110 0000 0010 1100 value = 1461.108154 Parent1 = 0 Parent2 = 46 Cross Site3	1100 1010 0001 0100 0100 value = 1828.391724 Parent1 = 15 Parent2 = 10 Cross Site17
0000 1100 1101 0100 1110 value = 264.669495 Parent1 = 25 Parent2 = 13 Cross Site8	1011 1111 1010 0101 0000 value = 339.499756 Parent1 = 18 Parent2 = 33 Cross Site8
0000 1101 0001 0100 0000 value = 1360.903687 Parent1 = 25 Parent2 = 13 Cross Site8	1011 1111 1100 1110 0000 value = 3434.122559 Parent1 = 18 Parent2 = 33 Cross Site8
1011 1111 1100 1110 0000 value = 3434.122559 Parent1 = 2 Parent2 = 45 Cross Site1	0110 0010 0010 0101 0000 value = 2330.462646 Parent1 = 27 Parent2 = 20 Cross Site3
1001 0000 0011 1101 0110 value = 1752.050171 Parent1 = 2 Parent2 = 45 Cross Site1	1101 1111 1100 1110 0000 value = 3397.762695 Parent1 = 27 Parent2 = 20 Cross Site3
1100 1010 0010 0101 0000 value = 2166.496094 Parent1 = 4 Parent2 = 4 Cross Site2	1010 0010 0000 0101 0000 value = 2347.312012 Parent1 = 26 Parent2 = 20 Cross Site11
1100 1010 0110 0101 0000 value = 379.255554 Parent1 = 4 Parent2 = 4 Cross Site2	1100 1010 0011 0100 0000 value = 2276.889404 Parent1 = 26 Parent2 = 20 Cross Site11
0011 0111 1010 0100 1110 value = 5.950563 Parent1 = 16 Parent2 = 13 Cross Site13	0000 0100 0010 1101 1110 value = 1295.282593 Parent1 = 40 Parent2 = 40 Cross Site10
0000 1101 1101 0001 0001 value = 743.005981 Parent1 = 16 Parent2 = 13 Cross Site13	0000 0100 0011 1101 1100 value = 2106.509766 Parent1 = 40 Parent2 = 40 Cross Site10
1001 1000 0000 0001 0000 value = 3026.196289 Parent1 = 47 Parent2 = 19 Cross Site14	1000 0001 1111 1001 1000 value = 1497.41394 Parent1 = 4 Parent2 = 38 Cross Site18
1010 0110 0010 0110 1100 value = 1396.44104 Parent1 = 47 Parent2 = 19 Cross Site14	0001 1011 0011 1010 0100 value = 757.921631 Parent1 = 4 Parent2 = 38 Cross Site18
1010 0010 0001 0100 0000 value = 2462.170654 Parent1 = 45 Parent2 = 42 Cross Site3	0110 0111 1110 1110 0000 value = 3035.79541 Parent1 = 2 Parent2 = 48 Cross Site3
0111 1111 1100 1110 0000 value = 3452.429199 Parent1 = 45 Parent2 = 42 Cross Site3	0000 0110 0010 0101 0000 value = 2013.141357 Parent1 = 2 Parent2 = 48 Cross Site3
0001 1000 0101 0110 0010 value = 82.998642 Parent1 = 1 Parent2 = 6 Cross Site9	1000 0110 0000 0010 1101 value = 335.019623 Parent1 = 15 Parent2 = 4 Cross Site19
1000 0010 1010 0101 1000 value = 462.834534 Parent1 = 1 Parent2 = 6 Cross Site9	1000 0001 1111 1001 1000 value = 1497.41394 Parent1 = 15 Parent2 = 4 Cross Site19
1001 1001 0000 0101 0000 value = 1456.256226 Parent1 = 47 Parent2 = 19 Cross Site11	1011 1110 0010 0101 0000 value = 1827.748169 Parent1 = 1 Parent2 = 41 Cross Site0
1010 0110 0010 0010 1100 value = 1419.860474 Parent1 = 47 Parent2 = 19 Cross Site11	1100 1100 0001 0100 0000 value = 2714.975586 Parent1 = 1 Parent2 = 41 Cross Site0
1010 0110 1100 1111 0000 value = 1383.536255 Parent1 = 19 Parent2 = 45 Cross Site8	0001 1000 0010 0100 0100 value = 2607.161621 Parent1 = 44 Parent2 = 15 Cross Site17
1011 1111 0010 0101 0000 value = 822.751526 Parent1 = 19 Parent2 = 45 Cross Site8	1000 0110 0001 0010 1000 value = 1861.133789 Parent1 = 44 Parent2 = 15 Cross Site17
1100 0010 1101 0100 0000 value = 1268.063354 Parent1 = 6 Parent2 = 25 Cross Site12	0001 1000 0000 0010 0100 value = 2579.331055 Parent1 = 47 Parent2 = 44 Cross Site18
0000 1100 0001 0110 0010 value = 1756.69812 Parent1 = 6 Parent2 = 25 Cross Site12	0001 1000 0010 0100 0000 value = 3142.484863 Parent1 = 47 Parent2 = 44 Cross Site18
0110 0010 0001 0100 1100 value = 1763.261719 Parent1 = 42 Parent2 = 31 Cross Site15	0110 0010 0001 1111 0000 value = 2251.985107 Parent1 = 36 Parent2 = 27 Cross Site12
1001 0111 0011 0010 0000 value = 972.525513 Parent1 = 42 Parent2 = 31 Cross Site15	0111 1111 1100 1100 1100 value = 2691.199463 Parent1 = 36 Parent2 = 27 Cross Site12
0001 1011 0011 1010 0100 value = 757.921631 Parent1 = 10 Parent2 = 46 Cross Site6	1000 0010 0001 0110 0010 value = 2516.42334 Parent1 = 15 Parent2 = 26 Cross Site3
1001 0000 0000 0010 0100 value = 2815.0625 Parent1 = 10 Parent2 = 46 Cross Site6	1010 0110 0000 0010 1100 value = 1422.801636 Parent1 = 15 Parent2 = 26 Cross Site3
0000 0100 0011 1101 1 110 value = 1289.677856 Parent1 = 37 Parent2 = 41 Cross Site5	1011 0111 1111 0101 1000 value = 2815.221191 Parent1 = 48 Parent2 = 6 Cross Site1
1000 1110 0010 0101 0000 value = 1827.748169 Parent1 = 37 Parent2 = 41 Cross Site5	0000 0111 1100 1110 0000 value = 2938.804688 Parent1 = 48 Parent2 = 6 Cross Site1
0000 1011 1101 1110 0101 value = 718.334961 Parent1 = 30 Parent2 = 9 Cross Site2	0100 0010 0001 0100 1000 value = 2259.015381 Parent1 = 2 Parent2 = 8 Cross Site1
1001 1000 0010 1000 0100 value = 2607.902832 Parent1 = 30 Parent2 = 9 Cross Site2	1110 0110 0010 0101 0000 value = 1934.777954 Parent1 = 2 Parent2 = 8 Cross Site1
0001 1000 0010 0100 0000 value = 3142.484863 Parent1 = 30 Parent2 = 5 Cross Site12	1011 0111 0000 0001 0000 value = 920.499084 Parent1 = 14 Parent2 = 24 Cross Site9
1010 0110 0001 1000 0100 value = 1648.934448 Parent1 = 30 Parent2 = 5 Cross Site12	1001 1000 0001 1010 0100 value = 2540.563965 Parent1 = 14 Parent2 = 24 Cross Site9
0001 1000 0000 0000 0100 value = 2643.164063 Parent1 = 10 Parent2 = 10 Cross Site7	0001 1000 0010 1000 0100 value = 2623.132324 Parent1 = 47 Parent2 = 43 Cross Site4
0001 1000 0000 0010 0100 value = 2579.331055 Parent1 = 10 Parent2 = 10 Cross Site7	1001 1000 0010 0100 0100 value = 2564.229736 Parent1 = 47 Parent2 = 43 Cross Site4
0000 0111 1100 1110 0000 value = 2938.804688 Parent1 = 38 Parent2 = 45 Cross Site5	1001 1000 0000 0001 0000 value = 3026.196289 Parent1 = 24 Parent2 = 43 Cross Site18
1011 1010 1101 0110 0010 value = 764.585754 Parent1 = 38 Parent2 = 45 Cross Site5	1001 1000 0010 1000 0100 value = 2607.902832 Parent1 = 24 Parent2 = 43 Cross Site18
average fitness 1611.138428 min. value 5.950563 max. value 3452.429199 generation = 1	average fitness 2110.324463 min. value 335.019623 max. value 3434.122559 generation = 2

convergence is solved practically. In next section we are going to investigate various coding procedures, we use to map with the solutions in implementing of GA. Until now we are using binary encoding mechanism so far.

5.5 CODING

Until now we had used binary string coding for mapping the parameter or parameters value to the finite length string in case of our simple optimization problem. Here we had concatenated 0's and 1's i.e initially i^{th} value will have 0 value in case of flip of a coin we had head and 1 value if we got a tail value. A binary string then represent a unsigned integer i.e a string a_i, a_{i-1}, ...a_3, a_2, a_1 will be decoded using formula $X = \sum a^i * 2^{i-1}$. Though this types of binary encodings gives us a lot of flexibility and power for many types of twists and turns and a large number of options to represents a solution. Past researchers has actively used these type of binary encoding almost in every type of problem representation in the field of science, engineering and technology spectrum. In this section of the book we will see number of other coding designs for problems in different areas. In the end we look for binary string that represents not a single parameter but n numbers of parameters.

It is seen that coding in GA search requires a lot of mind's eye and thought process. Coding of the solution should be such that every permutation and combination of various positions should be addressed. A programmer is blessed to chose from various choices of coding available. If our coding system is not efficient then it will not affect our solution quality as GA's are robust in their working. Our coding system should be such that short and high showing schemata should be applicable to the basic problem and it should select the unimportant alphabet that represents the solution of the problem. In our earlier example, we had laid stress on binary coding. We can also try many non binary encoding mechanisms. Comparison between the two is given in Table 2.

For example we had mapped 6 bit with the combination of alphabets and numbers (Table 3).

Coding Corresponding Table (Binary to Non Binary)

It is seen that in binary encoding there a number of similarities between high order schema, which could be exploited, but in non binary codings, there is nothing to exploit. Thus our coding system should be such that we could pin point the similarities, so we could exploit them when we run GA code.

Table 2. Comparison between the two decimal value and Non binary value.

Binary String	Value	Non Binary Coding
11000	24	Y
11000	17	Q
10011	19	S
00111	7	G

As we have discussed to code effectively for a GA. So in order to code for a particular problem, the researcher has to find a way keeping these principles in mind.

In our previous problem, it was an unsigned fixed point integer. But to convert this unsigned integer $(0, 2^l)$ to a specific interval $[U_{min}, U_{max}]$. The precision of this coding is given by the formula:

$$\prod = (U_{max} - U_{min})/ (2^l - 1)$$

Since l = 5,

$$00\ 000 = U_{min}$$

$$11\ 111 = U_{max}$$

Other values lies between them.
Multi parameter coding (10 parameters)

Table 3. Mapping of 6 bit with the combination of alphabets and numbers.

Binary	Non Binary
00 00 00	A0
00 0001	A1
00 0011	A2
000101	A3
.	.
.	.
.	.
11 11 11	A63

00001	00110	....	11110	11111
U_1	U_2		U_9	U_{10}

Here each of the five bits represents one parameter so in total of 50 bit. Code in C++ language is given below:

```
int value = 0; int i; a[10];
for(i = 0;i<10;i++)
{ if (a[i] = = 1)
value = value + pow(2,i);}
```

5.6 CONCLUSION

In this chapter we were able to solve the puzzling working steps of GA by probing various steps, data structures to implement GA practically. We had implemented SGA in C++ programming language. Our code can be run on commonly available computers by using C++ compiler.

Our initial data structure discussed is strings of population. Two non overlapping populations are also represented such as oldp[i] and newp[i]. The population itself is a structure that consists of binary strings, fitness value and other parameters related to them. A simple SGA consists of three basic steps selection, crossover and mutation. In case of selection we had used stochastic roulette wheel selection. Simple crossover and mutation are implemented as discussed before. This whole process is done and is called generation, which generates a new set of strings, called population. After implementing and running GA code for a simple function F(x) = x/c, where c is a normalized vaue. We found out that GA find better or optimal results after few successive generations. Various other and not so important details of implementations are also been discussed. Various other coding procedures and possibility has been discussed. So the source code for the crossover, mutation and selection will be same for all the problems, but the fitness function will vary from problem to problem. In our later chapters we will take more comprehensive look at the GA procedures and the parameters values of the operators that affect the GA performance.

REFERENCES

Deb, K. (2000). *Optimization for Engineering Design: Algorithm and Examples*. Prentice Hall of India Private Limited.

Goldberg, D. E. (2002). Genetic Algorithms in Search, Optimization and Machine Learning. Pearson Education. *Asia*.

Haupt, R. L., & Haupt, S. A. (2004). *Practical Genetic Algorithms*. John Wiley and Sons, Inc.

Rajasekaran & Vijaylakshmi Pai. (2007). *Neural Networks, Fuzzy Logic, and Genetic algorithms, Synthesis and Applications*. Prentice-Hall of India Private Limited.

APPENDIX: SIMPLE GENETIC ALGORITHM (SGA) PROGRAM IN C++

```
// Genetic Algorithm program for Function f1 in C + +.
# include<iostream.h>
# include<conio.h>
# include<stdlib.h>
# include<math.h>
# include<time.h>
float objfun(int a[]);//Calculate Objective Function
void initialize(); //Generate Initial Population
void writereport();//Print Whole Population & their objective
function values & parents p1 & p2, cross over site
void statistics();//Calculate & print max., min. & avg.
objective function values of a generation
void generation();//Crossover & Mutation
void calcobjfun();//Assign objective function values
int selection();
struct population
{
int a[30];
float value;
int p1;
int p2;
int crosss;
} oldp[50],newp[50];
 int i,j;
 float m;
 int s;
 int cross;
 float sumfitness = 0;
void main()
{ clrscr();
cout<<"Enter mutation probability"<<endl;
cin>>m;
cout<<m<<endl;
//s = m*50*8;
cout<<"Enter crossover probability in percentage"<<endl;
cin>>cross;
```

```
for(i = 0;i<50;i++)
{ oldp[i].p1 = 0;
 oldp[i].p2 = 0;
 oldp[i].crosss = 0;}
initialize();//Generate Initial Population
writereport();//Print Whole Population & their objective
function values & parents p1 & p2, cross over site
getch();
statistics();//Calculate & print max., min. & avg. objective
function values of a generation
for(int z = 0;z<50;z++)
{
generation();//Crossover & Mutation
for(i = 0;i<50;i++)
oldp[i] = newp[i];
//writereport();
calcobjfun();//Calculate Objective Function
statistics();//Calculate & print max., min. & avg. objective
function values of a generation
cout<<"        "<<z<<endl;
getch();
 }
getch();
}
void initialize()//Generate Initial Population
{ int x,i,j;
time_t t;
srand((unsigned) time(&t));
for(i = 0;i<50;i++)
{ for(j = 0;j<30;j++)
{ x = rand() % 100;
if (x < 51)
oldp[i].a[j] = 0;
else
oldp[i].a[j] = 1;}}
                }
void writereport() //Print Whole Population & their objective
function values & parents p1 & p2, cross over site
{ cout<<"Initial population generated is"<<endl;
for(int i = 0;i<50;i++)
{ for(int j = 0;j<30;j++)
cout<<oldp[i].a[j];
//cout<<endl;
 oldp[i].value = objfun(oldp[i].a);
 cout<<"value = "<<oldp[i].value;
 cout<<"Parent1 = "<<oldp[i].p1;
 cout<<"Parent2 = "<<oldp[i].p2;
```

```cpp
cout<<"Cross Site"<<oldp[i].crosss;
cout<<endl;
}        }
float objfun(int a[]) //Calculate Objective Function
{long int value = 0; int i; float value1;
for(i = 0;i<30;i++)
{ if (a[i] = = 1)
value = value + pow(2,i);}
value1 = (float) value/1073741823;
return value1;}
void statistics() //Calculate & print max., min. & avg.
objective function values of a generation
{
 sumfitness = 0;
float avgfitness;
int i;
for(i = 0;i<50;i++)
sumfitness = oldp[i].value + sumfitness;
 avgfitness = sumfitness/50;
 cout<< "          "<< avgfitness;
 float min;
 min = oldp[0].value;
 for(i = 0;i<50;i++)
 { if(oldp[i].value< min)
 min = oldp[i].value;
 }
 // cout<<"min. value"<< min;
 float max;
 max = oldp[0].value;
 for(i = 0;i<50;i++)
 { if(oldp[i].value>max)
 max = oldp[i].value;
 }
 cout<<"        "<<max;
 }
 void generation()//Crossover & Mutation
 { //static int f = 0;
 int g;
 g = random(101);
 if(g<cross)     //Crossover
 {
 for(i = 0;i<50;i = i+2)
 {
 int crss = random(30);
 // cout<<"crossover site is"<<crss;
 // cout<<endl;
 int p = selection();
 int q = selection();
```

```
newp[i].p1 = p;
newp[i].p2 = q;
newp[i].crosss = crss;
newp[i+1].p1 = p;
newp[i+1].p2 = q;
newp[i+1].crosss = crss;
for(j = 0;j<crss;j++)
newp[i].a[j] = oldp[p].a[j];
for(j = crss;j<30;j++)
newp[i].a[j] = oldp[q].a[j];
 for(j = 0;j<crss;j++)
newp[i+1].a[j] = oldp[q].a[j];
for(j = crss;j<30;j++)
newp[i+1].a[j] = oldp[p].a[j]; }
for(i = 0;i<50;i++)    //Mutation
{
for(j = 0;j<30;j++)
{ int g1;
 g1 = random(1000);
 if(g1<m)
 { if(newp[i].a[j] = = 0)
 newp[i].a[j] = 1;
 else
 newp[i].a[j] = 0;}
      }
} }
 else
{ for(i = 0;i<50;i++)
newp[i] = oldp[i];
for(i = 0;i<50;i++)
{
for(j = 0;j<30;j++)
{ int g1;
 g1 = random(1000);
 if(g1<m)
 { if(newp[i].a[j] = = 0)
 newp[i].a[j] = 1;
 else
 newp[i].a[j] = 0;}
 }
}
   } }
void calcobjfun()
{   for(i = 0;i<50;i++)
oldp[i].value = objfun(oldp[i].a) ;
}
int selection()
{int i; float r1,r, partsum, rando;
```

```
partsum = 0; i = 0;
r = random(100);
r1 = (float)r/100;
rando = r1*sumfitness;
while(partsum< = rando && i<50)
  {
partsum = partsum+oldp[i].value;i = i+1;
}
return(i-1);}
```

Chapter 6
Understanding Genetic Algorithm (GA) Operators Step by Step

ABSTRACT

In today's world of soft computing, GAs are a hot topic. Researchers developed this fascinating application to face or to counter many difficult problems which cannot be solved through traditional approaches. We have seen that in the published work of GAs, an author does not reveal the working of the GA as a whole. In this chapter, the authors tried to untwist the GA methodology. This knowledge will be helpful in applying GAs for various applications (i.e., in the fields of science and technology and business). In the case of business-related problems, the use of GAs will have viable value. This chapter is a guide to using GAs vs. other soft computing techniques. Later in the chapter, the authors explain the working and comparison of GAs by using question and answer format.

6.1 INTRODUCTION

Optimization is an essential feature for real world problems (Deb, 2002). In financial or stock trading system it is a key feature. Here we optimize the profit. There are several traditional techniques that are in use for past few decades. Since then a lot of new technique have comes into existence, one difficulty that comes into picture is to find optimal value. Traditional or

DOI: 10.4018/978-1-7998-4105-0.ch006

standard optimization techniques do not give good results and it is seen in past that got stuck to a local optima often. Soft computing based optimization techniques such as GA simulated annealing gives better results than these statistical based optimization techniques (Deb, 2002). GA's are an adaptive heuristic based algorithm. Here encoded population which represents solution, self-evolve generation after generation. GA's are invented by John Holland of University of Michigan in 1960's. GA's are gaining popularity as a non-conventional optimization technique. It is seen in past researches that the use of GA in combination of traditional techniques gives better results. For example first use GA to find a global optima ridge, after it we will use traditional technique to climb this peak. Thus in this way we improves our result quality.

6.2 ADAPTIVE COMPUTATIONAL MODELS OF NEWER GENERATIONS

Research and practises in forecasting financial or stock market domain is characterised by a vast use of experimental data for the case of model development (Bauer, 1994). Chapters in part one of our books gives a detail examination of theoretical improvement, taken place in the past and recent researches. It is seen that financial and stock markets consists of a number of diverse agents. These all agents interact with each other in a multifaceted manner. Until this date it is very difficult to explain non equilibrium or chaotic condition of the stock or financial market in a single inclusive, theoretical and mathematical model. No financial model is self explanatory and work properly in every up and down. In today's scenario financial and stock trading models are computationally adaptive in nature. Development of these soft computing techniques by passes the theoretical formulations by applying mathematical formulas that fit best to data by using the modus operandi of optimization. These adaptive computational models are generally used to 1. Take a deep insight about the working of the internal structure of the market. 2. To make accurate predictions about the future values of the market. Here we apply adaptive computational models on large amount of data and fine tune the discrepancies. In this we validate model scientifically. This is not the case with usual theoretical models. In adaptive models we describe the whole process in form of mathematical formulations.

Past researchers have shown that these adaptive models have given promising results. One of the examples of these adaptive statistical tools used for optimization of various models if Genetic Algorithms (GA's). Now a day's use of GA has conquered in almost all the system analysis and relevance. GA is one of the most popular types of adaptive optimization technique which is used to optimize parameter set of a mathematical function or a rule set also. To my knowledge of past researches, these new approaches has achieved only 5% of their budding and a lot more work is to be done to fine tune them. To my study these soft computing based techniques such as Neural Networks (NN), Fuzzy logic, Genetic Algorithms (Gas) has only just arrived. These techniques require a large processing power to get accurate results and perform experiment on a large amount of data. With the availability of cheaper and higher processing power computers experimenting on a large amount of data and finding accurate results with the use of these soft computing techniques has become easier. GA's working or processing are always parallel in nature. Here each iteration is independent to each other. Thus here n number of multi processors and computers can be used to run these iterations parallel, which results in saving of time.

Past theories or assumptions about market tell us those stock market posses a property of randomness in its working. Based on this assumption Efficient Market Hypothesis (EMH) states that market absorbs all the information in it. Investors and traders try to optimize their profits.

Optimization is widely used in stock trading model. It is a basic building block in it. Classical optimization procedures are used for several decades. They occur with a problem of local optima. In case of multiple optima function they may get stuck to local optima assuming it to be a global optima. But advancement in optimization procedures leads to the development of more advanced soft computing procedures such as Genetic Algorithms and Simulated Annealing. GA's are self adaptive procedures, which generates a fixed number of solution generations after generation. GA's are first invented by John Holland of University of Michigan in 1960's. Now a day's GA's are becoming popular optimization procedures in all fields.

It is seen that combination of classical and neo soft computing based optimization procedure has come into the picture. These are known as hybrid procedures. Here GA working is used to obtained global scenery. And then we turn to classical technique to fine tune it. Hybrid procedures are future optimization procedures. These advances in optimization procedures were notice by market forces. Several readymade commercial software's packages had come into existence for example Evolver is most popular amongst them.

6.3 GENETIC ALGORITHMS

GA's are more advance optimization procedure or algorithm (Rajasekaran et.al, 2007). GA are generally used as solution provider and their procedures are self evolving in nature. GA's uses the logic of biological nature and is based on Darwin theory of natural selection or survival of fittest. In biology spices evolve and fittest of them adapt to the environment. Thus a GA program generates solution and adapts and fit to the problems with perfection generation after generation. Now a day's GA's are widely used in a number of engineering problems.

It was experienced that copying the concept of imitation of natural evolution into mathematical formulas are mind blowing. In nature we had seen the success of evolution. The species which are present are well adapted to the environment by considering all criteria's. In GA's procedure we had copied biological evolution process into algorithm procedures. GA produces a number of solution and them improves their solution quality generation after generation. While in case of classical optimization technique only one solution is generated at a time in the optimization path.

In GA population a number of solutions are generated. These possible solutions are mapped or represented in form of array of binary strings i.e 0's and 1's. Each member is known as chromosome. Thus each chromosome is a binary series of 0's and 1's, which represents a solution. Thus encoding any possible solution into a string of 0's and 1's is one of the limitations in GA. After initial random generation of population we apply two operates on it i.e crossover and mutation. These two operators represent process of reproduction in natural case. These two operators represent process of reproduction in natural case. The whole process of GA is as follows: Let there be a initial random population generated at a particular time t. After selecting individuals with higher fitness function value, these two operators' crossover and mutation are applied to it. Thus a new population with higher fitness function is generated. Schematically whole process is a s follows:

P (t) Population at a particular time t

Selection

Crossover

Mutation

P (t + 1) Population at a particular time t + 1.

Thus after a reproduction phase a new population of individuals with same size is created. Thus considering the number of individuals of population be 'n'. The process of reproduction i.e selection, crossover and mutation is done repeatedly, n number of times and a new population with same number of individuals is created. The nature of selection operator is that individual having fitness function more than average will be selected repeatedly. The population of individual having fitness below average is bound to be left out. This selection process clearly imitates the Darwin process of survival of fittest.

To start with the GA we will have to define the nature of fitness function. Fitness function actually defines the solution quality. It is the ranking of a individual in the population. It defines the goal or parameters or number which we want to achieve i.e it can be a maximization or minimization value. In other words fitness function defines the goal which we want to achieve. In GA procedure to implement it we first define the fitness function, then we generate a random population and represent it in form of binary string. After this we calculate fitness function of all individual members of population and selection operator is applied. On the selected individual we apply crossover and mutation operators.

Crossover operator is used to transfer or exchange information between two chromosomes. Simpliest form is uniform crossover. Process of crossover is shown below:

Chromosome 1 : 00000 00000 00000 11111 *Offspring* 1

$$\longrightarrow$$

Chromosome 2 : 11111 11111 11111 00000 *Offspring* 2

Applying crossover on population depends upon a certain probability (P_c). This probability P_c is the design parameter defined by the individual. A random number r is generated and if its value comes below the crossover probability set. Then crossover is performed. Here pair of chromosomes are selected. A random point is generated having range between 0 and maximum length of chromosome. Chromosomes are divided and their positions are exchanged. Thus two newer individuals are generated and they are replaced by the older one in the population. This whole process is shown above.

After crossover operator mutation operator is applied. Nature of mutation operator is to add a new information or diversity in the population. Mutation operator is applied bit by bit. Here also a probability of mutation operator P_m is defined. A random number between range (0, 1) is generated for each binary bit. If the value of this random generated number of below P_m then the binary bit is mutated or its value is changed from 0 to 1 or 1 to 0. Thus all these three operators' selection, crossover and mutation are applied sequentially and in a repeated manner. After the applying of these three operators fitness function is calculated for each individual. Based on its values we decide, whether we should go for next GA cycle or not. There are a number of criteria's which decides the termination of GA. One of them is desired result obtained, other ones are convergence of the fitness values, predefined the total number of generation can also be another criteria.

Efficiency and efficacy of GA has been proved theoretically and practically by researchers. Practical results shown by various researchers who had applied GA in almost in every walk of life and engineering application shows that results obtained by GA completely out performs the results obtained from traditional techniques. It is also seen that GA works well for complex optimization problems which consists of large number of local maxima and minima. GA works parallel at many points in the search space. Due to this feature, GA does not stuck to local optima.

GA explain above is its simplest form Many other different form of GA has come into picture. There is a different version of problem representation and various different forms of crossover and mutation operators can be applied to it. It is seen that binary representation of problem is mathematically and practically easy. Various other representations such as floating point and alpha numeric representation is also done. In floating point representation of problem, mutation is done by replacing the floating point number by another random floating point number. Many other advanced and specialized GA operators have been invented which will be discussed in coming chapters. Main aim of these operators is to make GA more effective and lethal to optimize parameter of a specific problem (Goldberg, 2002).

John Koza of Hopkins University discovers an innovative application of GA i.e Genetic Programming popularly known as GP. In Genetic Programming (GP) programs are encoded as strings of digits and their fitness function is represented in a numerical way. This concept was used by Koza to run various LISP programs. Similarly this type of implementation leads to the discovery of Neural Network and much other type of algorithms.

6.4 QUESTIONS AND ANSWERS ABOUT THE WORKING OF GA, ITS MYTH VS ITS REALITY

Q- 1 Genetic Algorithms (GA's) are used for which type of optimization types?

Ans: Here the main aim of GA is to optimize. GA is a optimization strategy. By optimization we means that we can either found minimize or maximize value of a system. As working of GA is incremental and they do not find the best solutions, but better solution as obtained from the traditional approaches or solution closed to the optimal ones. These solutions will have some monetary or exchange value. Performance here is of comparative in nature i.e better than the previous one.

Another terminology that comes into picture is that if a NP hard problem, which has a huge space, which means almost infinite, set of solutions. Then applying brute force technique i.e to apply each and every combination is time consuming. This procedure will require high processing power as problems of this type are of complex in nature. So for this type of problems GA is the answer, as you can parallel search the space from a large set set of existing solutions.

Q- 2 How does a problem be represented so that we can apply GA on it?

Ans: It is the toughest part in GA implementation. In order to represent problems stings are used. Binary string coding is the most popular method to represent a problem. Binary strings which consists of 0's and 1's are represented and mapped to the real problem solution. Many other type of string representation are also used for example, string have alpha numeric characters, alphabet or tree representations are also used. Past research papers gives a fair idea about it.

Representing solutions to a problem in form of string requires a lot of thought process. We should keep in mind such that every permutation and combination of the solution parameters should be taken care of. This whole process could be both entertaining and irritating simultaneously. Trying for various probabilities could be time consuming also. Thus after a lot of calculation you could see light at the end of the tunnel.

Q- 3 What do we optimize in a GA and when we stop?

Ans: At first sight, GA tries to find best or optimal string. Since string represents the solution itself. In a twist it finds the best possible solution found until now. If our string represents a set of parameters, then our GA will try to find the parameter set which gives us best solution. In other way our solution is represented by fitness function in GA>

After the procedure of string representation is finalized, we will start thinking about performance calculation or fitness function formula. We had to give a thought that what we want to optimize. If fitness function formula is not crafted carefully then we might end up in faulty result. This will not be the fault of computer or GA but it will be of ours. We just are sure to properly derive the fitness function formula.

Q- 4 In GA base optimization we means that we want to maximize something. What will be the case if we want to minimize something?

Ans: For this a small change in fitness function formula is to be done. In general we had tried to maximize the fitness function $f(x)$, so in a reversal to minimize it following changes will be made:

$$F(x) = 1/[1 + f(x)]$$

In case of stock related problem, in order to maximize fitness function, we find trading rule that gives maximum profit or return. Thus in the reverse case, we find trading rules which gives negative rate of return. This could be beneficial if we find such rule, then in our real world we will do the reverse what the rule says in order to get the profit. Thus if fitness function is negative then we could change minimum fitness to maximum fitness by just subtracting it by maximum absolute value and it will maximize. Thus by a simple change in a fitness function code we could achieve our goal. Alternatively if we design GA for minimization problem, it will be a mammoth task.

Q- 5 What is the process to calculate string fitness or its achievement?

Ans: It is a known fact that computer programs are a set of commands. We just have to give right commands to get desired results. Since fitness function represents a string. Hence a correct fitness function will decide which string will be selected for next generation or not. Proper care should be done to formulate fitness function formulas.

In case of stock investment problem, fitness function is the profit we had earned from our investment. Since each string has a fitness function value of its own. The set of parameters values obtained from the string will be calculated. The binary position of strings will give decimal equivalent, which in turn gives the value of set of parameters. These parameters will be put in the trading model designed, which will operate on the historic data to find profit or return, which in turn will give fitness function of the particular string. In all there are infinite numbers of ways or coding procedures in which solution to the problems can be represented as a string and fitness function can be calculated.

Q- 6 Can there be a comparison between Chaos theory and GA?

Ans: It is tough to equate these two techniques. Chaos theory is descriptive or clarification in nature. Rather than it is used to forecast or to do some trading. Chaos theory requires some initial sensitive parameter to give us indication about the chaotic degree of the system. Chaos theory does not comprises of any formula that will help in forecasting. Chaos theory explains the system behaviour or its stability. Whereas GA requires some knowledge of system in order to optimize forecasting value or trade with it. Chaos theory does not require any assumptions in the beginning.

We can develop a hybrid system which comprises of both chaos theory and GA. First we will test the system stability or chaotic mess in it. If noisiness in the system is less and system is stable in nature, then we assume that we will be able to predict market with a better accuracy. After this we will use GA to find best trading rule or optimize parameters of a pre defined trading strategy. If market is in chaotic state then we will abandon it as our all efforts are going to be proved futile.

Q- 7 In what way chaos lacks in comparison with GA?

Ans: Chaos theory only let you know that if the system is in chaotic or in stable state. But after that what?. System degree of stability is the only result that this theory gives. There are many equations or formulas with the help of which you could forecast. But what if system is chaotic? You cannot go in a reverse direction. You cannot make mathematical formula from a noisy data patterns. It is virtually impossible. If this could be possible then in both cases when the system is chaotic and stable, we will be able to forecast the data. By going in reverse direction is not practically possible in chaotic system.

Q- 8 Do lessons from the chaos theory will help in applying GA?

Ans: In past researchers who had applied chaos theory to the past market data has found that stock market data trend or patterns repeat after every five years. Thus for more accurate results, a training system has to developed by taking data from the recent past. This could be helpful for applying GA. whereas chaos theory helps to find the regions among the whole data, where market is noisy as it will not be for best trader to predict it.

Q- 9 How does a Neural Network gives more accurate results as compare to GA?

Ans: In comparison to GA Neural Network is a more black box based technique. Neural Network relies more on experimentation then upon the system knowledge. In case of neural network we tell the specified inputs and desired outputs also. Rest all is done, without allowing you to know what is done between the input selection and output results. But in case of GA a little amount of knowledge is needed to start. In Neural Network prior knowledge about the system is crafty.

GA needs the solution should be mapped on to a string. Formula to calculate fitness function will require some knowledge about the system. After this is done GA will optimize from set of population of solution in a black box way. Thus main advantage of Neural Network over GA is that less knowledge about the system is needed.

Q- 10 What are the main disadvantages of Neural Networks?

Ans: In case of Neural Network from input to output they are linked via a certain network of nodes which are loosely connected to each other. Working in a neural network is just like enlighten occult practice ie mysterious and black box in nature. It gives good results but what is the modus operandi, it is not known.

Other drawback is that a lot of experimentation is to done for more accurate results. Experimentation can be done in a number of of types as there are n ways by which we can apply neural network to forecast data i.e possible parameters that can be varied is node connection, total number of hidden layers etc. Hence neural network can be applied in infinite number of ways. Since neural network working is of iterative in nature, so they are time consuming and require a lot of processing power and memory when applied on a stock market data to get more accurate results.

Q- 11 How is GA better than Chaos theory and Neural Networks?

Ans: Though GA is a black box technique, but to start with a GA, we have to take some knowledge of the system. For stock market investment GA can be applied to optimize set of trading rule or a parameter of a pre define trading rule itself. Main advantage is that we test results on various parameter or rule set and interpolation can be made from it. In contrast to neural network no elucidation of the system can be done, since they are total black box technique. In case of chaos theory only system stability or degree of noise of the system is generated. Here from the starting argument or reasoning claims will be made or we will justify some result. This is also a disadvantage of the system architecture.

Q- 12 What level of programming skills do a GA practitioner need to know in order to implement GA?

Ans: Quick answer is a little bit. Almost all steps of GA procedures are of similar in nature and are same for all problems. In GA steps like selection, crossover and mutation are applied in a repetitive manner on the strings. Only system information that is needed is the fitness function calculation of the string. So the process that changes from problem to problem is the fitness function formula and data interrogation. Various function codes of GA such as selection, crossover and mutation and all other minor function such as initial population generation etc. does not changes from one system optimization to other. Exception is that if we use some advance GA operators, as we are going to discuss them in later chapters of the book. Otherwise coding does not have to change. We can use any high level computer language such as Pascal, FORTRAN, C, C++, Java or Mat lab to write a GA code. If you are not good in knowledge of programming languages or programming itself, then there are many free GA code made available by GA practitioners, which makes your task easier.

Where as in case of other soft computing techniques such a s neural networks, many open source and paid software's are available, which are good for users who are not good in writing codes. Though there are infinite number of combinations or variations among GA operators and n number of ways in which strings can be represented in GA. So developing a all inclusive GA intercession is very difficult.

Q- 13 Where is all popular GA packages arc available to us?

Ans: As interests of many researchers are growing in GA, Many open source and paid software's are available to us. Apart from these many major book written on GA by well known authors such as (Goldberg, 2002), (Deb, 2002) in their book also provide code written on GA in various languages.

Q- 14 Can GA be used for complicated or large search space problems?

Ans: GA works with a great speed. Within a short period of time they are able to search large spaces heuristically. Thus they are perfect for large search space complex problems. GA is also useful for small search space problems i.e small string size, but where fitness function calculation is complex and time consuming. In case of small search space one of the other search procedures is to us e brute force technique or enumerative search. But if time is a constraint the GA will be the best technique to use it. Thus crux of our discussion is that GA is not only good to be use for large search space and complex problems, but also good for small search space and complex fitness function problems also where time is a constant.

Q- 15 How will you find or test quality of solution find out by GA?

Ans: In case of NP hard problems we do not know the best or optimal solution. Hence in this case we compare the solution found out by GA with the solution found by other traditional techniques. There is no way to find optimal solution for large and ill defined problems. Other procedure to find weather solution found out GA is optimal or not is to apply GA with same operators and parameter settings, a number of times on the problem itself. If we run for 15 trials and out of which 10 trials results are same. Then we consider it as a optimal result. But what if results all 15 trials are different. Then in this case if time and computational power is not constraint, then we will go for more number of trials. After the quality of results obtained, we will decide in run time to go for more trials or not. There may be other procedures to improve solution quality. One is to change the parameter settings and other is to make design changes in the algorithm itself.

In case of stock market investment problem, the real optimization is to fine most profitable strategy until so far. This profitable strategy should outperform other strategies found so far. Thus in case of stock market the word "Optimal" is not absolute but relative. It means that parameters or rule which may be optimal today may not be optimal in future. It means, it may change from time to time.

Q- 16 What if solution found by GA is poorer in solution quality as compare to the results found out by other traditional techniques?

Ans: It may happen. First reason for it is that GA solution may converge after few generations. This happens if selection technique is of greedy in nature and number of generations and population size are not adequate. Other reason may be faulty string representation and not so perfect fitness function formula. Hence to implement a GA we right a computer code. As computer program is a set of instructions. Poorer or faulty instructions will not give us not so good results. Last but not the least is bad luck. As GA are heuristic based techniques, so if we start with some poorer solution randomly selected. It may happen that after certain successive generation's solution quality remain poorer and may not recover. A lot number of different trials may give better results.

Q- 17 What is the rate of GA parameter settings in running a GA code?

Ans: GA from past researches has shown that GA working is of robust in nature, no matter what parameter settings we use. In our coming chapter we are going to discuss in a large way the effect of GA parameter on the solution quality. But for the beginners more attention should be paid on the string representation, fitness functions etc. Usually high crossover rate with low mutation rate will give better optimal solutions.

Q- 18 What is the speed of GA?

Ans: Speed is a relative term in our search procedure. Our earlier program was coded in C++. As processing power of computers are increasing for several years. Time require to do excessive data access and their calculation is decreasing day by day. With better data analytics approaches, programming approaches and newer problem representations and fitness function calculation, time required to run GA code for a given number of generations is decreasing. With the addressing of these bottle necks, GA speed is increased significantly.

Q- 19 How much solid is the theoretical foundation of GA?

Ans: As father and inventor of GA John Holland has provided a solid base of the theoretical proof of GA. Searching many search spaces parallel at a given point of time makes GA a very effective and efficient search technique. Mathematical representation of GA is very complex and tedious. A lot of theoretical mathematical representation work has to be done in GA.

Q- 20 Is GA more popular than Chaos theory, neural network or any other soft computing technique?

Ans: Work of GA in stock trading system is in initial phase. In comparison to other techniques such as neural network, fuzzy logic work has been started many years before GA comes into existence. These all techniques are simple and appealing than GA. Due to this GA will take more time and research to become popular. It is seen that as more and more complex problems are encountered in investment applications, the use of GA is gaining popularity. GA can be applied to potentially all types of optimization problems. Computation power has accelerated the development of many GA applications. So with the use of faster computers more NP hard and data centric problem can be executed by using GA's. Easy availability of other mercantile software packages available in neural network and other soft computing techniques, there i.e no advancement in their research. Neural network is a black box technique, so it does not require any thought process as required by GA. Due to this reason other techniques are more popular than GA. But as time is passing by GA are gaining popularity day by day. Results obtained by GA are more acceptable then results obtained by other techniques relevant. But for a absurd case combination of two algorithm to solve a problem will give us better result as compare to implementation of a single algorithm in isolation.

6.5 CONCLUSION

The main aim of this chapter is to give a brief reference about Genetic algorithms (GAs). Frequently asked questions are answered satisfactorily. In question and answer format reader will quickly absorb the working of Genetic algorithms (GAs) and its comparison with other soft computing techniques.

REFERENCES

Bauer, R. J. Jr. (1994). *Genetic Algorithms and Investment Strategies*. John Wiley and Sons, Inc.

Deb, K. (2002). *Optimization for Engineering Design: Algorithm and Examples*. Prentice Hall of India Private Limited.

Goldberg, D. E. (2002). *Genetic Algorithms in Search, Optimization and Machine Learning*. Pearson Education.

Rajasekaran & Vijaylakshmi Pai. (2007). *Neural Networks, Fuzzy Logic, and Genetic algorithms, Synthesis and Applications*. Prentice-Hall of India Private Limited.

Chapter 7
Operator Control Parameters and Fine Tuning of Genetic Algorithms (GAs)

ABSTRACT

Genetic algorithms (GAs) are heuristic, blind (i.e., black box-based) search techniques. The internal working of GAs is complex and is opaque for the general practitioner. GAs are a set of interconnected procedures that consist of complex interconnected activity among parameters. When a naive GA practitioner tries to implement GA code, the first question that comes into the mind is what are the value of GA control parameters (i.e., various operators such as crossover probability, mutation probability, population size, number of generations, etc. will be set to run a GA code)? This chapter clears all the complexities about the internal interconnected working of GA control parameters. GA can have many variations in its implementation (i.e., mutation alone-based GA, crossover alone-based GA, GA with combination of mutation and crossover, etc.). In this chapter, the authors discuss how variation in GA control parameter settings affects the solution quality.

7.1 INTRODUCTION

In previous chapters we had explained basic steps of GA's by working it on a simple problem (Goldberg, 2002). In a whole we came to know that GA is a search process which can find better solution for large, NP hard problems

DOI: 10.4018/978-1-7998-4105-0.ch007

a s compared with solution obtained from classical techniques. There are a number of GA control parameters for ex. Crossover, mutation, population size, number of generations etc. Based on these there can be n number of variations in implementation of GA. Thus it is a matter of study that which control parameter or which variation will give better solution quality with minimum number of iterations and with speed. We are going to explore these questions in this chapter. Here we are going to understand about the robustness and power of GA in solving various ill defined problems.

Considering the research in recent hot topics, those who has got some work or research finding have two choices 1. Share my research work with others i.e. Get it published. 2. Don't share it and takes a front position in the competition of GA practitioners. It is seen from past research papers that a lot of working amongst the parameters in GA is kept secret from the GA practitioners. Researches on the various GA applications do not reveal the correct picture. Since GA is a black box technique, it is getting popular day by bay and more GA work is coming into picture than ever before. In this chapter we will discuss about the internal working of GA and how changes in the internal settings affect the solution quality and GA robustness. The distinction between the internal working parameters of GA is a very tricky matter. It is a pure form of GA research whose results has got huge potential. Since GA belong to computer science field, but its application is in every other field of engineering and non engineering areas.

It was very difficult to write this chapter. Here we try to reveal the research findings of various researchers on GA internal working in a simple and naive way. Our real focal point is to find effect on the result, if we give a twist in the internal GA parameter settings. Knowledge of this type of working on GA will be useful in solving variety of NP hard problems. This will also be helpful in applying GA with better control parameters settings, which will give better results in minimum number of iterations. So to solve any business of engineering problem, we must learn about its internal working.

Working of Genetic Algorithms' is of smart in nature (Deb, 2002). By the term rich we mean that they are able to solve problem in a diversified number of fields such as from engineering to business etc. We are also going to discuss various historic works done on GA and current state of GA. Just by seeing the diversity and variation in which GA can be applied, we will come to know the robust working in various conditions. GA working is parallel and blind in nature. We will start the chapter with the simple working of tripartite GA. Then we will investigate the effect of GA control parameters i.e Crossover probability, mutation probability, population size, number of generations etc. In results obtained from GA from experimental stand point.

7.2 GENETIC ALGORITHMS (GA'S) IN TEST

GA's belongs to a class of evolutionary algorithms. Evolutionary algorithms are basically heuristic techniques. GA's uses operator such as crossover, mutation and selection which imitates rules of natural evolution. By this way GA tries to find better or optimal solutions to various NP hard and illogical problems. In our explanation we are working on classical GA. Here our solution to the problem is encoded into a binary string of 0's and 1's of fixed length. These binary strings are known as chromosomes and every bit of strings is called a gene. There are other types of encoding techniques such as floating point numbers representation or alpha numeric representation etc. In these all cases applications of crossover and mutation operators will be different from the previous binary string representation. For example if we apply mutation operator on binary bit string, we will generate random number range (0,1). If the value of the random number comes below the mutation probability P_c as decided by the GA practitioner, then we will reverse the bit value i.e from 0 to 1 or 1 to 0. But in case of floating point number if we apply mutation operator, then this floating point number will be replaced by any other floating point number generated randomly. Thus in this way better performance of GA will be achieved. Present day researchers are also trying to find best formulas for application of crossover and mutation operators in various solution representations. It is seen that fixed binary string length is most popular amongst GA practitioners. Before starting with GA we define the parameters of the system we want to optimize. We spell out the range of values i.e minimum and maximum. After the computation of the number of bits, this defines the parameters. Thus on concatenating these number of bits finite length or array of binary strings are generated, which represents particular solution to the problem or they are called chromosomes. After this our evaluation function calculates fitness function of each chromosome generated randomly. Fitness function tells the solution quality of the chromosome i.e how close is the chromosome is near to the optimal parameter setting we want to achieve. In short it is the solution quality of the problem. Initially GA calculates fitness function of all chromosomes generated randomly in the initial phase. Thus after it, based on the fitness function of the chromosomes they are selected i.e they will be able to pass their binary string information to the next generation of string. Thus chromosomes of the next generation will be formed by the transformation of the strings selected by the use of selection operators. This transformation process consists of operation or implementation of two operators' i.e crossover and mutation (Deb, 1999). Thus from the previous population newer population is created.

This selection method is an algorithm which picks up the individuals or chromosomes from the population of string in generation n. It is seen that some higher quality chromosomes are repeatedly selected while other lower quality chromosomes are not selected at all or sparingly. After two pairs of chromosomes are selected, we will go for crossover operator, which will depend upon the crossover probability as decided by the GA practitioner. We will generate a random number, if its value comes below the crossover probability, then we will go for crossover otherwise not. In crossover operator crossover point will decide the way bits will be swapped in the pair. If the crossover point value is zero then the both strings will be passed into next generation unaltered. If crossover point is more than zero, then bits of the binary strings will be swapped from that point and two newly transformed strings are generated and passed to the next generation of strings. This process is done repeatedly until termination criteria are met or maximum generation fixed by the GA practitioner is reached.

After this we will apply mutation operator. Mutation is done bit by bit. Mutation is just an inversion of binary bit. Mutation probability P_m will decide whether the particular bit will be mutated or not. Thus mutation probability of all the binary bits in the population will checked and applied. This new string obtained will pass into the next generation. Fitness function of each individual generated again and this whole process is done to obtained strings for next generation. This process is done repeatedly until maximum number of generation is achieved or desired solution quality is achieved or fitness function of the individuals of population converges to a particular point.

Past researchers had done a lot of experiments to investigate the internal workings i.e complex interactions among various control parameters for effective results of GA. This is due to the fact that crossover probabilities, mutation probability, population size, number of generations are decided by the GA practitioners before starting the programme. These operators interact with each other in a very complex way. Values of these control parameters vary from problem to problem. A full investigation among the interconnection of the working of various control parameters is done in this chapter. We have taken these control parameters as pair wise and in single usage also i'e mutation only, crossover only,, mutation with crossover, Population size with number of generations keeping number of function evaluations constant. A lot of experimental work is done by researchers is done in past. In a real world NP hard problem in order to find best possible solution or optimal result, we have to evaluate function evaluation of various points. Thus for optimization and search problem a number of function evaluations have to be done interactively and it consumes 99% of the optimization algorithm time. Our aim in any optimization algorithm or GA is to get near to or true optimal solution in minimum number of function evaluation. Since there are n variation in the parameter settings of control parameters and 99% of GA time is consumed to calculate fitness function evaluation. Our aim is to find those parameter settings that give optimal or better results in a less number of function evaluations, thus saving time and space as we have limited processing power. There are in general three criteria for a GA program to get terminated 1. Optimal solution reached, 2. Population converge to particular good solution, 3. Numbers of generations that are fixed are reached. Our parameters settings should be such that population converge towards an optimal solution in a minimum number of generations. Our discussion in this chapter is based on the explanation of results which are borrowed from my own research work (V. Kapoor et. al, 2010), (V. Kapoor et. al, 2011) and research work of various other researchers (Goldberg, 1989), (Kalyanmoy Deb et. al, 1999), William Spears, 1993), Annie, 1997). This leads us to gain a valuable insight into the complex and randomized working of GA. Once this working of GA control parameters is understood, GA practitioners will have no difficulty in fixing values of GA control parameters i.e crossover probabilities, mutation probability, population size, number of generations. The above study is a must for successful run of a GA. Apart from this parameter settings a fine tuned representation scheme to code the solution is needed. The representation scheme should be efficient and flexible, rather than tight. Thus with the proper combination of these two factors GA will give us results with flying colours. As shown in past researchers. Thus to test GA the formula of total number of function evaluation is: Total number of function evaluations (S) = Population Size (P) * Number of Generations (N).

We are running GA for a fixed number of function evaluations, not in an infinite mode. Now we are going to discuss various potholes or difficulties that a NP hard problem inherits within itself.

Most common of the difficulty factors are multi-modality, Deception, Isolation and Collateral noise. To explain each of these factors in multimodality there are many false peaks which causes an algorithm to get attracted towards there and stuck up there only. In case of deception GA get stuck in not so good solution space. In case of isolation, information about the solution quality is not available; hence it is just like finding a needle in a haystack. This may lead GA to search nowhere. In case of collateral noise, it may deceit the bad solution with the good solution. Thus larger sample size is needed to clear that deception. By surveying the NP hard problems it is found that the level of above difficulty factors may be low or high depending upon the problem. These all factors are also interrelated to each other.

In the coming section we will apply many variations in GA and discuss their results. We will see how changes in crossover probability, mutation probability, population size and number of generations keeping total number of functions evaluations constant effect solution quality. We had experimented for various crossover rates starting from 0.1 to 0.9.

It is seen that there is a variation in convergence rate for different crossover rates. Detail will be discussed in next section. After this we will try mutation for various probability i.e from 0.1 to 0.1.

Low mutation rate leads to poorer solution, while higher mutation rate leads to better solutions but randomly. Since mutation is a disruptive operator. It leads to the disruption of convergence. Third but not least we had tried GA with 1. High mutation and high crossover rate, 2. High mutation and Low crossover rate, 3. Low mutation and low crossover rate, 4. Low mutation with high crossover rate. Fourth we apply GA with varying population sizes from 20 to 100.

Rate of convergence is higher for small population size and vice versa. We had modified different control parameter setting based on our intuition. Results can be forecasted but proper empirical test has been made. In the end our conclusion is that changes in GA parameter settings do not restrict us to get attractive solution. There may be a case that in some case that speed to find better solution is less otherwise speed is more. Thus robustness of GA ids proved.

7.3 EXPERIMENTATION WITH VARYING GA PARAMETERS IN USE

In the working of GA, there are two main working operators' i.e crossover and mutation. There are a large number of past studies which explain the role of these operators. Still there is no one study which gives us a correct answer, that any one of these operator is powerful than other. Both of these operators are powerful when compared. Both of these operators have different roles to play in GA working.

It is that mutation alone with some adjusted rate along with selection operator has given better results. It is a very important operator and it gives better results in an less time, when used with some adjusted rates. There are two camps in GA practitioners; one say mutation has an edge over crossover, other say vice versa.

A lot of theoretical and empirical studies have been done to examine the effect of these operators on solution quality. Most of the researchers consider crossover as a frontline operator with primary importance and mutation as a background operator. They believe that use of mutation alone is not sufficient. These all studies are deceptive in nature and results obtained by one researcher contradicts or dispute the result obtained by another researcher. Until this date there is no fixed analysis that validates the belief of crossover and mutation camp. To my sense one cannot say that any of the two operators is more powerful than other. Both operators have different functions to perform when applied in combination or isolation. There is no doubt that both operators are integral part of GA. Here we validate the claims of both these camps. There are two roles of a GA operator, one is disruption or disordering or disturbance, and other is construction or building block. Both the operators consist of both of these properties but with a varying intensity. It is seen that disruptive property is more in mutation as compare with crossover operator. While ability to preserve a building block is more in crossover operator as compare to mutation operator. It is seen that crossover is a working of two individuals while mutation is working of one individual. Mutation of a single bit does not affect the mutation of another bit. Results of crossover produce two offspring, while results of mutation produces only one offspring.

John Holland (1975) in his book "Adaptation in Natural and Artificial Systems" gives us a detail working of behaviour of these constructive and disruptive rates of these operators. For both crossover and mutation the disruptive rates depends upon their probabilities. In case of crossover another parameter i.e number of crossover points will decide its disruptive rates. Higher probability of crossover and larger number of crossover points will lead to higher disruption rate. Thus in no way crossover has a lower disruption rate than mutation. The difference is the way by which we apply crossover operator. Mutation is an operator that selects a bit depending upon the mutation probability and then flips or change that bit from 0 to 1 or vice versa. This proves that though disruption rate of mutation is higher in any case, but higher rates of disruption in crossover can be achieved with its proper implementation as described above if needed.

7.4 CONSTRUCTION VS DISRUPTION THEORY

Disruption is a process when the building block in the binary strings is broken down. Thus disruption somewhat leads to exploration towards newer search spaces. It is seen that crossover with many points or uniformity is more disruptive or explorative than crossover with single or two point crossover.

Now comparing this power of disruption or exploration with mutation. In mutation a bit is changed if it is selected. If mutation rate is 0 then no disruption or exploration will takes place, but if mutation rate is 1 then disruption is at its peak. Better and higher level building blocks will be lost due to high rate of mutation. Thus in both of these operators same rate of exploration or disruption can be obtained provided mutation and crossover rates are adjusted properly.

Suppose two hyper planes have bit position in common. Then in crossover there is a guarantee that positions are similar in two hyper planes will preserve and these building blocks will cross to next generation for sure. While in case of mutation it is not sure that higher level building blocks is not disrupted. Thus by studying the behaviour of GA working of GA is anticipated. From the above theory it is clear that mutation has got higher disruptive rate as compare with crossover. In some cases crossover has limitations for disruption or exploration as an operator, no matter what the crossover rate or crossover points are there. Crossover conserves alleles at the cost of mutation. While mutation does helps in protecting the building blocks. Until now crossover is considered to be a disruptive operator. In contrast crossover is constructive in nature. Here higher order building blocks are made from lower order building blocks. When disruption level is more in the population, higher level of construction can only be obtained through the use of crossover operator. This leads to the convergence of population. Hence mutation at this stage can add much needed genetic diversity. In comparison with mutation, crossover has higher construction rate and survival. Thus in this way crossover is one up to mutation operator. In mutation we can obtain higher construction level, but rate of survival or passing of important alleles to next generation is compromised. This is not the case with crossover.

In case of construction mutation cannot perform to a degree to which crossover is a go getter. In case of disruption no matter by what settings crossover is implemented it cannot achieve the results obtained by mutation. Since GA is a black box technique, our attention in GA working is to get higher order building blocks with a better fitness function.

Mutation operator main aim is to generate diversity in the population and to prevent population from converging. By this means GA search many new spaces. While crossover operator is a smasher, that preserves the alleles. Hence issue is to which operator we should pay more attention. We cannot advocate the use of only one operator. Both of these operators has different role to play in search process. Importance of these operators varies from problem to problem. Balance between them should be made for the purpose they are used and to obtained good results. Use of any of these operators is deleterious and leads to lower solution quality. Only higher rate of mutation leads to somewhat close to optimality, but it results in lower average fitness function. While in case of higher rate of crossover higher maximum fitness function has to be made. Thus for getting better optimal results

All the factors such as construction, survival and diversity or disruption is required in GA. Another conclusion is that an isolated use of any operator is of no use. They applied in combination with each other with a proper rate and settings.

7.5 ROLE OF MUTATION OR MUTATION RATE

(Goldberg,2002) in his book "Genetic Algorithms in search optimization and machine learning" explains that mutation is an independent operator. Applied bit by bit i.e if applied on a particular binary bit, value will change from 0 to 1 or vice versa. Past researchers have considered mutation as disruptive operators. Some of the researchers has considered mutation as constructive operators, as it is used to construct certain building blocks or recover desirable genes or alleles which are broken during crossover operator application. Apart from this mutation, is also used to explore newer search areas by adding much needed much needed genetic diversity in the population. Now the question comes about the advisable rate of mutation, which is to be applied. It is seen that in case where there is high allele coverage, convergence rate, lesser diversity in the population, complex coding method used for representation of solution in GA higher rate of mutation is used.

Though mutation is always considered to be secondary operator but its usefulness cannot be ignored. Importance of mutation comes into picture when the greedy approach of selection operator in combination with crossover operator leads to the loss of much needed genetic diversity in order to effectively run GA simulations for further few left over generations. Generally high mutation rate is a random walk. It helps to regain desired building blocks which have lost in initial generations. In general frequency of mutation is kept very low i.e 10 mutation bits per 1000 bits in total i.e P_m in this case is 0.01. It is also known that rate of mutation depends upon various other factors i.e encoding mechanism, type of optimization problem, greediness of selection operator in use, population diversity or its size etc. It is not the working of mutation operator that improves the fitness, because results in a random walk. It is the selection operator that improves the fitness function as it selects the individuals with higher fitness values and discards less fit members, which increases the average fitness function of the population, thus improving the overall fitness function of the population. In this way generation after generation there is a continuous improvement in the maximum and average fitness of the population.

A popular view about mutation is that it is a background operator, disruptive in nature and must be used infrequently or cautiously. It tends to destroy binary pattern in the string and generate random noise in the population. Thus in order to avoid danger to eliminate highly fit schema, which is present in the population, mutation is used with caution. So possibility of the schema to get survives increases. In contrast if crossover point accidently fell in between the highly fit schema, mutation is used to retrieve the building block which has been lost. Thus the role of mutation can be constructive or destructive depending upon the rate to which it is applied.

If in a particular problem tie to calculate fitness function is more, than number of iteration in a GA to be run should be kept low i.e compromise in the population size has to be made. So to add genetic diversity in the population higher mutation rate has to be applied. Otherwise GA will run with a slow improvement rate. It is also seen foe normal problem if mutation rate is kept high, then GA run resembles like a random walk and preventing GA population to converge. In case of tripartite GA as discussed in previous chapters low mutation rate is sufficient. If convergence in GA population is not reached after subsequent generations is not reached, than there is no need for higher rate of mutation.

Hence to conclude mutation may develop a new building block, but may disrupt many other higher level building blocks or high level schemata already present in the population. Mutation also includes diversity as well as new information in the population.

7.6 CROSSOVER ROLE

This section focuses on the individuals effects of crossover or GA applied alone with crossover operators. It the generation of building blocks that controls the GA performance. Role of the crossover operator is to preserve the schemata. Crossover operator is more exploitative in nature in comparison to mutation operator as discussed above. Main nature of crossover operator is to preserve the higher level building blocks. Crossover has got higher construction or preservation ability. It helps in transferring the present entire desired schemata to the next generation population. Crossover operator mainly combines various low order building blocks randomly, and selects them randomly through selection operator. In this way higher order and desired building blocks is generated. There is one drawback in crossover operator, though it it constructs, newer bit patterns through recombination, there is no way it adds new information to the population. Result is that exploitative power of crossover is compromised, due to which solution quality diminishes. Though GA parallel search in many areas, if there is no heterogeneity in the population all the efforts of search will go in vain. Thus in this way power of GA is compromised. Crossover helps in construction of building blocks, there is a very much possibility that a desired building block can reach premature death if chromosome or individual that consists the desired building block is not selected by the selection operator or if crossover point lie in between that building block. So it is seen that disruptive power of crossover is less than mutation. Main work of crossover is to transfer desired building blocks or schemata from one generation to other. It is generally drawn from the GA run results that almost 50% of building blocks in the population die in a generation for various reasons. These results in a effect that GA results often get biased as generation passes by.

Thus GA's operators, crossover and mutation are a combination of exploitation and exploration. Exploitation leads to better solution quality and better parallel searching of space, while exploration results in adding newer diversity in the population as without it GA would become stagnant. It helps in refreshing of entire population. Hence both of these operators are necessary for efficient working of GA to robust results. As seen that a variety of researchers recommend higher crossover arte with combination of lower mutation rate for a successful GA run.

7.7 POPULATION SIZE

In GA if total numbers of function evaluations are kept constant. Hence proper balance between population size and number of generations has to be made. In case of larger population size, genetic diversity is large, which leads to better solution or optimal solution must be close to optimal. If population size is less then high rate of mutation operator must be applied to get much needed genetic diversity. There is a threshold value in case of population size below which GA will not give us desired results or find optimal solution. Higher mutation rate in small population size may lead us in wrong direction, thus further delaying the GA to find optimal result. GA will give better result only when proper population size is allocated. In smaller population there is a possibility that GA will converge towards a local optima or to a particular search space. Increase in population size will leads to increase in average fitness and overall population solution quality. Larger population sizes help GA to search parallel in many search area of the problem. This is more feasible in solving complex problem for which GA id=s build. Larger population sizes also helps in minimizing the role of mutation operator. Thus our conclusion is that proper population size has a major effect in GA working.

7.8 CONCLUSION

We should select and tune GA operators in such a manner, that they do not affect, GA success rate. Though GA working is robust in nature, as GA with only one operator in isolation will give better result than traditional numerical based method. In order to fully exploit the GA working, proper use of selection, crossover, mutation operators with above threshold population size is needed. In the end of this chapter a large amount of important information is obtained by studying the working of these operators and how to fine tune them. Our questions about the importance of GA control parameters and their best settings are altogether given by reading this chapter.

REFERENCES

Deb, K. (2002). *Optimization for Engineering Design: Algorithm and Examples*. Prentice Hall of India Private Limited.

Deb, K., & Agrawal, S. (1999). Understanding interactions among genetic algorithm parameters. *Foundations of Genetic Algorithms, 5,* 265–286.

Goldberg, D. E. (2002). *Genetic Algorithms in Search, Optimization and Machine Learning*. Pearson Education.

Kapoor, V., Dey, S., & Khurana, A. P. (2010). Empirical analysis and random respectful recombination of crossover and mutation in genetic algorithms. *International Journal of Computers and Applications, 1*(1), 25–30. doi:10.5120/1530-133

Kapoor, V., Dey, S., & Khurana, A. P. (2011). An empirical study of the role of control parameters of genetic algorithms in function optimization problems. *International Journal of Computers and Applications, 31,* 31–36.

William, M. (1993). *Spears* (Vol. 2). Crossover or Mutation, Foundations of Genetic Algorithms.

Wu, Lindsay, & Riolo. (1997). Empirical Observations on the Roles of Crossover and Mutation. *Proceedings of the 7th International Conference on Genetic Algorithms*, 362-369.

Chapter 8

Advance GA Operators and Techniques in Search and Optimization

ABSTRACT

Genetic algorithms (GAs) are the latest technique to solve problems. A huge amount of research work is available but still there are a lot of newer avenues which have to be explored. In this chapter, the authors discuss variations in the GA operators that can be done and various other background operators that can be use to improve the efficiency and efficacy of GAs. It is not just like a mathematical or statistical technique. In this chapter, the authors discuss various procedural variations, twists and turns, and special meaning they could give to the GA operators in order to improve the solution quality. These newer operators and variations might be useful for researchers in the implementation of GAs to find better solutions.

8.1 INTRODUCTION

Use of science and technology is to make human life simple. Basic science and technology extract the laws of the nature. The invention of electronic machine called computer is the most feasible development in the past. With the help of large processing power provided by computer, our power of prediction and decision making capability has increased many fold. We have to make decision in every sphere of human activity weather in engineering field or

DOI: 10.4018/978-1-7998-4105-0.ch008

technical field. This affects the end product or the desired result we need. In any problem there consists of large number of solutions. Some solutions have large pay off values as compare to other. The engineer should be able to pin point the solution with a larger pay off according to its feasibility. Then he should search feasible solutions to get the optimal value. Searching the solution area is of two types, Deterministic and Stochastic. Deterministic search technique uses steepest gradient method while stochastic method uses randomization as a process to reach towards the optimal value. Various other non traditional methods have also come into picture and has become popular now a days. These methods or algorithm are: simulated annealing, particle swarm optimization, ant colony algorithm, Genetic programming, Genetic algorithms etc. We are going to discuss all these algorithms in the last part of this book. GA is based on the Darwin theory of natural selection and survival of fittest (Goldberg, 2002).

In past computer scientists develop some evolution strategies in which evolution is used to optimized the design parameter fir the given engineering problems. In evolutionary population approach, population of solution for the given problem is generate and by applying various operators which were inspired from the nature to generate newer population of solutions with higher fitness and acceptability. Evolutionary optimization is a popular and active research area now days. Concept of evolutionary programming was first developed by I. Recenberg, a German scientist in 1960's. He published his work named "Evolution Strategies". GA's are soft computing based search and optimization procedures based on the concept of natural genetics and selection. GA's are invented and developed by John Holland and his colleagues and students of University of Michigan USA in 1960's and 1970's. GA's is a general purpose optimization search procedure and is not design to solve specific problem. They can be applied in any field of engineering and technology. Holland in his work published as a book "Adaptation in natural and artificial systems" in 1975 explains the theoretical working of GA. After that a lot of work is done by (David E Goldberg, 1989), (Kalyanmoy Deb, 2002) were published in the public domain. In GA we move from one population of chromosomes (i.e array of strings of 0's and 1's) to another newer population by applying genetic naturally inspired popular operators such as selection, crossover, and mutation. A selection operator selects chromosomes having fitness value more that the average fitness value of the population. Crossover exchanges part of string in two chromosomes with each other. Mutation when and where applied changes the binary value of the chromosome i.e from 0 to 1 and from 1 to 0. These procedure developed by Holland were a major breakthrough in the field of search and optimization. Popularly it came to be known as Genetic Algorithms. Theoretical foundation of GA is based on the concept of Schemas and building block hypothesis as explained in the previous chapters. Based on this theory GA procedure are explained as below:

1. A set of building blocks is producing randomly which is known as initial population set.
2. A new building block is generated by using crossover as a operator, which exchanges the sub part of the building block of two chromosomes (Parent1 & parent 2) selected.
3. A new building block is generated using Mutation operator.
4. Selection operator is applied to select chromosomes in the population with higher fitness function for further application of crossover and mutation operators.
5. Process from point number 2 to 4 is repeated until a termination criterion is met.

With the invention of GA, computation evolution has been put on a firm footing empirically. Until now theoretical foundation was in picture. With the wide spread research in GA's, boundaries between GA and evolutionary computing now over lap each other. GA is now represented as evolutionary computation in a majority way (Hupt et.al, 2004).

GA is generally guided in many directions by the use of these three operators: selection, crossover and mutation. In our passion to keep working of GA simple, we are introducing several variations in these operators as well as many other interesting operators. This will help us to improve efficiency of GA and we will be able to prove GA as a robust search and optimization technique. These advance and low level operators will be helpful in improving GA's working. Some of these operators may be problem specific dependent (Rajesekaran et.al, 2007).

8.2 ADVANCE OPERATORS

8.2.1 Encoding

There are number of ways to represent a chromosome. Coding mechanism depends upon problem to problem i.e being solved. Most popular encoding mechanism amongst the researchers is binary bit encoding or strings.

One thing I want to make it clear is that it is not at all compulsory to code the variables which are being optimized. In some of the cases we can directly apply GA operators on the variables itself. But these cases are of exceptional problem cases, which come into picture. Popular ways to encode the variables are given below:

1. Binary Encoding: Binary encoding is the most popular encoding mechanism. John Holland (1975) in his research mainly worked with binary string encoding. Representation in binary string encoding is shown below:

```
Chromosome A: 1100010101
Chromosome B: 0011011011
```

Here solution to the problem is represented by the use of 0's and 1's. The total length of string gives the accuracy. More the string length more is the accuracy, less is the length less is the accuracy. Representation of 3 bit binary string is given as below:

```
3- bit string    Numeric Value
000                          0
001                          1
010                          2
011                          3
100                          4
101                          5
011                          6
111                          7
```

For example:

$$101 = 1 * 2^0 + 2^1 * 0 + 2^2 * 1 = 5$$

Suppose there are two variable X_1 and X_2 which we want to optimized. The upper and lower limits are defined as:

$$X_i^L \leq X_i \leq X_i^U$$

If three bit strings are used then (000, 000) and (111, 111) are the lower and upper limit. (X_1^L, X_2^L) and (X_1^U, X_2^U) representation. The formula for decoding value of binary string is given below:

$$(x+a)^n = \sum\nolimits_{k=0}^{K=n(i-1)} 2^k SK$$

S_k is the binary string value. So S_1 S_2 S_3.....Sn-1, Kis the bit position.
If we know the lower limit and upper limit of the string i.eX_i^L, X_iU equivalent value of a string is given below:

$$X_i = X_i^L + ((X_i^U - X_i^L)/ (2^n i - 1)) * \text{(Decoded value of a string)}$$

X_i^L&X_i^U value of a 3 bit string is (000) & (111).For example consider a string 101, decoded value is 5.

$$X_i^L = 5, X_i^U = 19 \text{ Then}$$

$$X_i = 5 + ((19 - 5)/ (2^3 - 1)) * 5 = 10$$

2. Octagonal Encoding: Below here is procedure to convert a integer into octal string and vice versa.

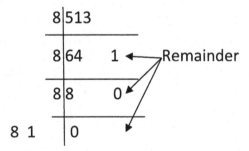

Octal string is 1001

1 0 0 1

$-1 * 8^0 = 1$

$-0 * 8^1 = 0$

$-0 * 8^2 = 0$

$1 * 8^3 = 512$

Total = 513

A three bit octal string represents number to a range from 0 to 511. Thus (000, 000) and (777, 777) are the lower limit (X_1^L, X2L) and upper limit respectively. The decoded value of the string formula is:

K= n-1

$\sum 8^K{}_{SK}$

K=0

Where K = bit position
SK is the octal bit value.
Accuracy formula is $((X_i^U - X_i^L)/ 8^n i$

3. Hexadecimal Encoding: It is similar to octal encoding, but the only difference is that in octal encoding we go on dividing the integer to be converted into octal encoding by 8. In hexadecimal we go on dividing the integer by 16. A three digit hexadecimal code represents integers range from 0 to 4095. Thus (000, 000) and (FFF, FFF) will represent lower limit and upper limit points. The decoded formula for a hexadecimal string S_i is calculated as:

K= n-1

$\sum 8^K{}_{SK}$

K=0

Where K = Bit position

SK is bit value at position k

Accuracy formula is $((X_i^U - X_i^L)/16^n i$

4. Permutation Encoding: In this type of encoding every gene or allele is represented by a integer number. This number can be weight or sequence. This type of encoding scheme is used by researchers in solving travelling salesman problem. Representation in permutation encoding is shown below:

```
Chromosome A: 5 7 6 2 9 7 1
Chromosome B: 2 9 3 7 6 8 5
```

The integer number can represent the order of city or distances between the city in case of travelling salesman problem.

5. Value Encoding: In this type of encoding, allele or geen in chromosomes represents any value that can be mapped to the solution of a problem. Here allele or gene can be numbers, objects, floating point numbers etc. This type of encoding is problem specific. For example it is usedto represent the weights of neural networks. Example of value encoding representation is shown below:

```
Chromosome A: 1.072  1.204  1.629
Chromosome B: avpbpqrspz 9 3 7 6 8 5
Chromosome C: High Low Moderate Big Short
```

6. Tree Encoding: This type of encoding mechanism is wiely used by researcher John Koza in his work on genetic programming. Tree encoding is shown below:

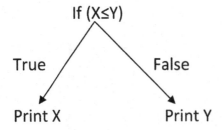

8.2.2 Reproduction

We start with GA by generating random population of chromosomes. Reproduction is the first operator we encounter with. It selects the strings or chromosomes based on the fitness function. Nature of selection operator is to select chromosomes for mating. String which are not selected will face death and string which are luckier to get selected will face life. The modus operandi to select a string or chromosome varies. Some selection operators are greedy in nature; some are explorative in nature etc. After selection operator crossover and mutation operator are applied on them to produce offspring's. Thus reproduction operator is known as selection operator also. There are varieties of selection operator (Bauer,1994). In this sub section we are going to discuss majority of these operators based on their strength and weakness. A common practice in all these operators is that they pick above average strings multiple times from a population for mating. We are going to take a detail review of their working and their finding.

1. Roulette Wheel Selection: It is the most popular selection scheme used by researchers. It is also known as roulette wheel proportionate. To explain this scheme in a simplified manner we start with a example. Let there be a population of 10 chromosomes or strings. If there are five similar strings with fitness value 13 and labeled as A and 5 similar strings with fitness value 7 and labeled as B. Thus label A captures 65% of the total fitness space. And label B covers 35% of total fitness space. If we spin the wheel 10 times to generate 10 chromosomes. Approx. About 7 members will be of A type and 3 members will be of B type. Since we spin randomly in physical space and in case of computer implementation it is done by generating a random number. In fact A/B lable will end between 0/10 and 10/0. Thus in this way higher fitness strings will be selected for mating.

In case of computation implementation, probability of ith string is calculated by formula:

$$Pi = Fi / \sum_{j=1}^{n} Fj$$

Fi = Fitness of ith string

$\sum_{j=1}^{n} Fj$ = Total fitness of the population.

Thus cumulative probability Pi represents the range from Pi-1 to i. Cumulative probability range of 1st string is from 0 to P1 and last string is $P_{n-1} - 1$. Where n is the total population size. Thus cumulative probability of a string is always in between 0 to 1. Thus if we want to select a string then a random number between o and 1 is generated by calling random number generator function called as rand() in C++ programming language. Thus matching of random number generated is done from the string. The random number generated lies in the string having that cumulative probability range, that string is selected and kept for mating. It is obvious that string having higher fitness value will have larger cumulative probability value range. Thus in this way random number generated will have higher chance to fall between this range and thus having higher probability to get selected. The same is the case with string having lesser fitness function. In this way working of roulette wheel selection technique is clear. In this way inferior string in each generation will be replaced or eliminated. We thus ensure that all the string selected is of superior in nature. Thus implementation of roulette wheel selection is very simple and easy. Decimal part of probability distribution is also considered in roulette wheel selection. If decimal part is not considered then it will reduce the noise generated by roulette wheel selection. This new selection technique is known as stochastic reminder selection.

Previously we have shown that expected number of count for label A and label B is 6.5 and 3.5. If we concentrate integer part, that for label A & B is 6 & 3.Thus for the tenth part it can be A or B i.e equal weight age. Thus split between label A & B will be either 7/3 or 6/4.

2. Genitor Selection: It is basically a ranking selection process. Here individual members of the population are ranked by their fitness value. After their better fitness individuals will be replaced by lesser fitness individuals.

3. Rank Selection: This selection technique is used when there is huge difference of fitness function in the population. Suppose there is a population size of 5. If string 1 fitness is 85%, then it will occupy 85% of the circumference. If we spin the wheel according to roulette wheel selection, there will be very little chance for other strings to get selected. So rank selection is best for this type of problem. An assignment function will give rank to the chromosome in the population. The best string

will be given rank n (as total population size is n) and worst string or chromosome will be given rank 1. Thus a new roulette wheel is constructed with rank or assignment functions as their slots. This type of selection procedure added much need noise in the next generation population and thus decrease rate of convergence.

4.   Tournament Selection: Tournament means a match between two or more than two members. Winner member will be selected for mating. In tournament selection two members are selected randomly from the pool of the population. Fitness of these two populations is compared. String having better fitness is selected and copied into the mating pool. It means that its allele will be part of next generation. This whole process is repeated until mating pool is filled up by desired number of strings. In this way newer mating pool will have higher average fitness function than from the previous one. As winner string is selected. Due to this selection pressure quality of strings will improve generation after generation. This will automatically leads to optimal solution in the end.

5.   Steady State Selection: This selection process is different from the previous ones. Here in every generation few chromosomes or individuals having higher fitness function are selected from the population. They are going to replace some bad or worst chromosomes and a new set of individuals for mating pool is created.

6.   Elitism Selection: In this type of selection procedure better fitness chromosomes are copied to form a new population. This increases overall efficiency of GA and best solution is not rejected. Elitism technique selects better fit individuals for mating pool. Better fit individual will be selected larger number of times, while lesser fit individual will be selected lesser number of times. Some of the worst fitness string will be rejected and eventually die off. The factor or parameter which will decide which individual will be selected or rejected is $F/\dot{f}$ where F is the fitness of the string and $\dot{f}$ is the average fitness of the population from where strings are selected.

Thus from above section we came to know diversify procedures to select string for mating. After this various operators are applied on these strings to generate newer better fitness strings or offspring's. The basic of selection operator is to ensure that mating pool is filled up by the individuals having above average fitness function. The efficiency and efficacy of a selection procedure is based on two parameters i.e population diversity and selection pressure. Population diversity is the diversity or rate of exploitation for newer areas of search space. Selective pressure means the rate of level by which better performing string is captured. In other words it defines the greediness of the selection procedure.

Both of these parameters are inversely proportional to each other. Higher rate of selective pressure will lead to the loosening of population diversity. And this results in convergence of population quickly or prematurely. Thus in this way we stuck up in a local optima as diversity in the population is lost at an early stage. Selective pressure is decreased in order to reduce the convergence rate. Thus GA will take some more generation to find a global optimal solution. Thus in a selection operator proper balance between selection pressure and population balance must be made. Thus higher rate of selection pressure or greediness in the selection procedure will lead to the stagnation and quick convergence of the population towards the local maxima. The selection operator should be able to add noisiness in the mating pool. Thus choice of selection operator should have balance between exploitation and exploration. Exploitation leads to quick convergence, lesser fit solution. While exploration leads to not so quick convergence, but higher quality of search.

In simple GA crossover and mutation are the two main operators. We will discuss variation in these two operators first and then we will discuss various other low level operators also.

8.2.3 Crossover

After selection operator fills the mating pool with better fit individuals, Crossover operator is applied. Crossover operator is a critical operator. It is of disruptive in nature. Better strings patterns will be broken. If crossover frequency is more and crossover points are more than search is just like a random walk or noisy in nature. It will leads us to nowhere. It will stuck us to the narrow regions of the search space. Crossover is a recombination operator. A crossover site is generated randomly and string values are swapped. There are many variations in crossover process in GA. They are discussed in the coming section:

1. Single Point Crossover: It is the most simplest and basic form of crossover operator. Here a point is chosen randomly between the starting and maximum length of the string. Binary bits after that points in both of the strings are exchange as shown below:

Chromosome 1 : (*Parent*)	11110	11001
Chromosome 2 : (*Parent*)	11000	00001

Chromosome 1 : (*Offspring*)	11110	00001
Chromosome 2 : (*Offspring*)	11000	11001

If chosen with caution application of crossover will produce better building blocks. Since crossover points are generated randomly, there is a possibility that crossover string quality or may disrupt already developed higher order building blocks. Better fitness score strings not produced by crossover will have little chance to get selected for mating pool for next generation.

2. Two point Crossover: It is similar to single point crossover. Here instead of one crossover point two crossover point are generated and binary strings between these two points in the two chromosomes are exchanged as shown below:

Chromosome 1 : (*Parent*)	11	110110	01
Chromosome 2 : (*Parent*)	11	000000	01

Chromosome 1 : (*Offspring*)	11	000000	01
Chromosome 2 : (*Offspring*)	11	110110	01

3. Multi point crossover: Here in contrast to one or two points, multiple points in the chromosomes or strings are generated either in even number or odd number. The binary bits between the two crossover points are exchanged alternatively. The whole process is shown below:

Chromosome 1 : (*Parent*)	00	000	0000	00000
Chromosome 2 : (*Parent*)	11	111	1111	11111

Chromosome 1 : (*Offspring*)	00	000	0000	00000
Chromosome 2 : (*Offspring*)	11	111	1111	11111

4.   Uniform Crossover: This process is extreme case of multi point crossover. Here we go bit by bit. Every bit is selected with a chosen probability. If the value falls within the number, then we exchange that bit from the bit of other chromosome selected for crossover. Whole process is shown below:

Chromosome 1 : (*Parent*)	000000000000
Chromosome 2 : (*Parent*)	111111111111

Chromosome 1 : (*Offspring*)	↓ ↓ ↓ ↓ ↓ ↓ 100100100101
Chromosome 2 : (*Offspring*)	↓ ↓ ↓ ↓ ↓ ↓ 011011011010

5.   Matrix or two dimensional Crossovers: Until now we have seen crossover over a single dimension array. Here there will be crossover over a two dimensional or multidimensional array. Here strings are arranged in a multi dimensional array and multiple random sites are generated and binary bits positions are exchanged.

The crossover operators should be designed in such a way that it leads to proper search. It is seen from above study that starting from single point crossover to multi point crossover intensiveness in the search increases manifold. A lot of research is being done to find better crossover operator. It is not left to individual GA expert to choose the type of crossover operator he wants to implement in his GA.

8.2.4 Mutation

After crossover the whole mating string is put on to mutation. Mutation is a bit wise operator that changes the value of binary bit from 0 to 1 and vice versa. Generally mutation probability is kept very low. It is considered to be secondary operator. It is used to add genetic diversity in the population or to generate some genetic structures in the population. If GA population stuck in a local minima, then mutation operator help us to recover from it. How mutation creates genetic diversity is shown below. Suppose there is a population of 4 with 4 bit string:

```
1000
1100
1010
0100
```

Now in all those strings right most strings have a value 0, if global optima requires value 1 in that position. Crossover cannot add this diversity in that position. It can only be added by the use of mutation operator. Though secondary, it is the important operator in the GA search. Mutation operator can be applied bit by bit or string by string. In string case whole binary string values are reversed, if mutation operator is applied.

Bit by Bit mutation operator

```
↓     ↓
0001001
```

After Mutation

```
1001000
```

String by String mutation operator

```
0001001
```

After Mutation

```
1110110
```

Mutation operator rate is generally kept low i.e0.01, that means 1 bit per 100 bits or 10 bits per 1000 bits. Apart from these basic operators, there are a lot more number of various not so important low level operators. When used strategically these operators gives us better results and add much needed power to GA. Some of them are listed below:

1. Inversion.
2. Dominance, Diploidy.
3. Deletion.
4. Intra chromosome duplication.
5. Translocation.
6. Segregation.
7. Speciation.
8. Migration.
9. Sharing.
10. Mating.
11. Bit wise operator.

In more detail:

1. Inversion: In case of inversion we generate two random sites. The bits between the two random sites are inverted as shown below.

```
1111 | 0000 | 1111
1111 | 1111 | 1111
```

There are various variations in inversion process which are explained below:

a.   Linear end inversion: Here we apply probability to apply it. If the inversion is not performed then end inversion is performed with a equal probability i.e 0.125 at the end of the strings (right or left). In this type of inversion either left end point or right end point of the string is selected. After this another point which is not far away from tm the half mark of string is selected. Thus binary value between these two strings is reversed. This linear end inversion is valuable, because it reduce the tendency of operator to disrupt the highly desirable building block in the centre of string.

b.   Continuous Inversion: Here in this type of inversion binary chromosome is selected, probability P_i is applied and if value falls within this probability, then the whole string is inverted.

c.   Mass Inversion: Here after creation of new population of strings, half of the population i.e first half or last half is selected and linear inversion using two points between the strings are taken and strings are inverted.

2.   Deletion and Duplication: Here some number of random bits is selected and duplicated by just previous bits as shown below. This operator reduces the rate of mutation as and when required in GA.

101	0100	101	*Initial string*
101	01 _ _	101	*Deletion*
101	0101	101	*Duplication*

3.   Deletion and Regeneration: Here two points in the string is selected randomly. The binary bits are deleted and new bits are placed randomly here.

100010010001	*Initial string*
10 _ _ _ _ _ _ _ _ 01	*Deletion*
101010111101	*After regeneration*

4.   Segregation: Here bits are selected and rearranged to produce new string.

↑ → ↓
10 0 000 0 1
↑ ← ↓
10010000   *New string*

5. Crossover and Inversion: Here it is combination of two operators. Two random crossover sites are chosen. The binary bits between these two sites are exchanged and new strings are obtained. After that bits between these two points are inverted by using inverter operator. The whole process is shown below:

01	001001001	01	*Parent* 1	*Before Crossover*
01	111011011	01	*Parent* 2	
01	111011011	01	*Parent* 1	*After Crossover*
01	001001001	01	*Parent* 2	
01	000100100	01	*Parent* 1	*After Inversion*
01	110110110	01	*Parent* 2	

6. Various other Bit wise operators: It is seen in GA literature binary based encoding is very popular amongst GA practitioners. Here solution to the real world problems are mapped into binary strings and GA operators explained until now works on it. In past chapters we had write GA code in C++ language. There are a number of build in functions which operates on these strings directly, easily and efficiently. Popular bit wise operators are:

    a. Complement operator: It is a unary type of operator represented by the sign ~. This operator inverts binary string values. It is always applied before the string as shown below:

~ 1000110110

After Complement operator

0111001001

    b. Logical bitwise operator (Bitwise AND, Bitwise OR, Bitwise XOR): This types of operators requires two operands and can be used as a substitute of crossover operator. These operators are applied on bit by bit basis. Workings of these operators are shown below:

144

```
String 1    String 2    AND    OR    XOR
    0           0         0      0      0
    0           1         0      1      1
    1           0         0      1      1
    1           1         1      1      0
```

    c.   Shift operators: There are two types of shift left shift («) and right shift (»). Operator here is applied on to the string. Apart from string it requires number of positions the binary bits has to be replaced. This number is given as unsigned integer.

        Shift left («): It is shown below

```
A = 111000111
A « 3 = 000111000
```

        Here bits are shifted by number of position given in second operand i.e unsigned integer. Thus the left most bits are lost and right most positions are filled by zeroes. Same is the case with the right sift operators but in a reverse direction as shown below:

```
A = 1110000111
A » 3 = 0001110000
```

        Here the bits are shifted in the right direction by the position given in the number. Thus the left most vacant position is filed by zeroes.

    d.   Masking: Here given bit pattern is changed to another bit pattern by using logical bit wise operator. Here two operands are used. One operand is original bit pattern, while second operand is the mask i.e a selected bit pattern that does the transformation.

        These all bit wise operator can be used in GA to produce new population or children of next generation. Here in GA, operators are applied number of times in order to keep population size constant.

7.   Dominance and Diploidy: These two operators are the most important operators, but they are being discussed at last. In biology books, chapter on genetics start with the work done by Mandel on peas plants, with mention of dominance (Goldberg, 2002). We in our book are explaining dominance and diploidy in last because we want to systematically explain the role of selection, systematic recombination and other operators first. In nature organisms are diploid and polyploidy in their genetic structure. This lead us to make assumption, that we cannot applied them in artificial genetic search i.e in Genetic Algorithms. The coming part

of chapter explains the role of dominance and diploidy to find alternate better solutions which are restricted by the use of excessive selection.

Until now in our GA search we had considered simple genotype i.e haploid or single stranded chromosome. But it is well known that the working of nature is not simple. Natural organisms consists of more complex chromosome structures ie. polyploid or homogeneous chromosomes. Here we are going to understand only diploid chromosome structure i.e chromosome in pair. In this type genotype structure consists of one or more pairs of chromosomes, which consists the information about the same function. Now the question arises that if this redundancy or repetition is important or not. Why kept number of pairs of chromosomes that decode the same function, but with a different answer or values. Now from this pair of chromosome which portion we will pay more attention and select it. Let us understand this complexity by an example given below.

Let there be a two chromosome structure

```
P q R s t u
P Q r S T u
```

Here each letter weather upper case or lower case represent a alleles, but with different nature or character tics. Each allele represent different feature of organism. For example q allele represents a fair skin and Q allele represents dark skin. So a person cannot be fair and dark skin feature simultaneously. Nature has to choose from any of the one value. This allele value q and Q have different feature and offspring can have either q or Q feature. This will be decided by the genetic operators called dominance. In final string one allele takes over dominantly over the other. It is expressed in the final string. The rule is that if capital letters are dominant over lower case or small case letters then:

```
P q R s t u
                →     P Q R S T u
P Q r S T u
```

IT means

```
P → PP, q → QQ, R → rR, s → SS, t → TT, u → uu.
```

Now the abstract view is clear. The question arises what is the use to carry double information, and then we cut information to half and use it. By seeing it in vogues it seems to be an unnecessary and time consuming step. In real nature no process is wasteful. There should be rationale behind this step i.e repetition of previous chromosomes and applying dominance operator on it. In nature there is a requirement of such type of arrangement, as it protects genes of older generations against the rapid changes in the environment i.e from hot climate to cold and then to a bearable temperature, from darkness to light. Hence there are many rapid changes in the environment. Thus the organism which has diploid or polyploidy structure, will have greater chances to survive in the this extreme change in the environment. This due to the reason that previous generation genes are not lost and preserved in their diploid and poly diploid structures. Thus multiple combinations exist and only one combination is expressed. Thus old genes are not forever if not selected. In this way they come into picture when required by the use of dominance operator, which is used occasionally or sparingly.

In case of Genetic Algorithms i.e our artificial search, some building blocks in chromosomes are lost due to faulty or randomized selection operator. Diploidy and dominance operator help us to carry these chromosomes as they were useful previously and allow them to come into existence in the future generations or in some hostile environment, when they are needed the most. It is seen that these two operators must be applied rarely with a low degree. Thus it empowers GA larger number of other solutions, resulting in an increase of efficiency and efficacy. In this way GA allows many alternative solutions to pass from one generation to other, and prevent them from being lost, as compared with simpler implementation of GA presented earlier. We have seen that applying dominance is not an independent act. Rather there must be certain rule to apply it at a particular location. Researcher had suggested certain schemes which are explained below:

- Radom, fixed and global dominance: Here dominance of all binary alleles is measured by just flipping an unbiased coin for each binary value. Thus when pairs of chromosomes are selected, dominant allele is selected.
- Variable, global dominance: Here probability of the dominance of 0's and 1's is calculated by the proportion of 0's and 1's in the current generation. If number of 0's exceeded the number of 1's, then 0 is the dominant allele and vice versa.

- Deterministic, variable, global dominance: Here also number of 0's and 1's are calculated for each position and pair chromosomes with larger portion of 0's and 1's are declared dominant.
- Choose a random chromosome: Here in two chromosomes selected. An dominant chromosome is selected at the flip of an unbiased coin. In this war all the alleles of the chromosomes are considered to be dominant.
- Dominance of better chromosomes: Here the fitness of the two chromosomes in the pair is calculated. Chromosomes with higher fitness function are considered to dominant.
- Use of third party chromosomes for diploid adaptive dominance: Here values of another chromosome consists the mapping of dominance or rule for it. In this dominance operator is applied dynamically in nature rather than static.

In nature or biology human being carries 23 pair of diploid chromosomes. In the above section of this chapter we had discussed various low level operators that can be used in GA. Use of these operators in combination with diploidy and dominance add some of the much needed genetic diversity and power to search newer spaces in GA. In addition to this, these operators help in getting good string combination. If the higher order operator i.e crossover or mutation destroys important allele combination, then with the help of these low level operators we can recover them in a systematic way. Thus propagation or transfer of building blocks takes place from one generation to other.

8.3 NICHE AND SPECIATION

Uptil now we had applied GA for uni modal function i.e function with only one peak. It is seen from the results of researchers that GA was very effective in finding a single global optimum and converging its population around it. In other domain where there are multiple optima's GA may find best peak and converge population around it. It is unable to find other rules or lesser peaks. Traditional GA are difficult to work for multi modal function.

It is seen for problems with equal multiple peaks traditional GA will converge towards a single peak. Thus GA to find best rule, GA will converge towards a single rule. Thus to allow or force GA to search for multiple peaks and avoid converging its population to a single peak, various population diversity schemes are suggested. Thus application of these schemes helps GA to fetch multiple optima for a multi modal domain instead of single optimal. This helps us to obtained both number and quality of optima.

To start with a multi modal domain, each peak or optimal point is called as niche. Every niche consists of number of rules for the system to find best rules of set of parameters. As there are number of niche with varying peak, number of individuals in these peak should be directly proportional to niche peak fitness as compare to other niche peak fitness values. Thus GA should populate niche in proportion to fitness relative to other peaks. One problem that occurs in implementing these population diversity schemes is that we do not know the multiple peak of the location of the system. Due to this it is difficult to populate each niche. Thus in order to identify various niche location and proportional population values various mechanisms are devised and discussed in next section.

- Crowding: In this process convergence capability of GA is reduced, by diluting the changes in the population, as it passes from one generation to the other. In crowding we select a part of population to reproduce next generation. The resulting generation of population is replaced in given manner. Here certain random number of individuals is selected from the population and most similar members is replaced by offspring. This results in minimizing the changes in the population as it passes from one generation to other and slowing the tendency of GA to converge at a single point in coming generations. Due to this exploration capability of GA is reduced to a significant level. Crowding technique may not be very useful to find multiple optima.
- Sharing: In this mechanism we reduce the fitness of individual chromosomes intentionally that have large number of similar members in the population. This results in exploitation of other areas in the search space or domain as well as reducing number of similar chromosomes on the population.

Other population diversity measures are standard sharing and dynamic sharing methods. Thus we had discussed these advance GA techniques to pin point multiple optima in multimodal area. Here niche formation and mating restriction methods such as crowding, sharing has been discussed.

8.4 MULTI OBJECTIVE OPTIMIZATION

Until now we are discussing objective function with single criteria. This criterion is translated into fitness function. After this we apply various GA operators to find the best or close to best solution founded until now for a given problem. But in some problem multiple criterion are present at a given time. Hence they all cannot be represented in a single function. These types of problems are known as multiple objective optimization problems. Many researchers in past has applied traditional process of optimization and search to find best possible solutions find until so far. As stated that there are multiple objective function in multi objective problem. Thus to represent multi objective in one equation is:

$$F = X_1 f_1 + X_2 f_2 + \ldots \ldots X_n f_n$$

X_1, X_2, X_3... are the weights and f_1, f_2, f_3... are multiple objective function. Here the solution is finding various optimal solutions of various single objective function using different weight vectors. These various solutions are called Pareto Optimal solutions. In latest GA is used to solve multi objective problem.

8.5 GENETIC ALGORITHM (GA) IN A NUT SHELL

Until now we all are very well versed with the working of GA. GA works with the coded string of variables, not with the variables itself. GA need function values for different variables. GA works with a population of chromosomes or solution not with a single solution. This makes GA very effective search methods as search parallel through various points. In GA multiple optima solutions are found in a single run. This is not the case with the traditional optimization and search methods. However there are various issues related to GA while implementing them. They are:

- Representation of solution in binary string.
- Population size Vs number of generations.
- Crossover rate vs mutation rate.
- Termination condition.
- Performance issues.

These issues have been successfully discussed in previous chapters. However various benefits of using GA are:

- Easy to absorb.
- Support multi objective optimization.
- Favorable for noisy environment.
- After every iteration solution quality improves.
- Parallel search.
- Exploitative and explorative in nature.
- Best suited as a alternative for hybrid application.
- Popular among researchers and lot of research has been done until so far.

GA are used when search space is very large, as brute force attack cannot be applied, where traditional techniques is too slow and hybrid methods are a failure.

8.6 CONCLUSION

Here we had discussed various not so popular advance operators, which can be used to improve GA working. Various unary and binary operators has also been discussed. Working of inversion, segregation, duplication, deletion and various other types of selection, crossover a mutation operators been examined in depth. Dominance and diploidy has been discussed at length, which uses long term past population memory. Key theories of niche and there sharing and crowding techniques has been briefly discussed. The literature we had discussed so far is the tip of the ice berg of GA research available so far. It is sure implementation of these advance GA operators will surely lead us to improve GA performance and increase its efficiency and efficacy.

REFERENCES

Bauer, R. J. Jr. (1994). *Genetic Algorithms and Investment Strategies*. John Wiley and Sons, Inc.

Deb, K. (2002). *Optimization for Engineering Design: Algorithm and Examples*. Prentice Hall of India Private Limited.

Goldberg, D. E. (2002). Genetic Algorithms in Search, Optimization and Machine Learning. Pearson Education. *Asia*.

Haupt, R. L., & Haupt, S. A. (2004). *Practical Genetic Algorithms*. John Wiley and Sons, Inc.

Rajasekaran & Vijaylakshmi Pai. (2007). *Neural Networks, Fuzzy Logic, and Genetic algorithms, Synthesis and Applications*. Prentice- Hall of India Private Limited.

Section 3
Genetic Algorithms in Finance

Chapter 9

Genetic Algorithms (GAs) and Stock Trading Systems

ABSTRACT

Recent advances and improvements in hardware and software technology have benefitted research in the field of finance. It has made research even more interesting. A large amount of data can be processed with lightning speed. Investors are now eagerly looking for small models and algorithms of a lucrative value and with better accuracy. Earlier, the decision to enter the market or to exit is taken emotionally with fear then by any rational thinking. Due to this, a lot of bad decisions were taken, and a huge amount of capital was lost. With the help of this computational system, a computer program will decide when to enter and when to exit the market without any human intervention. The decision here will be taken by testing a large amount of permutation and combination of various parameters associated with the system. This chapter briefly explains the scope and agenda of various algorithms for computation research in finance.

9.1 INTRODUCTION

Advancement in computation technology had made a dent in every strata of society. In the field of stock trading this effect is very large. In past we always had a large amount of data. But manually it was impossible to process the data. It would take days sometimes even months to process such a huge amount of data. With the advancement of hardware technology i.e increase

DOI: 10.4018/978-1-7998-4105-0.ch009

in processing power, results are obtained with a faster speed. Computational power also helps us to formulate complex models and to simulate them with accuracy. We can run them by writing a simple program. This helps us to explore newer opportunities to invest capital with a lower risk. Thus a new area to study finance has come into picture. Present and coming chapters will make a detail analysis of these newer computation methods. Advancement of machine learning techniques, soft computing techniques (Genetic algorithms, Neural Networks, Fuzzy Logic etc.) help us to formulate newer models, found newer parameters of these models and help us to analyze data with an efficiency. Thus a new area of research based on these newer computation models has come into picture in the field of finance and economics.

With this computational power we will be able to do number of experiments on the past or historic data. Computation models are unbiased and are not driven by emotions. With a squeeze of time, to perform such test we would be able to find which model really worked well and will be a value generator. Thus this testing of past data will help us to find the profitability of various models. It is seen that data sets and the models are very complex and we cannot do calculations of it by the use of human mind only. Various attempts to find a pattern to enter the market by eying the charts will not give good results and decision taken will be wrongly biased. Hence validity of the decision taken is somewhat questioned. If we use these soft computing methods, these patterns would be found out by the program which is an implementation of that particular algorithm and the computer will do all the work. The program code will run on the past years of data, look for the pattern which will give us profits when we enter the market. Thus in the same way exit pattern will also be found.

With in invention of these newer soft computing based approaches, they challenge the fundamental concepts of market behaviour and economic principles (Bauer, 1994), (Rajasekaran et. al, 2007). In some past researches, researchers have tried to formulate newer more profitable strategies, while some researchers have tried to gain insight of the working of financial markets. Proper use and utilization of these methods will help us to make and test newer models and with different parameters. This will help a trader or individual to make more accurate decision with rationality. This in turn will reduce the risk and increase the competitiveness.

Now the question arises that what we should study in computation finance. The topic meaning will vary from person to person. In order to make the whole thing popular we should be able to give a precise definition of computation finance, which should be accepted by the people from every area who want to try it for value addition. A working definition of computational finance is that all these machine learning techniques and soft computing algorithms are general purpose in their procedures. They can be applied to any system and to any field, interfacing these algorithms with financial system or stock trading system and applying it to a past stock market data, will leads to capital gain or profit. There must be acceptance and consensus about the working of computation finance, which will lead to the avoidance of any criticism and will focus on their implementation. Initial stages of research in this area and boundaries were close. But as the research in this area increases, the boundaries of it changes considerably. Our chapter does not give full survey of the topic, but it gives an insight of it with special emphasis on evolutionary algorithms i.e Genetic algorithms (GA's). Full survey of various computational techniques is beyond the scope of this book and it requires a large space to work on it. This field is still young and is in the infant stage as compare with other traditional statistical methods applied in the field of finance research. Computational finance challenges to fundamental theories in economics, finance and market.

In market if we take a decision to buy or to sell, to enter or to exit, we should take decision on the basis of some reasoning. Decision makers here can be individual's persons or analysts etc. They should have rational thinking in taking the decision, otherwise they will make losses. In a simple or naive or layman case, if we want to purchase anything. If two prices are quoted for it then we will go for lower price. This is a simple rational reason for taking any decision. For some complex problem to make any rational decision, it may take more mathematical efforts. It depends upon person to person. Some persons have larger brain capacity to solve the problem and some has less. Some may solve the problem quickly, some are lethargic in nature. So as the complexity of problem increases, calculation to make any decision also increases. Our brain also has certain limit. Some of the problems where there is a explosion of combinations, these are known as NP hard problems. They cannot be solved just by the use of human brain and manually. For example the case of travelling sales man problem. If we start with a few cities then it is okay. But if there are few hundred or thousand cities then it is very difficult to solve them manually. In case of finance or stock trading model, we create a system which tells us when to make an entry and to make an exit. There may be explosion of combination of parameters in the model. So we have to find which parameter setting is best i.e optimized value of parameters of the model have to be found. In case of running and random test we select a set of parameters randomly and then test it. If result obtained is not appropriate then we adjust them according to our intuition and see how model behaviour changes according to it. But if we follow some process, several traditional optimization processes are there. Manually we change parameters settings and see in which direction we get good results. We manipulate the parameters and see effect of interaction of parameters on the solution quality. Another process is brute force optimization (Lederman et.al, 1995). Here every parameter setting from the starting to the nth setting is applied on the model and solution quality is checked. The best solution quality obtained from the set of parameters is taken for future use. There is problem with this approach, if search space is large enough, then it will take years to check each and every solution and then to find an optimal one. Brute force technique is workable when search space is small. But brute force optimization technique is a complete search technique found so far. So for large search space problems heavy duty optimization methods such as genetic algorithms have proved successful. GA's when applied properly can find a optimal solution or close to optimal solution when number of parameters involved are more. A GA based strategic system is an important tool in the hands of stock trader or analyst when applied properly.

It is seen that some algorithms find better solution in a lesser time. As we are having constraints in data size and processing power. In order to be more rational it depends upon which algorithm you use and how much processing power your computer has. Better selection of algorithm and faster computer can give better solutions as it will involve more rationality in making decisions and thus lowering overall risks. Thus our rational reasoning depends upon the type of algorithm we use and computation power we have in hand. It also depends upon the cognitive reasoning and resources we had at our door step. For ex. Nature of algorithm, processing power of our machine and time we had got to make a decision. Here rationality of all the mathematical and computation based models depends upon the quantification of resource available. Hence for the best practice we should use fastest computer and better or latest algorithm proven so far to value add in our results.

9.2 THE EFFICIENT MARKET HYPOTHESIS

Now as in previous section we had understood one feature associated with the market i.e rationality. Here we are going to examine Efficient Market

Hypothesis (EMH) which is the basic assumption behind most of the analysis to predict the market (Focardi et, al, 1997). The statement of Efficient Market Hypothesis (EMH) dates back to early 1990's i.e with the start of financial markets. Efficient Market Hypothesis (EMH) conventionally states that markets are efficient and absorbs all information i.e the market indices reflects all the information available.

Now the question arises can we predict the market. By seeing the past work of various researchers this question is discussed in a very detail manner. Popular hypothesis in finance such as Efficient Market Hypothesis (EMH) comes into picture, which states that we cannot beat the market; and in no condition we can make profit from it by forecasting the market. Efficient Market Hypothesis (EMH) in detail states that all information related to the market is already shown in its prices and if any new information comes into picture, market corrects itself according to the information. So market is efficient and we cannot predict it by using any methodology. In fact there are three types of Efficient Market Hypothesis (EMH):

- Weak: It states that, we cannot forecast the market based on the use of past historic data.
- Semi Strong: It states that w cannot use any publishes or known information to forecast the market.
- Strong: It states that any available information known or unknown in public domain cannot be used to forecast it.

We are considering weak form of Efficient Market Hypothesis (EMH) as we try to earn abnormal profits by analysing past historic data, their trading volume, charts etc. Weak form of Efficient Market Hypothesis (EMH) states that any type of technical analysis will not bear any fruits. In stock market as we know that it is a zero sum game. If somebody makes a gain than somebody makes a loss also. Weak form of Efficient Market Hypothesis (EMH) is related to Random walk Hypothesis. Random walk Hypothesis states that returns on investment are of independent in nature. Next day return is not dependent on previous day returns. As new information from various resources keeps on pouring, market absorbs all the information which is shown in the market indices. It does not depend upon the past return. Random walk model is stated as below:

$$Y(t) = Y(t-1) + Rs$$

$Y(t)$ = Value of market indices at time t.

Rs = Independent and identically distributed variable.

A lot of research is done by researchers by using historic prices of stock market indices in order to falsify weak form of Efficient Market Hypothesis (EMH) and see if market prices are predictable. Some studies are more precise and some are vague in nature, which gives no confirmation about the predictability of the market and daily returns are not a random walk. Past researches have shown some self contradicting statements about random walk and Efficient Market Hypothesis (EMH). So to counter these anomalies newer methods and theories are to be invented to contradict weak form of Efficient Market Hypothesis (EMH).

9.3 GETTING AN INSIGHT ABOUT THE FINANCIAL AND STOCK MARKET

There is a common feeling among the investors and non investors that a large amount of capital is at stake throughout the stock markets of the world. Stock market indices not only show the strength of a nation's prosperity and vice versa. They both are strongly linked with each other. Today in the age of Information technology market is simply approachable not only to the strategic experts but also to the common and naive investor also. The ups and down of stock market effect our living every day. It has a direct impact on our social life also.

A non desirable feature which is associated with the market is doubt, about its state. This feature defines the nature of market and is inescapable in nature. So our whole research in building of newer model is to reduce this ambiguity feature. This model tries to tap the noisiness or randomness of the market. Some researchers have attempted to predict market on daily basis, while other say that market is efficient for long term. As we all know that power of money derives not everything, but many things in this world. So this is the main reason researchers are attracted towards the forecasting of stock market. Fundamental is the monetary gain. There are many challenges in prediction, since market is volatile and market data is of high frequency in nature. This main feature of forecasting has been a main topic of discussion amongst the researchers, and academician's worlds wide. In field of finance a hypothesis that has been formulated is very popular is Efficient Market Hypothesis

(EMH), which states market absorbs each and every information related to it and by no means can we forecast it. Many researchers and academicians reject this hypothesis out rightly, many accept it. Till date Efficient Market Hypothesis (EMH) has not been accepted undisputedly or no consensus has been made on it.

By seeing this type of case of stock market forecasting, there are two groups of researchers and agents. One says that we use various mathematical and computational processes to predict stock market. So they challenge Efficient Market Hypothesis (EMH) theory. Other group validates Efficient Market Hypothesis (EMH), and says that market is efficient, as it absorbs every new piece of information in it and corrects itself according to it. So there is no way we can predict it. This group also lay emphasis on the fact that stock market run is of a random walk and stock data is of very high frequency i.e of noisy in nature. So best way to forecast the tomorrow opening price is by use of human intuition only. A researcher from the group that contradicts Efficient Market Hypothesis (EMH) uses a lot more number of methods to forecast the stock indices. These methods or process are divided into four types

1. Technical Analysis for prediction
2. Fundamental analysis for prediction
3. Traditional Time series analysis for prediction

4. AI Based and soft computing based various machine learning procedures. Now start with technical analysis. Technical analysts are chart readers, which reads the charts based on past data. They try to make an insight about the market just by discovering patterns in the chart. The charts are made from past historic data of the market. Next comes the fundamental analysis. It is the detail study of the inherent or essential merit of the particular stock. By this data decision to invest or divest from the stock is to be made. In traditional time series model to find bearish and bullish run in the market is based on the past daily market indices. These models are of two types: Univariate and Multivariate type. If we use one variable then it is univariate and if we use more than one variable then it is multivariate model to forecast the market. Last come to the machine learning based or soft computing based models. Machine learning techniques are actually algorithms which try to find pattern more accurately in the past data. The degree of accuracy of these all four procedures depends upon the way, by which they are applied and past data sets which are used. From past work we found that none of these techniques are consistent in working, so that an investor or stock trader could blindly

follow it. Our study in this chapter and coming chapters is concentrated on the soft computing based machine learning techniques, with special emphasis on Evolutionary based computation i.e Genetic Algorithms (GA's).

9.4 STOCK MARKET PREDICTION AND INVESTMENT THEORIES

This section gives us a brief survey of some of the practices and notion that are practiced in the stock market for prediction. An investment theory to predict the market is based on the parameters which one should take into account while entering or exit from the market (Bauer, 1994). Investor generally see's, thought and react. It is that this process which does the capital allocation to the market.

It is of no doubt that majority or almost all of the investors enter into the market to make money or to achieve profits. In order to make profit, we should put capital in the stocks that have good future. This can only be done by forecasting the market indices. An investor invests or divests money in the market, depends upon the information they have, which is shown in the market indices. According to fundamental analysis, the real or actual value of stock depends upon the condition of the firm. While technical time series prediction model investor action depends upon the investor behaviour or actions. It does not depend upon the actual or factual value of the firm. Hence in fundamental analysis there is 90% logic and 10% intuition or psychology. While reverse is the case in traditional time series prediction. It believes that market is driven only by psychology.

Market Data: The market trend i.e bearish or bullish run is predicted by the detail analysis of the past or historic data. Data can be classified into three parts:

1. Technical Data: It is the data which is directly associated with the stock. For example closing price, opening price, day high, day low, volume of shares traded per day, delivery volume etc.
2. Fundamental Data: It is the data which is directly related to the company. For ex. Profit of the firm, Earning per share (EPS), trade orders etc.
3. Derived Data: This type of data is generated by changing or combining various technical or fundamental data to generate a new data. For example rate of return, volatility etc.

A systematic analysis of all these all data helps us to make an insight into the market working. We will be able to deduce or conclude various rules from it. It is that conclusion which all the above methods discussed briefly is going to do. The process is different for various prediction models.

9.5 PREDICTING OR FORECASTING THE MARKET

Definition for prediction or forecasting of market is that we have search and analyse past data, find association and correlation between these data. After these rules for prediction has to be made. Then these rules have to be tested on another set of data to find their accuracy. If accuracy level is found to be permissible then we will use it to predict future market. So the past data which is used to prepare any rule or model is divided into two parts. First is training set and second is testing set. In this whole process we will be able to find the degree of randomness of the market.

9.5.1 Various Forecasting Methods

Predicting any stock market indices is a very tedious and fascinating process. Through the whole process your senses are on your toes. Various stock market forecasting models vary from casual or relax way (i.e study of chart mode from past data) to a more conventional or official way (i.e time series analysis or regression analysis). Earlier in this chapter we had classified various forecasting techniques as given below:

1. Technical analysis Methods.
2. Fundamental Analysis Methods.
3. Traditional Time Series Forecasting Methods based on Technical indicators.
4. Machine Learning or Soft Computing Methods.

These above classification are different from each other in their type of procedures and data type on which their experimentation is to be done. Only thing that is common in them is that they forecast market indices for the benefit of the investor. No one technique stated above is consistent in prediction, so that the investor or trader can rely on it. Each technique has been in question in some or the other way.

1. **Technical Analysis:** Technical analysis is used to forecast market i.e when to buy and when to sell by seeing various charts and finding useful patterns in them. Main notion in technical analysis is that share prices move in a trend which is due to the changing behaviour of the investor due to the reaction of the information that has pour in. Using the stock data i.e closing price, day high, day low, volume, opening price a technical analyst tries to predict the coming stock indices movements. By analysis of these charts we can detect movement in which direction market is going. These bullish, bearish or noisy movements are noticeable in nature. They are often repetitive or cyclic in nature. By study of these charts certain rules are inferred for market prediction. A technical analyst is also called chartist popularly. Almost all of the researchers in this community believe that market is 90% based on psychology and 10% based on logic. So a careful and minute study of market charts will give us an insight what majority of traders is doing and what will be the market future. Though popular in use this type of prediction is generally criticized by the researchers. Firstly that formation of various rules just buys seeing the charts vary from researcher to researcher. These rules are of subjective in nature. Hence this procedure if often criticized by researchers from other areas. Technical analysis is used to predict market on a short term or daily basis.

2. **Fundamental Analysis:** This type of analysis is based on firm foundation theory to select individual stock. Here a fundamental analyst generally use fundamental data as stated before such as growth, company profit, tax rates, bank interest rates etc. To get a clear picture about the company, whose stock is being traded? This will help him to find how strong foundation of company is? Here the real or actual value of the company stock is being calculated. Here the main activity of the analyst is to find the inherent or real value of the stock or company. So the simple trading model or rule is: If the inherent or actual value is more than the value of the stock which is being traded, then buy signal is generated otherwise do not enter that stock or it will be termed as bad or gone investment. In a reverse to technical analysis a fundamental analyst believes that market is 90% logical and 10% psychological. In our later chapter we are not going to emphasize on this type of study. Main difference with other studies is that here data changes on quarterly or yearly basis not on daily basis. This type of analysis is good to predict the market on long term basis.

3. **Traditional Time Series Prediction or Technical Analysis:** Here analysis of various past or historic data related to the stock is being done. Various combinations of these data series is being made and from this future value of time series is predicted. This branch of time series study is known as econometrics. Basically there are two types of time series classification: 1. Univariate (With single explanatory variable) 2. Multivariate (With more than one explanatory variable). This process to predict any time series data is known as regression analysis. In regression there are two time series i.e one is of dependent variable. It means the series of parameter which we have to forecast. Other series if one in number or more than one in number are called independent variables. So the factors that influenced the dependent variables or the series which we want to predict are searched. Then mapping of values of the series of dependent variables and independent variables is being done. If we get a higher degree of correlation for it weather positive or negative. Then we will go for regression based analysis (Simple or Multiple). These regression based models are being used to predict stock market indices. A very good attempt is made by the author (V. Kapoor et. al 2020). In his work on modeling the effect world stock markets on India's NSE Index. (V. Kapoor et. al 2020) in his work has perform simple and multiple regression to forecast India's NSE index. The data we use was from 2001 to 2008. In his work closing prices of London Stock exchange (FTSE), New York Stock Exchange (NYSE) and Australia's All Ordinates are being taken as independent variable time series. The dependent variable or series that we want to predict is the closing prices of India's NSE index. Due to the time lag, as these all stock are in different time zones, prediction by taking into account of closing prices of these stock exchanges, simple and multiple both type of regressions are applied. Results obtained were satisfactory in nature. This regression model is one of the techniques to forecast the market. There are many other technical procedures which are used to forecast the market. They also come under time series prediction. Some of the popular technical indicators are moving averages, Moving Average convergence Divergence, Exponential Moving Average, Relative Strength Index, Stochastic Oscillator, Bollinger Brands etc. So prediction is done with the help of regression tool and to make a profit from that prediction a trading rule by combining one or more than one indicator is being made, which gives buy or sell signal. These all techniques are

helpful in prediction of market on daily basis. It is also widely used by economist and stock traders.

4. **Machine Learning Methods:** Though Efficient Market Hypothesis (EMH) is strongly placcs and put up by various analyst. This has not stop many researchers to falsify this hypothesis and to perform forecasting with a larger accuracy. This return will help us to garner profit from the market. With the advancement in computer hardware technology, processing power and abundance of fast memory drive at cheap rates, we have been able to access vast quantities of stock market data and store them and access them, whenever we required. Due to high availability of processing power at a cheap rate we are in a position to simulate complex soft computing procedures such as Neural Network, Genetic Algorithms, Fuzzy Logic etc. On the available huge stock market data in minutes and find inferences from them. A large amount of computational power is needed for this procedure to get implemented. Thus a new field which comes into existence, which is known as "Data Analysis". To see whether the market is predictable or not is the answerer of the question we need. This same answer which is needed by the analyst or the forecaster. For this answer of the questions stated below should be known:

    a. **Q-** 1. Does our stock data contains pattern in them?
    b. **Q-2.** If there are pattern, are we are in position to locate them?
    c. **Q-3.** If we are successful in locating the pattern then how many times or frequency that the patterns are repeated in the past data?

These all soft computing techniques to forecast the data comes under the classification of "Machine Learning Methods". These soft computing technique locate or pin point various unseen or hidden data patterns and find certain useful inference from the data. Though this book is about application of Genetic Algorithm in stock market, but we are going to discuss neural networks in brief here. These two methods Neural Networks and Genetic Algorithms are widely used in stock market prediction, but by seeing past we have got a rich literature available in the public domain to study with. They both have been used for stock market prediction individually in various permutations and in combination with each other also known as hybrid techniques.

9.5.2 Neural Network in Forecasting

It is a very important type of soft computing technique used for forecasting. Here we choose certain input variables to find the defined output variable. This picking of results input variable results in forecasting success. A neural network is a data process procedure in which certain input data streams is given and desired output stream is obtained. Working of neural network is of regressive in nature (Lawrence, 1997), (Walczak, 2001). Hence it is more accurate in its working. Neural Network is made up of nodes or neurons which are divided across various layers. The distribution and linkages of these nodes or neurons with each other defines the structure or framework of the network. All the linkage between these neurons is characterized by the weight value. Basically a neuron does the processing which receives some input and gives us the discrete output. This input can be specified by certain function. These functions can be linear, sigmoid, Trans sigmoid etc. Basically there are three layers in which neurons are distributed i.e input layer, hidden layer and output layer. Each layer can have one or more then input but it will have only one output. The total number of hidden layer can vary from 0 to any number. Input layer does not consist of any transfer function. Thus there are varieties of combination in which these hidden layers can be placed. Thus neural network can be applied in a large number of ways for same input data and the desired output. After defining the architecture and function of each neuron, values of weights should be explained. Thus this process of adaptation of weights is known as training process of neural networks. This training process i.e adjustment of weights fit the network to the training set data. Thus after desired output value is obtained, this network consisting of input layer, hidden layer, output layer, transfer function and weights are applied to testing set. For example in case of stock market prediction, if we choose previous day closing prices and opening prices as input, in order to forecast the next day opening price. Neural network architecture is set. Since neural network is a supervised based. Network is trained and weights are adjusted to get the desired and more accurate output series. Our accuracy will depend whether the input which we are considering has an impact on the output which we are going to make. If such a relationship between the output and input variables does not exist, then it is unlikely that we are going to get the desired result or accurate predicted series. So the main feature here is that input series should be selected with caution. Past researches has used neural network to forecast stock market data, mortgage risk management, find credit score of a person, economic forecasting etc. By now it is clear that neural network work is of black box in nature. Due to this feature neural network is criticized by many other researchers. As evolutionary computation is of less black box in nature, researchers has turned towards it, to forecast the stock market prices. Genetic Algorithms (GA's) can be used to search best or optimum architecture or topology of a Neural Network or it can be used to define A Neural Network structure.

9.5.3 Evolutionary Computation in Stock Market Forecasting

With the increase in popularity of evolutionary computation, initial research was done by Richard Bauer, 1994. He used Genetic Algorithms (GA's) to find various investment strategies. Results obtain motivated researchers from other areas to take evolutionary computation especially Genetic Algorithms (GA's) to be applied in financial forecasting area. Prominent researchers were: (Mahfoud et. Al, 1997) uses Genetic Algorithms to forecast the prices of various stocks. Koza, 1992 in his work uses Genetic Programming to forecast foreign exchange prices by using various technical rules. (F. Allen et.al, 1998) uses Genetic Programming process to search technical rules. Data taken of Standard and Poor index from 1928 to 1998. (J. Korczak et. A)l, 2002 uses Genetic Algorithm's with moving averages to forecast stock market prices of French stock market. List of researches is not limited, as a lot of researchers are using Genetic Algorithm's in financial forecasting. Some researchers has used Genetic Algorithm's (GA's) in combination with Neural Network or Fuzzy Logic. Genetic Algorithm's (GA's) are used to define their structure.

Now to get a brief glimpse of Genetic Algorithm's (GA's). Genetic Algorithm's (GA's) was discovered and first use by John Holland in 1975. Genetic Algorithm's (GA's) is based on Darwin theory of survival of fittest i.e stronger species is likely to survive in a competitive and hash environment. Genetic Algorithm's (GA's) have been successfully used to optimize a large number of domains. In a conventional Genetic Algorithm's (GA's), it consists of three major constituent. The first component is for generation of random set of initial population. This randomly generated is called first generation of population. The second constituent is defining fitness function, which is also known as objective function. It tells us about the solution quality or how close our solution is towards optimal. The third constituent is to generate next set of individuals with better fitness function values. This new generation formation depends upon the solution quality of individuals in the previous generation. Thus in the previous generation individuals three operators selection, crossover and mutation are applied to get a new set of individuals. Selection operator selects the members with more than average fitness function to be passed into next generation. It does not do any changes to it. Crossover operator requires two highly fit individuals, selected by selection operator and exchanges the character tics of the individuals in a random way. This two offspring created will have character tics of both 1st individual and 2nd individual. In the end mutation operator selects all individuals by its probability and changes all its character tics in a random way. Thus number of individual's which comes out of this transformation or changes are passed into the next generation. Then again this whole three operator's i.e selection, crossover and mutation are applied until termination criteria are met. There can be a number of termination criteria's i.e from total number of generation reached, amount of variation of individuals in two generation is minimum or population of individuals converges to a particular point, optimal value or pre defined fitness we want to achieve is achieved.

Genetic Algorithm (GA)

```
{
Create a random population of individuals
Calculate fitness function
While (Termination Criteria as decided is not met)
{   Apply Selection Operator
    Apply Crossover Operator
    Apply Mutation Operator
}   }
```

Apart from Genetic Algorithm, Genetic Programming (GP) is also a typical classification of evolutionary computation. Genetic Programming (GP) popularly known as GP is an advancement and a type of variation of Genetic Algorithm. It uses trees type data structure in contradiction to strings or chromosomes to represents the individuals in the population. Various high level computer languages such as LISP support Genetic Programming (GP) to solve various problems.

It is seen that both evolutionary computation technique is potent and naive in nature. Working of them is flexible in nature and a large number of search spaces are effectively searched parallel in a few iterations. They have been applied to the problem which is NP hard, complex, non linear and multi dimensional search spaces are there. In case of Genetic Algorithm (GA) binary representation of chromosomes is done by default, while tree based encoding is done in case of Genetic Programming (GP). Evolutionary algorithm work or search many spaces parallel. Due to this feature they do get stuck to local optima. This feature is desirable, but comes with a lacuna i.e increase in computational time and requirement of more processing power. As compared to Neural Network, Fuzzy Logic they are much slower in nature. This slowness of algorithms can be checked by making efficient parameter and coding settings or by use of advance operators in the algorithm as discussed in previous chapters. One of the variations in Genetic Programming (GP) is forest GP. Here each strategy is a set of various sub strategies. Each sub strategy has different objective function. Thus each sub strategy is called a tree and whole set of this sub strategy is called a forest. This type of strategy is used for multi objective optimization. So each chromosome here is a forest, which is a set of multiple trees. Each tree has its own objective function which is totally different and independent from other trees. If all tree in the forest Genetic Algorithm (GA) has same objective function then multiple objective function will be changed to single objective function.

Evolutionary algorithms, Neural Network are intelligent tools which are used in financial and stock market applications. Where these technical analysis, fundamental analysis, time series forecasting are considered as mechanical tools. These intelligent tools are heuristic based and posses the feature of artificial intelligence in it. Various other type of evolutionary algorithms are Genetic algorithms (GAs), Genetic Programming (GP), learning classifier systems, evolutionary programming etc. Genetic algorithms or Evolutionary programming cannot be applied in a single way. They are applied in combination with a trading rule. This technical trading rule is made up by combination of various technical indicators. On this technical rule Genetic Algorithm (GA) is applied. This in return represents a whole investment procedure. Here one half parts is mechanical driven and other part is evolutionary driven. Mechanism or mechanical driven is a part when we develop a trading strategy by combining various technical indicators by using if else statement. The parameters of this predefined trading rule is generally optimized by the use of evolutionary algorithm especially Genetic Algorithms (GA's). There is also another version in applying Genetic Algorithm (GA) is that to generate a new rule from the set of rules already present. This process is known as rule generation and its optimization using Genetic Algorithm (GA). Various researchers have optimized parameters of a trading rule made with the combination of various technical indicators. They applied their finding on the past historic data and promising results has been obtained. Until this date Genetic Algorithm (GA) applied on to the stock market is showing better and promising results as a whole.

9.6 MODEL SELECTION

In the previous literature we have discussed various procedures in brief such as mechanical mechanism (Time series models, fundamental analysis etc.). So no one model is found to be consistent and can be applied in all condition. It is generally seen that these mechanical tools are largely used by economists and traders. They are not computationally intensive. A large amount of literature is available in the public domain. Drawbacks from these mechanical tools are that they fail in non linear patterns, ands their performance degrades in the noisy environment of the market. Whereas these intelligent tools, when applied traces various hidden patterns in the past data. Draw back are that to implement them additional knowledge of programming language and algorithms are needed. To implement them a high degree of processing power is needed. They neither are nor radically accepted by the traditional economist or analyst. Performance degrades if we choose wrong parameters setting or when we apply them improperly. Hence each strategy has its pros and cons. We are not in a position to select one or neglect the other. In a middle path we choose both of them and build a simple and practical module which combines this mechanical tool with Genetic Algorithms (GA's).

It is seen among researchers that closing prices of any stock is considered to be a reliable data for any forecasting. These data of any stock for any indices are available in the public domain. Various other stock related data such as day high, day low, opening prices, volume etc. are also available and can be used in various permutation and combination to forecast. As in today scenario, a lot of data, memory to store the data and processing power is available to all the economist and analyst. So the question arises how do we use our expertise, this is more important question. It is not advisable to consider all the variable types available in our model. This is going to create a hanging state unnecessarily. Some variables are not so important and degree of interference in forecasting is very less. These variables can be discarded. In this way our model will have less computational complexity and will take lesser time to forecast. So both processing power and time required will be less. It is also seen that researcher's uses derived certain variables which are obtained from calculation of these original variables. These dependent variables have also been proved useful in forecasting stock data with more accuracy.

9.7 ARTIFICIAL MARKETS- AGENT BASED

Efficiency of market is challenged by many researchers. This is questioned by many researchers. Some says investors are efficient. If some information comes into existence then all the investors or majority of them comes to a same conclusion and thus this is reflected in the market indices. Some say that homogeneity in the decision taken by the investor is not there and market are efficient. So to study the market behaviour, attempt is made by certain researchers to create an agent based artificial market. In artificial based markets, agents are the computer programs. Some programs are written in the straight forward fashion, while some display artificial intelligence in them. The behaviour exhibited by these programs is dependent upon the code written by the programmers. So the programme has a large degree of freedom to apply artificial intelligence in the code. Hence these programs behave like an artificial agents or humans in the stock market. A very influential artificial stock market was developed by Santa Fe Institute (1997, 1999). Here several artificial agents would do trading i.e take decision to buy or sell based on various market conditions. Hence two interesting behaviour in the market was noticed, one is a herd mentality i.e actions taken without any rationality and other is regime switching. These two approaches are also tested. Thus in this artificial modelling agents or traders were represented as programs with varying degree of intelligence in it. In a way market movement or behaviour is explained artificially.

9.8 CONCLUSION

Due to advancement in processing power, memory and hardware technology there is an exponential rise in research in this area of computational finance. Due to this we can challenge Efficient Market Hypothesis (EMH) in a proper way. Since this field requires knowledge of both computer science and economics, it requires a lot of hard work and thought process to capture it. There are constraints both in the field of economics and computation. So researchers are not in a easy position to combine both of these fields. With the passage of time computational finance is emerging as a new subject of research. A lot of researchers from the communities from the field of economics and computer science are joining to do research and develop newer models. Impact on the result obtained is immense. Due to this it is benefiting the society in a big way.

REFERENCES

Allen, F., & Karjalainen, R. (1998). Using genetic algorithms to find technical trading rules. *Journal of Financial Economics, 51*(2), 245–271. doi:10.1016/S0304-405X(98)00052-X

Bauer, J. (1994). *Genetic Algorithms and Investment Strategies*. John Wiley and Sons, Inc.

Focardi, S., & Jonas, C. (1997). *Modeling the Market-New Theories and Techniques*. Frank J. Fabozzi Associates.

Kapoor, V., Dey, S., & Khurana, A. P. (2020). Modeling the influence of world stock markets on Indian NSE index. *Journal of Statistics and Management Systems, 23*(2), 249–261. doi:10.1080/09720510.2020.1734297

Korczak, J., & Roger, P. (2002). Stock Timing using Genetic Algorithms. *Applied Stochastic Models in Business and Industry, 18*(2), 121–134. doi:10.1002/asmb.457

Lawrence, R. (1997). Using neural networks to forecast stock market prices. *University of Manitoba, 333*, 206–2013.

Mahfoud, S., & Mani, G. (1996). Financial Forecasting Using Genetic Algorithms. *Applied Artificial Intelligence, 10*(6), 543–566. doi:10.1080/088395196118425

Rajasekaran & Vijaylakshmi Pai. (2007). *Neural Networks, Fuzzy Logic, and Genetic algorithms, Synthesis and Applications*. Prentice-Hall of India Private Limited.

Chapter 10
Synergistic Market Analysis, Technical Analysis, and Various Indicators

ABSTRACT

Most of the stock and financial market analysis uses past or historic data in order to forecast the future market indices. This study of past or historic data in order to infer certain value addition from it is known as technical analysis. In this chapter, the authors study a large number of popular indicators. A trader uses these indicators individually or in combination with other indicators to make a trading rule. They test them on past data and choose particular parameters and indicators that gave more profit and drop those that are loss making in nature. Thus, the decision to make entry and exit is given by these technical indicators. This chapter gives a detailed explanation of the most popular technical indicators in use.

10.1 INTRODUCTION

In this chapter we are going to have a in depth analysis of technical indicators and their working, which will be helpful in making market predictions (Copsey, 1999). As popularly stated by T. S. Elliot "Present time series and past time series are the indicators of future time series and vice versa." Technical analysis is one of the oldest forms of analysis procedures with its origins goes back to 1800's. It is the most popular form of analysis as data of past stock

DOI: 10.4018/978-1-7998-4105-0.ch010

prices and volumes are publically and easily available as compare to the data of other systems. Technical analysis tries to find recognizable and repeated patterns, which will help them to find future movement of stock prices or indices. Various indicators have been invented by a number of researchers. This type of analysis defines Random Walk Hypothesis and weak form of Efficient market Hypothesis. Thus it is believed that a large amount of profits can be generated by the use of technical analysis. Technical analysis includes a number of processes such as chart analysis, pattern analysis, technical indicator analysis etc. Out of these technical indicators can be represented in a mathematical formula (Lento, 2007). Basic assumption in these indicators is that the patterns in the prices that have occur in past are going to occur in future also with same frequency. These technical indicators generate buy, sell or keep neutral signals depending upon the parameter values on which you simulate them.

From past researchers there is evidence that these stock market analyst, hedge fund managers rely on these various technical indicators to take their decisions on the daily basis (Fama, 1965), (Fama, 1970). This all thing suggest that a large volume of market trade is guided by these technical indicators. We should be cautious while using these technical indicators as we know markets are efficient and absorbs any information very quickly. All our efforts to use these technical indicators will prove futile, if we do not use them with proper parameters and in a quick manner. Though there is n number of technical indicators available in financial literature. Most popular of them is moving averages and various momentum oscillators such as Relative Strength Index (RSI), Stochastic Oscillators etc. A trading rule shall be able to tell when to enter, when to exit and stop loss i.e when to exit after losing a trade. If a rational decision on stop loss is not made then trader will face huge amount of loss. Thus these technical indicators gives us a entry price, exit price and stop loss price based on the mathematical calculations on the past price data and with a rationality. Technical indicators guide us to make decision on what we have to do. They makes detail analysis about the market direction i.e if in a uptrend then we buy, if in a down trend then we sell, if in straight line then we resist in taking any decision. Various attributes of technical analysis are:

1. Charting: Here graph of past historic prices such as bar chart, line chart, candle stick charts are prepared.
2. Back Testing: Here different strategies to trade are to be tested. Actually these strategies are some type mathematical formulas. They all are tested on past prices of various securities.

3. Optimization: Various parameters of these technical indicators are fine tuned or optimized to get maximum profit. These are again tested on the past historic prices.

Thus these all and many more qualities are possessed in technical analysis. So they are also popularly known as decision support system. Advance feature of technical analysis incorporates various soft computing and Artificial Intelligence (AI) based optimization techniques in order to optimize its parameter values. Now days the term technical analysis or indicators is used quiet often in media by the financial analyst and professionals. Technical analysis in contrast to fundamental analysis is used to forecast short term prices i.e on daily basis and use past prices. A lot of research work is already being done and is also undergoing on the issue of technical analysis. Detail of this is being discussed in coming section and chapters of this book.

10.2 INITIATION TO TECHNICAL INDICATORS AND VARIOUS MOMENTUM OSCILLATORS

In this section we will understand the modus operandi of the technical indicators and learn them to use in our forecasting process. Technical indicators are classified into two type's i.e leading indicators and lagging indicators. Both of them have advantages and disadvantages. Some of the indicators are also called oscillators. We will also learn them to use a s signal generators. In the later section of this chapter we are going to have a detail analysis of some popular technical indicators.

A technical indicator working is of susses ion or sequence of various data position or values that are obtained by imposing a mathematical formula to the past data of a stock or security. Data can be opening price, closing price, day high, day low etc. of a security. Some indicator works on only one series of data, while other works on more than one data series. The formula is applied on to the data series and data point is generated. Only one data point is of no use, so a series of various data points on various time lags between present and past is done to make a perfect decision. Most of the analyst shows the data point generated and price values by these technical indicators in graphical charts. Pictorial view will help us to take decision in an easy manner. Technical indicators are of varying perspective. Some are of simple to understand, while others are of complex in nature. For example moving averages have a simple formulation while Relative strength Index (RSI), and Stochastic Oscillators has complex formulas, which requires deep penetration of logic to be fully understood. Though starting from a simple technical indicator to a complex one, they always provide the direction in which stock prices are moving with a varying time lag and accuracy.

For example most popular technical indicator is simple moving average, in which average of closing prices is calculated for a particular data point. In this way series of data points are calculated. Moving averages are used to smoothen the data and to dampen the random noisiness in the data. If volatility in the time series is of very high degree then a trader will have difficulty to find a price direction. Then moving averages smoothens the fluctuations and help us to identify the direction of the price movement.

Basically indicators doe's three types of work: They awake us, they give confirmation and they are used to forecast the values. In case of alert we came to know about the momentum in the price of a stock. If the momentum is getting lost then there is no reason to enter it. Confirmation gives us strength to our rationality. If in a moving average price crosses it, then it is a confirmation to enter. Some indicators are used only for forecasting purpose i.e to find direction of a price of a stock. What does an indicator do? As the name suggest they indicate. They indicate an action which is to be taken on the price. This should be taken into consideration while making analysis. It is seen in practice that an indicator give us a buy signal, but if we use some other technical indicator then it gives us an opposite signal i.e a sell signal. So a detail study must be done to test the strongest of a signal given by the indicator. There are cases when an indicator gives us false buy signal by studying only the declining peak. To make useful and correct inference from an indicator is a art then a thing of a technical. Perfection in this art comes from a lot of experience. It is seen that some indicator works well for certain stocks and may not work well for other stocks as parameters of certain indicator works well for other stock or parameter for certain indicator may not work well for other stock. Expertise on indicator develops with experience. There may be hundred of indicators in the market. With passage of time more and more number of indicators is coming into picture. Publicity of indicators is there in the market, so select a correct indicator is a tough task. Though there are a large numbers of indicators in market, only some of them are fruitful in their working or merit in their working. For stock indices analysis purpose we have to choose the set of indicators very rationally and carefully. There has been attempt to cover all of the indicators and this has proven futile. Our main focus should be on one or two indicators from which we should draw various inferences. We should not choose any two indicators from same category. It should be kept in mind that indicator chosen from different category should give same signal at a point of time.

10.2.1 Lagging Indicators

As the name suggests lagging indicator go after the price movements. They stick up to the trend. They are not of leading in nature. They keep the traders into the market as long as there is strong trend weather upward or downward. In this way if market indices develop a steep upward or downward trend, these types of indicator gives us best results. When the trend of market is flat or sideways then these indicators gives us poor results. In case if noisiness in the market, these indicators will give false signals and thus will leads us to faulty decision or we will feel cheated. Some of the most liked lagging indicators by the analysts and researchers of this field are moving averages (Simple, exponential, weighted, moving average convergence divergence etc.). In this case we use two moving averages of variable lengths. If the shorter moving average crosses the longer moving average then we consider that there is an upward trend in the market and a buy signal is generated. If shorter moving average crosses below the longer moving average then down trend is detected and sell signal is generated. The length of the moving averages should be decided by hit and trial method or with the help of Genetic Algorithm which we will discuss in later chapters. It is generally seen that longer moving averages give more accurate results and less whipsaws.

10.2.2 Advantages and Disadvantages of Lagging Indicators

Main advantage of these trend backing indicators is to signal that trend weather upward or downward has been developed. The main lacuna is that the trend should be sustainable in nature. In these cases these trend backing indicators are of extremely useful in nature. If the upward and downward trend are strong and of longer periods then more profits will be generated and less trading signals will be generated. Drawbacks of these indicators are that as the name suggests, they give signals with a time lag or lateness. Hence significant amount of profit that can be captured is lost, as market has moved by and large portion. Thus there will be always delay in entry and exit points, which narrows out the profit and risks also.

10.2.3 Leading Indicators

As given in the name, leading indicators leads the price movements. Here the time period is decided and look back period stock market price action is recorded and reflected in the result. Most liked leading indicator is Relative Strength index RSI), Stochastic oscillator, Momentum, Commodity Channel Index, Williams % R etc.

10.2.4 Momentum Oscillators

Momentum oscillators are leading type of indicators. By meaning of momentum we mean that rate of change of the stock price over a period of time. As rate of price of a stock increases or decreases, momentum signal also increases or decreases with it. If rate of change is less then it means that momentum has slowed down or died. This means that price movement of a particular security is in a flat way. Reduce in momentum signal does not always mean that bearish trend has began, or there is a change in trend. It means that momentum has come to a centre level.

10.2.5 Advantages and Disadvantages of Leading Indicators

Major advantage is that in comparison to lagging indicator they generate an early signal of entry and exit. As compared to lagging indicators a large number of entry and exit signals are generated by these leading indicators. Thus in this way we trade more and earn more. Early signal means warning against the strength or weakness of the market. In case of trending markets, it means that if trend is upwards, then these indicators will let us know about the overbought position for selling. If trend is in downward direction then these indicator will give us oversold position for buying.

As signals are generated prematurely then there is a lot of risk as compare to the lagging indicator. Here the number of signals also increases, which means there are more false signals and whipsaws given by the indicator. So it may increase your losses and trading commission which will chew or narrow your profits.

10.2.6 Challenge Given by the Indicators

Proper balance between sensitivity and consistency must be made. If one is increased then other one is decreased. Ideally we want that an indicator should be sensitive in nature and should give early signal with a less false signal or whipsaws. Hence to increase sensitivity or to get early signal we should reduce the time periods of the indicator in use, but this will increase the number of false signals also. Hence in the same way if we reduce the sensitivity or increase the time period, then the number of false signals generated are also reduced. Thus a proper balance between risk and reward should be made.

In case of moving average, longer moving average will generate few signals and few false signals as compare to the shorter moving averages. Thus 5 day Relative Strength Indicator (RSI) will generate more signals then 20 days Relative Strength Indicator (RSI). So a proper balance between trading signals and false trading signals should be made for selecting the time periods of these signals.

10.3 TYPES OF OSCILLATORS

An oscillator is a type of indicator that vary above and below the centre line or in between certain levels over a period of time. The value given by oscillators is given at extreme points i.e overbought or oversold levels, but it does not remain there for a long period of time. As compare to other indicators their values fluctuates in a large way. Oscillators can be classified into many types. Mainly oscillators are of two types centred and banded. In centred oscillator the value fluctuates above and below a centre line, while in banded oscillator value fluctuates between the two extreme points i.e overbought and oversold points.

10.3.1 Centred Oscillators

These type of oscillators swings or oscillate below and above around the centre line or point. This type of fluctuation helps us to find the degree and direction of the momentum of the indices or the stock price. If the oscillator is above the centre line i.e we consider the price movements as bullish and if oscillator is below the centre line then we consider the price movements as bearish or in negative direction.

Moving average Convergence and Divergence (MACD) is a popular centred oscillator. Moving average Convergence and Divergence (MACD) is the difference between the two short term and long term exponential moving average (EMA) of a stock price. It is seen that extremely large and short distance between the two moving averages does not last for a long time.

10.3.2 Moving Average Convergence and Divergence (MACD)

Moving average Convergence and Divergence (MACD) is different from other indicator such that it has a nature of both lagging and leading indicator. For example it consists of moving average which is a lagging indicator and in order to calculate Moving average Convergence and Divergence (MACD) we calculate the difference of short and long term moving average. This difference is actually the measurement of rate of change. In this way rate of change or fluctuation in the stock value makes Moving average Convergence and Divergence (MACD) as leading indicator. Though there is time lag in its signal generation. Thus with the combination of both i.e moving averages and rate of change, Moving average Convergence and Divergence (MACD) has both the properties of lagging and leading indicator.

10.3.3 Rate of Change (ROC)

Rate of Change (ROC) is a example of centred oscillator. Here also its values vary or oscillates around the centred line. For example a n day Rate of Change (ROC) oscillator gives us a rate of change of values for last n days. Larger the positive value larger is the bullish momentum, and larger the negative value, larger is the bearish momentum. In contrast to Moving average Convergence and Divergence (MACD), there are no upper limits and lower limits in Rate of Change (ROC) oscillators. In this we cannot judge overbought and oversold levels and their reversals. This is the major drawback of these oscillators. Here in some cases upper and lower limits are fixed by the practitioners by the observations from the past. Which vary from security to security? In order to judge or empirically find these extreme upper and lower limits banded oscillators are used.

10.3.4 Banded Oscillators

Here the value of two oscillators varies between the two band i.e two limits in contrast to the centre line. Here lower band tells that there is an oversold position, while upper band gives us overbought position. Thus from these points reversal takes place. Upper band and lower band values changes from stock to stock and for different types of oscillators etc. Main advantage of this types of oscillators are that analyst are able to pin point over bought and oversold levels. Popular banded oscillators are Relative Strength Index (RSI), Stochastic Oscillators etc. In comparison with Moving average Convergence and Divergence (MACD) and Rate of Change (ROC) the calculation and logic on which Relative Strength Index (RSI) and Stochastic Oscillator are based are more complex, which we are going to discuss in the coming section of this chapter.

For Relative Strength Index (RSI) over bought and oversold levels are kept 70 (Overbought) and 30 (Oversold) but for Stochastic Oscillators these levels are 80 (Overbought) and 20 (Oversold). These values are recommended and they may change for security to security. It is the user preference that it may change these values for making any decision, considering volatility of the market.

10.3.5 Commodity Channel Index (CCI)

Not all banded oscillators are positioned between upper and lower limits. In case of Relative Strength Index (RSI) and Stochastic Oscillators, both are depending upon range. There upper and lower limit ranges are 0 and 100. Commodity channel indicator (CCI) is not a range bound oscillator. Here its compare present security price of the stock for a given time. Theoretically this oscillator has no upper and lower bound, but actually its upper and lower values falls between -100 and 100. This makes Commodity channel indicator (CCI) a popular and useful indicator, which helps us to find overbought and oversold positions. These levels -100 to 100 can be adjusted according to market volatility and price movement of a particular security.

Advantage and Disadvantage of Oscillators

Centred oscillators help us to find the strength and direction of the momentum of the stock prices. As in centred oscillator the reading vary around a centre line or point. While in case of banded oscillators the fluctuation is in between the two extreme values. It tells us the extreme levels that the stock price can get. We can also identify extreme readings in case of centred oscillators also. But in an ideal case we should use banded oscillators for this purpose.

10.3.6 Oscillators Signals

The main function of the oscillator is to generate buy and sell signal. In some case there is an early entry or exit, and some case it is just in time. These signals tell us the time when the positive or negative trend is going to reverse or change. In order to reduce the risk these signals should co exist with the signal generated by other technical indicators or by technical analysis process such as study of price patterns charts etc.

Divergence is a new concept in order to find a signal. Divergence gives us a warning that a positive or negative trend is about to change. In case of negative divergence the indicator gives lesser value then the actual value that security has achieved. It is an indication that high has been achieved and trend is about to get reversed. Not in all negative divergence there is a bearish movement. In case of positive divergence when indicator give a less low then the actual low point the security has achieved. From this point there is appositive reversal or bullish trend is going to be there. Not all positive divergence results into a bullish trend.

Overbought and oversold Boundaries: Banded oscillators help us to find overbought and oversold extreme values. The values given by these indicators swing between the extremes as their values are decided by the user. In case of strong positive or negative i.e bullish or bearish trend they fail. So if there is a strong upward or bullish trend then buying that stock will give more profit then by selling as the banded indicator gives an overbought signal. Hence for a strong trend oscillator working is not robust in nature and signal (Buy or Sell) generated are not valid in nature.

So in case of a strong uptrend i.e bullish, buying the stock will give much profit then by selling it, as if the indicator is giving an overbought position. Same is the case with strong bearish trend. Here buying an oversold position will not give us great returns. If a trend is detected then if you act against it then it will lead us to a huge loss. It is very tricky to find a trend. If the trend is strong then indicator will tell about overbought or oversold signals for a long time. In case of a strong bullish trend the indicator will give an overbought signal i.e to sell the sell but the security price will advance in the upward direction. A downward bearish divergence signal will be given. But this downward bearish signal should be considered as suspicious. As in the case with strong downtrend the oscillator will give oversold signal, but the positive divergence signal should be considered as false as stock price touches lower peak every day. This does not mean that oscillators are useless, but they should be used in conjunction with other technical indicators. So our first step in using banded oscillators is to find overbought and oversold levels. In case of Relative Strength Index (RSI) overbought and oversold extremes are 70 and 30. While in case of Stochastic Oscillators 80 and 20 are considered to be overbought and oversold extremes. If overbought and oversold signal is identified, then it should be treated as caution and should be verified by using other technical analysis procedures.

Common procedure is if a security price gives a overbought or oversold signal and turn around the upper band and lower band then only sell and buy signal should be generated. So to have a robust reading these banded oscillators should be used in conjunction with lagging indicators such as moving averages crossovers in order to be more positive about their result.

10.3.7 Centreline Crossovers

Here in centreline crossover the signals are generated as the oscillator swings above and below a centre line. Analyst and traders uses this centreline in combination with Relative Strength Index (RSI) and Stochastic Oscillator in order to get a robust signal. So to get divergence or turn around point we turn our study to centre line crossovers. As extremes are checked by banded oscillators and middle ground is checked by centreline oscillators. Popular centreline oscillators are moving average Convergence and Divergence (MACD) and Rate of Change (ROC) etc.

A centreline crossover will generate buy or sell signal if the indicator line crosses above or below the centre line. This is considered to be positive or bullish and negative or bearish momentum. So if we use centre line oscillator in combination with banded oscillator there will be more true signals with less whipsaws. So if we combine various indicators to generate the signal, we are going to get more robust signal for all cases. So our challenge to get a profit is met. Thus by combining two types of oscillators indicator with lagging indicator, then if all of them gives sell signal when banded oscillator reaches the extreme, and there is a negative movement to the below of the centre line in centre line oscillator and bearish moving averages cross in an reverse direction.

So by waiting the entire three signals to be generated at the same time, we are sometimes losing money. But as the reliability increases and risks lowers, gains also lowers. This will in turn trim down our profits. So in last if we sum up that banded oscillators gives us the overbought and oversold levels. But it is not true we buy or sell in these levels. They are the alerts given by the oscillators. So in order to take any decision analyst see whether the same signals are generated by other indicators also. If that is generated then there is a confirmation for buy or sell. So by relying on these three different type of indicator buy signal is generated, when there is an oversold condition, positive divergence and bullish crossover movement and sell signal is generated when there is a reverse condition. If the market has a strong bullish or bearish trend then it is not advisable to rely on the signal generated by the oscillator. A strong trend in the market falsifies the oscillator signal. It is judged that oscillators when used in combination with other indicators chart analysis, trend identifiers etc. gives an effective result. Thus in this way chances to get a successful reading is increased.

10.4 MOVING AVERAGES (MA)

It is a basic and most commonly used technical indicator in technical analysis. Moving averages (MA) are simple in calculation and it's working. We are going to make a detail analysis and inspection of moving average in this section.

Moving averages (MA) flattens the price data and is a typical trend generating and lagging indicator. We cannot forecast a price of a stock but we can judge the direction in which prices are going. Moving averages (MA) flattened the noisiness in the data. Moving averages (MA) are the basis of many advance technical indicator which we are going to discuss later in this chapter, such as Moving average Convergence and Divergence (MACD) etc. various types of moving averages (MA) are weighted moving averages, exponential moving averages etc. Moving averages (MA) are trend finding indicator which gives us the value of support and resistance of the stock price.

Formula to calculate Moving averages (MA) is to add the closing prices for a specified period and then divide the whole sum by that number of specified period. So formula for Moving averages (MA) is

$$(MA)n = \sum_{i=1}^{i=n} Ci / n$$

$$(MA)n = C_1 + C_2 + C_3 + \ldots\ldots\ldots C_n / n$$

Considering a short, medium and long term moving averages (MA). A short term moving averages (MA) is more sensitive to the price change as compare to medium and long term moving averages (MA). As short term moving averages (MA) embrace the changes in price more quickly. Thus any changes in the price action will be seen quickly as compare to medium and longer term moving averages (MA). Now considering moving averages (MA) of 10, 30, and 60 days. A 10 day moving averages (MA) does not move away from the price action. It fluctuates around the price, while 60 day moving averages (MA) do not touch the price of a stock. In order to eliminate the noise in price data and get a clear trend, we have to bear the lag. So as the moving averages (MA) time lengths are increased they trend to follow the price action with a larger slowness. Since it is the lagging indicator they show the changes in the price action with a larger slowness. Since it is the lagging indicator they show the changes in price direction with some lateness. So the question arises that why to use longer duration moving averages (MA) as shorter duration moving averages (MA) embrace price fluctuation more quickly. In shorter duration moving averages (MA) though time lag has been managed, they give more false signals and whipsaws as compare to longer duration moving averages (MA).

10.4.1 Weighted Moving Averages (MA)

In order to overcome the time lag, some analyst uses weighted moving averages (MA). We have seen that current price movement is more important than past price movements. So current price movements are given more weights as compare to past price movements in weighted moving averages (MA), as compare to simple moving averages (SMA) where all values are given same weights. Formula for weighted moving averages (MA) is given below:

Weighted moving averages (WMA) = $C_n * 1 + C_{n-1} * 2 + \ldots\ldots C_1 * n)/ (1+2+3+ \ldots..+n)$

Hence C_1 is multiplied by n, C_n is multiplied by 1 and so on. Once we add all these values, they are divided by the total of we have used. So weighted moving averages (MA) are closer to the price movement within a less lag time. So a longer duration weighted moving averages (MA) will give better results as comparison to the longer duration of simple moving averages (MA). Main drawback is that in absence of any strong trend they generate whipsaws more frequently and give false signals.

10.4.2 Exponential Moving Averages (MA)

Exponential moving averages (MA) are somewhat different from simple moving averages (SMA) and weighted moving averages (WMA). In case of weighted moving averages (WMA), we consider recent prices to be more important than prices in the recent past. Exponential moving averages (EMA) try to reduce the time lag by applying some weight to the most recent prices. The weight value depends upon the time period for which moving average is to be calculated. Difference between simple moving averages (SMA) and exponential moving averages (EMA) are that simple moving averages (SMA) value depends upon the past price value, while exponential moving averages (EMA) value depends upon the exponential moving averages (EMA) calculated for the previous day. If you will see any price chart which onsist of price line, simple moving averages (SMA) line and exponential moving averages (EMA), we will see that time lag is reduced in any type of reversal of time in exponential moving averages (EMA) line. Formula to calculate n day Exponential moving averages (MA) is:

Initial simple moving averages (SMA) = n-period sum / n

Multiplier = (2 / (n + 1)

$$Exponential\ moving\ averages\left(EMA\right)$$
$$=\left\{Close - Exponential\ moving\ averages\ EMA\left(Previous\ day\right)\right\} * Multiplier$$
$$+Exponential\ moving\ averages\ EMA\left(Previous\ day\right)$$

Initially simple moving averages (SMA) for n day is considered to be first exponential moving averages (EMA) value. It is seen that as the number of days i.e value of n increases in exponential moving averages (EMA), the weights or multiplier value decreases, so the multiplier value for shorter time is more than the multiplier value for longer time. This tells us that exponential moving averages (EMA) is sensitive to recent price changes then the past price changes. If we make a comparison between n day simple moving averages (SMA) is very easy to calculate. Here as we move forward old prices are left and new prices are taken into account. Here in exponential moving averages (MA) we first start with the calculation of simple moving averages (SMA) for its 1st exponential moving averages (EMA) value. After this the actual exponential moving averages (EMA) formulas for calculation is used. As it is seen in the formula of exponential moving averages (EMA). Present value depends upon the previous exponential moving averages (EMA) value. So the current value changes according to the past value. So the main aim of exponential moving averages (EMA) is to increase accuracy and reduce the computational complexity or calculation complexity.

It is seen that longer period moving average have more time lag while shorter moving averages (MA) will have less time lag. They are more sensitive to the price changes. Shorter moving averages (MA) are just like a small paddle boat while longer moving averages (MA) are like a big ship that are lazy in working and changes slowly. There are differences in the formulas of moving averages (MA) and exponential moving averages (EMA), so they are different in their signal generation. Exponential moving averages (EMA) is bound to have less time lag for the same time period, when compared with simple moving averages (SMA). Hence exponential moving averages (EMA) are more sensitive than simple moving averages (SMA). Simple moving averages (MA) will be used to find support level and resistance level in combination with exponential moving averages (EMA) which will generate optimal buy and sell signals. The length of the moving averages (MA) which we use depends upon the trader. If we trade short term or we are short term investor and trend is weak, then we will use short moving averages (MA) i.e between the range of 5 – 20 days. For medium investor and medium trend moving averages (MA) range is from 20 – 60 days. For long term investors, moving averages (MA) will be for more than 100 days.

The direction line of the moving averages (MA) gives us trend about prices. A upward movement of the longer moving averages (MA) moving average line gives an indication for a strong long term trend.

10.4.3 Moving Averages Crossover

Two moving averages (MA) i.e of shorter length and of longer length in combination will be used to generate trading signal. 5 – 35 day will be considered as short length and 5 – 200 day will be considered as longer length moving averages (MA). A bullish signal or buy signal is generated when shorter length moving averages (MA) cross longer length moving averages (MA) line,. A bearish signal or sell signal is generated if reverse happen. By nature moving averages (MA) are lagging indicators. Longer moving averages (MA) gives or confirms about the trend and shorter moving averages (MA) will give buy or sell signal. It is seen that in case of weak trend a lot of whipsaws are generated by the moving average crossovers. There is a triple moving averages (MA) crossover method also in use, where we use one short term moving averages (MA) and two longer term moving averages (MA). Here in short term moving averages (MA) crosses two longer term moving averages (MA) in upward direction then a buy signal is generated and if it crosses two longer term moving averages (MA) in downward direction then sell signal is generated. It is seen that moving averages (MA) crossovers are prone to whipsaws. That can be avoided if we use more filter to reduce noisiness in price data. Moving averages (MA) can also be used to find support and resistance for the case of uptrend and downtrend.

10.4.4 Summary of Moving Averages (MA) in Use

There are both advantages and disadvantages of moving averages (MA) in use. They should both be weighted among themselves. It is seen that moving averages (MA) are a lagging indicators which is a disadvantage, but they are also trend indicators also which a major disadvantage is. Since a trend is always our friend. Moving averages (MA) gives us the assurance that we are in line with the trend. Once we get a trend, moving averages (MA) with their time lag gives us delayed signals. So with the use of moving averages (MA) we are not able to buy at the bottom and sell at the top. So in order to avoid such lacuna we use moving averages (MA) in combination with other types of indicators.

10.5 MOMENTUM INDICATORS

In the stock market analyst are always looking for trend and momentum of that trend. Trend following indicators are moving averages which are simple in calculation. But the introduction of desktop computers, more complex indicators are invented and implemented to calculate the momentum of the price. A large number of momentum indicators are in use. In this section we are only going to explain the most common and popular indicators such as Moving average Convergence Divergence (MACD), Relative Strength Index (RSI) and Stochastic Oscillator. Momentum is measure of the difference of price between the current time and past time.

10.5.1 Moving Average Convergence Divergence (MACD)

Moving Average Convergence Divergence (MACD) was invented by Gerald Appel in 1970's. Moving average Convergence Divergence (MACD) is of simple and effective in nature. Moving average Convergence Divergence (MACD) converts two trend following lagging indicators i.e Moving averages (MA's) into a momentum oscillator. Here we use two Moving averages (MA's) of varying length i.e shorter Moving averages (MA's) and longer Moving averages (MA's). We then subtract the larger Moving averages (MA's) value from the shorter Moving averages (MA's). It give us the best of both the world features i.e trend and momentum. Moving average Convergence Divergence (MACD) is a centreline momentum indicator. It swings its value above and below the centreline i.e zero. Analysts see for centreline crossover positive or negative, convergence, divergence etc. and generate signals. Since there is no restriction in the values given by Moving Average Convergence Divergence (MACD), we can manually identify overbought and oversold levels in it. Moving Average Convergence Divergence (MACD) formula is given below:

Moving Average Convergence Divergence $\left(MACD\right)$ *Line :*
Short Term Exponential Moving Average − Long Term Exponential Moving Average.

Signal Line $= n\text{-}day$ *Exponential Moving Average of*
Moving Average Convergence Divergence $\left(MACD\right)$

Moving Average Convergence Divergence $(MACD)$ *Histogram*
$= Moving\ Average\ Convergence\ Divergence\ (MACD) - Signal\ Line.$

Moving Average Convergence Divergence (MACD) calculated the difference or fluctuation between the two Exponential moving Averages (EMA's). The length of short term Exponential moving Averages (EMA's), long term Exponential moving Averages (EMA's) and n – day Exponential moving Averages (EMA's) of Moving Average Convergence Divergence (MACD) is judged by the user. Many values can be taken and tested depending upon the price movements. These values are generally generated by using Genetic Algorithm's, Neural Network which we are going to explain later in this book.

- **Interpretation:** Moving Average Convergence Divergence (MACD) gives the convergence and divergence of the two Moving averages (MA's). When two v come close to each other convergence occurs, otherwise there is a divergence if they move away from each other. Here due to shorter length Moving averages (MA's) most of the Moving Average Convergence Divergence (MACD) movements occur. Moving Average Convergence Divergence (MACD) value fluctuates above and below the centre and zero line. Positive value of Moving Average Convergence Divergence (MACD) means that bullish momentum is increasing. Negative value of Moving Average Convergence Divergence (MACD) means that bearish momentum is increasing. Direction of Moving Average Convergence Divergence (MACD) line changes in case of crossovers.
- **Signal Line Crossovers:** n- day signal line crossover above and below the Moving Average Convergence Divergence (MACD) line is the signal generator. A bullish run is forecasted when Moving Average Convergence Divergence (MACD) line crosses signal line in the upward direction. A bearish run is forecasted when moving Average Convergence Divergence (MACD) line crosses signal line in the downward direction. These crossovers last for certain time, depending upon the strength of the momentum. A lot of precaution is required to fall on these signals. At the extremes weather positive or negative these signal should be read with caution. As we had stated that Moving Average Convergence Divergence (MACD) is unbounded, but the lower and upper limits can be fixed just by seeing historic data and by a

visual assessment. If the stock price movement are of volatile in nature or noisy in nature, then we will get a large number of crossover signals.

Divergence occurs when Moving Average Convergence Divergence (MACD) diverges from the price line. A bullish divergence occurs when stock price is lowest and Moving Average Convergence Divergence (MACD) forms higher low. Lowest price describes that security is in down trend and higher low of Moving Average Convergence Divergence (MACD) tells that lower momentum has been lost. Thus this slowness of down size momentum can be taken as trend reversal to the bullish direction. A bearish divergence is considered when a security price is having highest value and Moving Average Convergence Divergence (MACD) form lower high. This describes that the bullish momentum has been weakened. Weakening of upside momentum can sometimes take as trend reversal i.e bullish to bearish. This bullish and bearish divergence should be read with caution. Commonly bearish divergence occurs in a strong uptrend and bullish divergence occurs in a strong downtrend.

- **Summary:** Moving Average Convergence Divergence (MACD) is unique because it is a combination of two lagging indicator which generates momentum. There are many settings for shorter and longer term exponential moving averages (EMA's). Lesser the value more sensitive is the indicator. A less sensitive Moving Average Convergence Divergence (MACD) will fluctuate above and below the zero centre line, but the crossover of the centreline and signal line crossover is less frequent.

Moving Average Convergence Divergence (MACD) is unbounded, so we cannot find overbought and oversold values. These upper limit values can be manually set just by seeing the past historic data extremes.

10.5.2 Relative Strength Index (RSI)

It was invented by J. Welles Wilder. Relative Strength Index (RSI) is a momentum indicator that calculates the speed and change of the movement of stock price. Relative Strength Index (RSI) value fluctuates between 0 and 100. Relative Strength Index (RSI) considers overbought when its value reaches above 70 and oversold when its value reaches below 30. Relative Strength Index (RSI) also identifies the trend of the stock price. Relative Strength Index (RSI) as a momentum indicator is popular among the researchers community. A lot of work and literature can be found on Relative Strength Index (RSI) in the public domain.

Relative Strength Index (RSI) Formula:

$$\text{Relative Strength Index (RSI)} = 100 - 100 / (1 + RS) \tag{1}$$

RS = Average Gain /Average Loss

Calculation of average gain and average loss for simple n day averages is

First average gain = Sum of gains over past n days / n

First average loss m= Sum of loss over past n days / n

Second and further calculation are based on the previous averages and current gain or loss.

Average Gain = [(Previous average gain) * (n-1) + current gain] / 14

Average Loss = [(Previous average loss) * (n-1) + current loss] / 14

Here the equation 1 changes RS into a oscillator that swings between 0 and 100. If plotted both RS and Relative Strength Index (RSI) plots are of same in nature. Here when average gain is nil then Relative Strength Index (RSI) value is zero i.e all loss. When average loss is zero i.e all gain the Relative Strength Index (RSI) value is 100.

The default value of n in Relative Strength Index (RSI) indicator is used as 14. If we use 10 day Relative Strength Index (RSI) then we increase its sensitivity and if we use 20 day Relative Strength Index (RSI) then we decease its sensitivity. Overbought and oversold levels can be kept 70/30 or 80/20. These all parameter values depend upon the stock price volatility and noisiness.

- **Divergences:** Divergence gives us a signal of reversal of a trend. Bullish divergence comes into existence when security price is lowest of the low and Relative Strength Index (RSI) highest low reading. This means that Relative Strength Index (RSI) reading does not justify the lowest reading and there may be trend reversal from this point. Where as bearish divergence comes into picture when security price is highest high and Relative Strength Index (RSI) reading is the lowest high then there can be a reverse in momentum. We should not be very excited about the divergence as they may mislead us in case of a strong bullish or bearish trend,. This strong trend can show a lot number of false signals. It is seen that Relative Strength Index (RSI) oscillator generally do not travel between 0 and 100. In case of bullish stock market it may travel between 40 to 90. In case of bearish market it may travel between 10 and 60. So positive reversal is actually a bullish divergence.

- **Summary:** Relative Strength Index (RSI) is still a robust, adaptable momentum oscillator, which is tested in every stock market environment. The results given by Relative Strength Index (RSI) are encouraging in the changing times of stock market. Relative Strength Index (RSI) consider overbought levels to be sell signal and for bearish reversal and negative reversals. While oversold levels gives us a buy signal i.e for bullish and positive reversals. These readings will fail if there is an indication of a strong trend in stock prices.

10.5.3 Stochastic Oscillator

Stochastic Oscillator: was invented by George C Lane in 1950's. It is a popular momentum indicator. Stochastic Oscillator is a pure momentum indicator. It does not follow the price but speed at which price is increasing or decreasing i.e momentum. Rule says that momentum changes its direction before the price. So it is easy to find bearish and bullish divergence or reversals. There are upper and lower ranges in Stochastic Oscillator, which helps us to find overbought and oversold levels.

Stochastic Oscillator formula:

$$\% K = ((\text{Closing Price} - \text{Lowest low}) / (\text{Highest high} - \text{Lowest low})) * 100$$

$\% D = 3$- days Simple Moving Average (SMA) of $\% K$

Lowest Low = Lowest low for the period for which Stochastic Oscillator is to be calculated.

Highest high = Highest high for the period for which Stochastic Oscillator is to be calculated.

The default value for the Lowest Low = Lowest low for the period for which Stochastic Oscillator is to be calculated.

Calculated is 14. So % K is calculated for 14 period and % D is the 3 day simple moving average (SMA) of % K. So the % K line is the signal line.

- **Fast, slow or Full Stochastic Oscillator:** The original George C Lane formula is considered to be fast Stochastic Oscillator. Here % K is rather noisy and % D is 3 day simple moving average (SMA) of % K. Buy or sell signals are generated by % D, if there is bullish or bearish divergence in % D crossovers. Slow stochastic formula is

Slow % K = Fast % K smoothed with 3 period simple moving average (SMA).

Slow % D = 3 period simple moving average of slow % K.

Here % K value is smoothened by calculating 3 day simple moving average of fast % K. So % K of slow stochastic oscillator is equal to % D of fst Stochastic Oscillator.

Formula for full Stochastic Oscillator is:

Full % K = Fast % K smoothed with X period simple moving average (SMA).

Full % D = X period simple moving average of full % K.

The default values of is taken as (14, 3, 3). As there are upper and lower limits bounded in Stochastic oscillator. The value of this oscillator fluctuates from 0 to 100 in any case. Traditional values setting uses 80 as overbought and 20 as the oversold levels. Overbought condition does not always signal a bearish move. Price of a stock can remain at overbought level if there is a strong bullish trend. Same is the case with oversold levels. Oversold condition does not signal a bullish move always. Price may remain at a lowest point if there is a strong bearish trend.

- **Divergence:** It is made when a new high or low in the stock price value is not validated by the Stochastic oscillator. In case of bullish divergence, if a price touches a new low and Stochastic oscillator give a higher low. It means that downward momentum is weakened and it may cause bullish reversal. So is the case of bearish divergence, if a price touches a new high and Stochastic oscillator gives a lower high. It means that upward momentum is lost or weakened and it may cause bearish reversal.

- **Summary:** It is seen that momentum oscillators are used for trading ranges. They may fail in case of strong trend in the price. But Stochastic oscillator helps us to find the signal in case of strong trend also. It also helps us to find the support and resistance levels for bearish and bullish trends. The parameter settings of Stochastic oscillator depends on user preferences, volatility in the stock price. A shorter period Stochastic oscillator gives us many overbought and oversold readings as compare to longer period Stochastic oscillator. It is advisable to use Stochastic oscillator in combination with other types of indicator for better accuracy and forecasting.

10.6 CONCLUSION

Stock traders generally take their trading decision i.e entry, exit and stop loss based on these technical indicators. Though there are a large numbers of technical indicators used by the researcher and stock traders. Our chapter here explain only few and most popular ones. It is to note that technical analysis like any other type of analysis is not 100% accurate. The level of its accuracy depends upon the experience of the stock trader and analyst. Hence technical analysis cannot be mastered with the experience.

REFERENCES

Copsey, I. (1999). *Integrated Technical Analysis. John Wiley and Sons (Asia).* Pte Ltd.

Fama, E. F. (1965). The behaviour of stock market prices. *The Journal of Business, 38*(1), 34–105. doi:10.1086/294743

Fama, E. F. (1970). Efficient capital markets: A review of theory and empirical work. *The Journal of Finance, 25*(2), 383–417. doi:10.2307/2325486

Lento & Gradojevic. (2007). The Profitability of Technical Trading Rules: A Combined Signal Approach. *Journal of Applied Business Research, 3*(1).

Chapter 11
Using Genetic Algorithms to Develop Investment Strategies

ABSTRACT

Genetic algorithms (GAs) are a powerful search technique. The use of genetic algorithms (GAs) will help in the development of better trading systems. The genetic algorithms (GAs) help the researcher to explore various combinations of trading rules or their parameters, which the human mind is unable to find. This chapter explains genetic algorithms (GAs) in brief and gives insight on how they find better trading strategies. Some of the manual trading strategies are good in nature. Genetic algorithms (GAs) only addition to them. Interfacing genetic algorithms (GAs) with stock trading systems or developing a combined model requires a large degree of imagination and creativity. It is an art not a scientific invention. Genetic algorithms (GAs) make use of computers to find various interesting trading systems.

11.1 INTRODUCTION

With the availability of huge processing power and memory at cheap rates at your door step in past decades. It has been helpful to develop new trading strategies to forecast stock data. This has result in creating new generation Artificial Intelligence (AI) based systems which are known as expert systems popularly. Many algorithms has also comes into picture to support them. Genetic Algorithms (GA's) is one such type of technique which is used as an optimizer in common to generate various trading rules or their best parameters

DOI: 10.4018/978-1-7998-4105-0.ch011

(Bauer, 1994). These artificial intelligence based systems are so powerful that no human intervention can match their results, as human mind has limited processing ability or cognitive power. But by a large decision or results by these expert systems are much superior then given by traditional systems. Genetic Algorithms (GA's) based expert systems are of flexible in nature and changes their working according to the market conditions. They are of self evolving in nature and take their learning's from the past. Results or solution find by them are of superior in nature and we cannot dream of finding such solutions by traditional optimization techniques. Of all optimizers present and past researches has found that Genetic Algorithms (GA's) are of most innovative and powerful in nature. Results are of promising in nature as we had applied them in past data and Genetic Algorithms (GA's) is replacing past traditional statistical based traditional search methods firstly.

Genetic Algorithms (GA's) are simple in nature as they are inspired by biological evolution. Genetic Algorithms (GA's) process is generally a artificial simulation in nature i.e its selection and survival of fittest (Goldberg, 2002). It is based on Darwin theory of survival of fittest. Genetic Algorithms (GA's) has found its application in a large number of areas in addition to the stock market domain. Past researchers have shown that Genetic Algorithms (GA's) has been successful in each and every domain.

11.2 GENETIC ALGORITHMS (GA'S) PAST HISTORY

Genetic Algorithms (GA's) are based on Darwin theory of natural selection and survival of fittest (Rajasekaran et. Al, 2007). The stock market domain problems generally posses a large search with almost infinite combinations. Genetic Algorithms (GA's) basically search in many dimensions in a search spaces. In this procedure many new vantage points are found not just one. Genetic Algorithms (GA's) generate a large number of solutions. Thus selection in combination with other intelligent operators consistently improves the fitness function, generation after generation. Nature has got a lot of power to evolve itself under various changing circumstances. Genetic Algorithms (GA's) is just the mimic of nature evolution in a computer program. First attempt to mimic the working of nature was done in 1950's and 1960's. These attempts were unsuccessful as proper balance between the operators is not successfully done.

In 1960's John Holland along with his students in University of Michigan developed Genetic Algorithms (GA's) with selection, crossover and mutation operator encapsulated in it. He successfully make a program which implemented c Genetic Algorithms (GA's). Since then Genetic Algorithms (GA's) has been able to solve many difficult and NP hard problems, which are unable to be solved by human mind. Since then John Holland is known to be father of Genetic Algorithms (GA's). Hence from this point of time researches in Genetic Algorithms (GA's) has been increasing at an exponential pace and various researches had applied Genetic Algorithms (GA's) in almost all areas known to us, prominent one is stock market forecasting.

Genetic Algorithms (GA's) comes under the umbrella of evolutionary algorithms. Popular evolutionary algorithms are Genetic Algorithms (GA's), Genetic programming (GP), evolutionary programming etc. are based on Darwin theory of natural selection. Here random population is generated which undergo certain changes and their individual member of population fight with each other for their survival or passage of their genes into the next generation. Of all categories Genetic Algorithms (GA's) has its popularity at its highest level. Genetic programming uses tree structure as a chromosome instead of binary or simple strings. Evolutionary programming also uses not strings representation. Though it depends upon our imagination to represent a solution in the program, there is no restriction in it. A lot of modification has been done since then in the original John Holland Genetic Algorithms (GA's) developed in 1960's. Genetic Algorithms (GA's) are flexible in their working, since its inception a lot of new operators has been added to it and many hybrid form of Genetic Algorithms (GA's) has come into the picture. As parallelism is the basic property of Genetic Algorithms (GA's), it makes an effective optimizer. It is well suited for combinatorial explosive or NP hard problem. Genetic Algorithms (GA's) found better solution or close to optimal solution in case of problem where value of best possible solution is not known and of those problems which are difficult to solve with traditional process. Below is given a Genetic Algorithms (GA's) procedure:

Basic procedure of Genetic Algorithms (GA's)

```
Create a random population of n members
While (If termination criteria is not met)
{ Calculate fitness of each member in population
Loop
Select two members according to their fitness
Apply crossover operator with crossover rate to produce new
members
Apply mutation operator with mutation rate to produce new
members
Endloop
```

```
Replace the previous members with the new member obtained after
application of crossover and mutation
Endwhile }
Give us the best member with best possible fitness value
End procedure
```

11.3 GENETIC ALGORITHMS (GA'S) IN FINANCIAL DOMAIN

After the entry into the world of Genetic Algorithms (GA's), we are now examining its usefulness in the area of financial domain. A lot of literature is available of the application of Genetic Algorithms (GA's) in this area. Genetic Algorithms (GA's) are best suited for financial modelling to these reasons given below:

- Genetic Algorithms (GA's) has made considerable improvements in their prediction as a when compared with other techniques.
- Genetic Algorithms (GA's) procedures are quantitative in nature, so they are better used for trading rule optimization or parameter optimization of a trading rule.
- Genetic Algorithms (GA's) are black box technique. That means does not use any of the information related to the financial domain except the fitness function value.

Genetic Algorithms (GA's) can be applied in a number of ways depending upon the problem. Working of Genetic Algorithms (GA's) is of robust in nature and results have shown that balance between efficiency and efficiacy has been made.

Genetic Algorithms (GA's) in financial domain is used for bankruptcy prediction which is the cause of major stress in bank. Genetic Algorithms (GA's) find various based on the balance sheet data and have been successful in prediction of a bankruptcy of a firm.

Genetic Algorithms (GA's) are also used to determine credit scoring for a person or firm. Banks are using Genetic Algorithms (GA's) generated rules to find the credit score based on the past data. This has result into a saving in their investment of the banks.

Other Genetic Algorithms (GA's) in financial domain includes database mining, optimizing parameter of a pre defined trading rule, or creating rules that generates buy or sell signals in the stock markets. If Genetic Algorithms (GA's) based procedure gives a small amount of improvements, in last we are going to have a large pay off. Since trillions of dollars are invested in the stock markets. Only 1% increase in accuracy will result in billions of dollar profit.

In case of stock market we predict or forecast the time series of the stock price data. Usually we use various technical indicators to predict the time series or to generate buy or sell signal. The parameter values of these indicators can be generated by using Genetic Algorithms (GA's) rather than taking heuristically. In advance stage we form a technical trading rule by combining two or more than two technical indicators. In this case search space increases exponentially and brute force attack is time consuming. Genetic Algorithms (GA's) is used to get better parameter settings that generate huge profits. Various portfolio selections for the stock is done by using Genetic Algorithms (GA's). Asset allocation strategies are done by Genetic Algorithms (GA's). Past researchers has found that Genetic Algorithms (GA's) search large solution spaces in a very effective and efficient manner. Simple and flexible in nature are the two main features of Genetic Algorithms (GA's). Various hybrid models has also been generated i.e Genetic Algorithms (GA's) applied in conjunction with neural network and fuzzy logic. This type of hybridization requires a lot of experience and knowledge. Once implemented these model when run in a personal computer are computationally intensive. Genetic Algorithms (GA's) applied in real time trading application is propriety of the researcher. It is seen that a lot of this type of knowledge is under wraps and only implementation are in the public domain. Usually technical analysis is based on the past data or price information. These are the macroeconomic fundamentals and rules generated here give us prediction on daily basis. Hence Genetic Algorithms (GA's) are used to find optimal parameter of a pre defined rule or rule itself.

A Simple Technical Trading Rule Optimization: Genetic Algorithms (GA's) are used to search optimal parameter for the trading model (Latemedia, 2007), (Kapoor et. Al, 2011). A simple trading rule is moving average crossover. Moving averages are average stock price for n days. Here if shorter moving average crosses above the longer moving average then buy signal is generated. If it crosses it in downward direction then sell signal is generated. In order to get optimal lengths of these two moving averages Genetic Algorithms (GA's) are used to find optimal values with fitness function as the profit generated by using these moving averages lengths. Genetic Algorithms (GA's) are run multiple times in order to get many better optimal or close to optimal parameters.

Another variation of Genetic Algorithms (GA's) is Genetic Programming (GP). It is used for rule generation. Suppose there are three different rules:

If (n-day MA > 0) then buy else sell   (1)

If (n1-day MA > 0) then buy else sell   (2)

If (n2-day MA > 0) then buy else sell   (3)

Genetic programming will generate rule such as

If (rule 1 says buy) then buy else sell

If (rule 1 and rule 2 says buy) then buy else sell

If (rule 1 and rule 2 and rule 3 says buy) then buy else sell

Here the chromosomes are represented in form of tree structure. Tree data structure of varying length and complexity are generated. These all tree structures expand and shrink generations after generations. Here statements are shown in a way of binary tree structure. So Genetic Algorithms (GA's) are robust optimizers, which are efficient to solve many difficult problems. Genetic Algorithms (GA's) have been applied in all fields of engineering. Genetic Algorithms (GA's) are general purpose algorithms which can be mapped to a particular problem. Genetic Algorithms (GA's) has generated large profits when applied in financial domain. Genetic Algorithms (GA's) is used with interest by a variety of researchers. Development of Genetic Algorithms (GA's) is still far behind as compare to other soft computing techniques as neural networks, fuzzy logic etc. But there is a growing momentum for research in this area.

There are two approaches in Genetic Algorithms (GA's) classification. These two approaches are named after the universities where they had been developed. One approach name is Michigan approach and other name approach is Pittsburg approach. The difference between these two approaches is that weather population in Genetic Algorithms (GA's) represents a single rule or set of rule.

In Michigan approach, the whole population represents a single rule with different set of parameters. Advantages of Michigan approach is that it has a smaller memory requirement and they can be processed faster. Draw back is that we have to confirm conflict resolution as some number of paradoxes is created here.

In Pittsburg approach each member of population represents a different concept and best concept after the successful Genetic Algorithms (GA's) run is generated. Advantages of this approach are that it has easier conflict resolution. Drawbacks are repletion and increasing in processing time and power. So it is easier to handle population in Michigan approach then in Pittsberg approach. Popularly we are going to choose Michigan approach in our Genetic Algorithms (GA's) system implemented.

11.4 OPTIMIZATION AND OPTIMIZERS

Traditionally trading models are developed heuristically in which optimization plays a very less role. This was a trial and error activity, if we want optimized that model. Optimization of a model always plays an important role in increasing profits. So the question arises that what you mean by optimization and optimizers (Deb, 2002).

An optimizer is an algorithm or set of procedures which found best solution found until so far. A Genetic Algorithms (GA's) optimizer is implemented in any high level programming language such as C, C++, Java, Python etc. So the Genetic Algorithms (GA's) optimizers are a few line of code written and executed successfully. So any algorithm which does any type of optimization is known as optimizer. To implement these optimizers efficiently we need computers. By and large, human brain is the most powerful hit and trial optimizer, as its imagination can go to any extent.

Optimizers are used to find best solution or settings for the problem. So what if the "Best Solution" phrase mean. In stock trading system it is the set of trading rule or parameters of a particular trading rule. By the word rule we mean it is logic of the stock trading system. A trading system can have at least two rule on is entry rule and other is exit rule and it can have n number of parameter settings. Parameters give us the logic in which rules are expressed. Parameter setting s can be various lengths of Moving averages (MA's), weights of neural network etc. So a trading system is a combination of both rule and system parameters. In this way their performance is judged.

So to get a good performance sometimes rules are changed and parameters values are adjusted heuristically i.e in a trial and error process.

So a trading system is combination of rule and parameter. A trading system is judged by its trading property. This profit or loss generated by the trading system is called fitness. This fitness function formula is in form of a code implemented in any language. A higher fitness is desired by the all users and traders. So the best solution is the largest fitness obtained so far i.e more profit and least cost. Optimizers are used to find best possible fitness or solution of the problem. Optimizers are sometimes a trial and error activity when we use human mind. If used with sophistication, various algorithms act as optimizers. For example Genetic Algorithms (GA's) based simulation is used to find high quality solution for complex problems.

11.4.1 Types of Optimizers

There are a number of optimizer's presents; each one has its own strengths and weakness. Classification of optimizers can be done in various ways such as human optimizer's vs machine optimizers, simple optimizer's vs complex optimizers, analytic vs stochastic optimizers etc. These all optimizers do a search to find best solution for a particular problem on which they are executed.

11.4.2 Implicit Optimizers

A typical example of implicit optimizer is that if a trader find same rule as a trial and error activity. He then test the rule and found that rule gives us a very poor performance. So the stock trader rework on that rule and parameter set of that rule and then runs to get the performance. He found that performance has been increased. This whole process of trader is done number of times and found out a rule which he can use. In this way trader has got a somewhat optimized rule by using an un optimized way. Here he tests a large number of solutions by an trial and error activity. This means that system has optimized itself in a defacto way. Here more than one solution is tested and best solution is adapted. This is known as defacto optimization. As stated earlier our brain is best optimizer we have so far. He has mentally solved the problem by using a trial and error activity.

11.4.3 Brute Force Optimizers

A brute force optimizer test all possible solution of a problem that is present i.c all combination of rule and valid parameter set available to us. Due to this feature brute force optimizer are of slow in nature. This major drawback for these types of optimizers. They are not recommended for combinatorial optimization problems. If in a problem there is an search space of 30 bits then the total number of combination that are in existence is 2^{30} which comes out in trillions. If 1 sec is the time to check for each solution, then it will take years or your whole life to check all the solution. Brute force optimization is useful for problems with a limited or small search space. In this best possible solution will be generated in seconds or minutes. Here when implemented in a programming language, we start with the 1st solution and counter is incremented by one after every iteration and stop until last solution is tested.

11.4.4 Genetic Optimizers

Genetic Optimizers are ultimate type of optimizers we have got. It is based on the theory of evolution. Genetic Algorithms (GAs) is a computer simulation of natural evolutionary process. Of all the optimizers we have seen no one has the power and performance as Genetic Algorithms (GAs) optimizers has. Genetic Algorithms (GAs) are stochastic optimizers, such that they incorporate a lot of random activity in its operations. Thus the combination of large amount of randomization, selection, crossover and mutation results in giving Genetic Algorithms (GAs) optimizer a great power.

Genetic Algorithms (GAs) can be applied with speed and accuracy in combinatorial optimization problems. Here Genetic Algorithms (GAs) founds close to optimal solution in a few function evaluation as compare to brute force optimizer technique. Genetic Algorithms (GAs) blindly search almost every corner of the search space, which cannot be imagined by the human mind. Genetic Algorithms (GAs) does not stick up to the local optima as compare to the other analytical methods. Analytical methods start is always in the right direction, but they get stuck up to the nearest hill or the top. Hence Genetic Algorithms (GAs) are shining example when compared to the analytical optimizers. Hence Genetic Algorithms (GAs) are best suited for discontinuous, noisy irregularities. Only special purpose optimizers for special problem beat Genetic Algorithms (GAs) in their working.

Another type of optimization is by the use of simulated annealing method. Here the process is the copy of the thermodynamic process, where molten metal freezes and anneal. It is a powerful type of stochastic method. It helps in finding global optimal values for ill behaved fitness values. Simulated annealing method is best suited to solve combinatorial explosive problem such as travelling salesmen problem, circuit design of a chip etc. It is found that Genetic Algorithms (GAs) results always outperform simulated annealing results.

11.5 HOW TO MAKE A SUCCESS IN OPTIMIZATION PROCEDURE

If we want to achieve success in the optimization process, then we had to follow these three steps:

1st Step: Sample data size should be large.
2nd Step: Number of parameters set that is to be optimized should be kept small.
3rd Step: A large number of repetitive tests must be made on the sample data.
4th Step: Always judged the solution quality by statistically available methods.

Traditional Optimization: Traditional Optimization or analytic optimizers fail when solution space is filled up with a large number of local peaks. They get trap to the local peak when working to find the global optima. Thus in this way they fail to find global best solutions. This could be avoided by using traditional analytic optimizers in combination with Genetic Algorithms (GAs). This provides best of both the world features such as fastness, accuracy with global optimal solution.

11.6 BUSINESS MODELLING

Business or stock market environment is cumbersome and complex in nature. With the passage of time this property of complexity is increasing in an exponential way. As total number of alternate solutions are increasing and time to make any decision is very less. Second cost of making errors is expensive. Third the effect of any decision which is taken is not easy to predict due to noisiness in the environment. Finally the role of technology has not only benefitted the business, but also increased the risk and complexity. So we need a tool that can summary of this situation. So analyst uses certain models which help them in making decisions. These models help us to find relationship between various variables, find cause and affect relationship etc. It is of no guarantee that these models will predict a system with accuracy and will be a success, but they will help analyst to get a better understanding of the environment. They also reduce some degree of risk. This helps the analyst to have a significant advantage over other naive person in the noisy environment. Modelling a certain system is an art along with science. Perfection in it comes with experience.

11.6.1 Model Definition

A model is a simple version or an abstract view of the real world situation. A successful model take into account all the key parameters and relationships which are important to make decision. Hence there are three qualities that a model must have in order to be more effective: These three qualities are:

1. Validity: Which means how truly it represents a real world situation?
2. Usability: Is model is better to be used for that particular situation.
3. Value addition by this model to its client or user.

Other qualities that a model must have are the cost of running it, its sophistication and time required to make a model. These all features make a model effective. Some of the modellers are called positivists. They believe that their model will give better results which will help in value addition. Some of the modellers are relativists, they believe that model should view situation from the perspective of all stake holders. Hence both the modellers are successful in their working. To have best of both the worlds features we should be relativists when we develop a model and positivists when we judge our model. The following are the major benefits of the model:

*   Models squeezes the time i.e operation time can be simulated in a second while simulating the model.
*   In experimentation of model, changes in model are very easy as compare to changes done in the real world situation.
*   If an error is generated in a model. As model is and trial and error activity, then the cost of an error in model is very less as and when compare in the real world situation.

- In the era of uncertainty, modelling help us to take a lot of risk in decision making process.
- To conduct an experiment on the model is a cost effective as compare to conduct and experiment in a real world situation.
- Model helps the decision makers to increase their experience and learning.
- Modelling increases the rigorous thinking in the decision makers.
- Generally model helps us to test a lot number of permutation and combination of various parameters which was not possible in real world situation.
- Model helps us to have a better understanding of real world situation, in contrast to the working of real world system itself.

The main draw backs of the modelling are:

- Some time model preparation is time consuming, if real world parameters are large.
- Traditional analysts are resistive to accept these computer and mathematical based models.
- Sometimes the real world data, much needed to model a system is not radically available or it is expensive.
- A lot more of uncertainty in the real world situation cannot be incorporated in the model.
- 100% reality of the system is mimic in the model. Then it is found that it may give many errors in signals.
- The basic assumption that we have taken into account all the variables, but in fact there are a number of interrelated variables.

In case of stock market scenarios there can be adverse and diverse situations. Hence more level of abstraction is needed in making that model and to represent it mathematically. Since relationship between the various variables are so complex so that they cannot be expressed in a physical model. We need some mathematical formulas and soft computing methods to represent them. In case of mathematical model there are three types of variables:

1. Independent Variables: Variables whose values we are going to predict.
2. Uncontrolled Parameters: Here we have no control in governing them and they are beyond our scope.

3. Dependent Variables: They are the parameters which affect the independent variables.

If uncontrolled parameters and dependent variables are having a property of certainty then model is known as deterministic model. If their values falls within a certain rage, in accordance to probability distribution. Then they are called probabilistic model. If there is inadequate or less information about these values then it is called intuitive model. Main use of the model is to determine the optimal solution for the rule or opportunity, by taking case of assumptions. These models are also known as prescriptive. The process in prescriptive technique is of trial and error type and comparisons of various alternatives present so far. Various popular and successful prescriptive models are based on enumeration and algorithms, which gives us optimal solutions. If all the alternative solutions are checked then it is called exhaustive enumeration. This type of procedure is useful when number of possible alternative and combinations are less, otherwise in case of large search spaces, it is impossible to test each possible combination. In contrast to this exhaustive enumeration technique, algorithm is a step by step procedure, which search optimal solution after certain iterations. Here solution quality improves after every set of iterations. In contrast to various traditional algorithms, which test for a small portion of the search space, not all search space.

Alternate to prescriptive model is descriptive model. Here this model does not check all conditions, but only a small handful of conditions. They are applied where optimizations are not needed. Similarly simulation is a process in which we perform experiments on the system by taking various combination of the parameters and find the solution quality of it. Simulating the model with different combination of parameters will give optimal solutions.

11.6.2 Modelling Process

The three major step expert or modeller do when he does effective modelling are:

1. Identify a problem.
2. Validate or verify a problem.
3. Obtain key variables of the model.

In a broad way modelling is a five step process. The varios steps and time needed to execute them is given below:

1. Problem Recognition (Time spend is 14%)
2. Model Formulation (Time spend is 9%)
3. Data Collection (Time spend is 9%)
4. Analysis of model(Time spend is 16%)
5. Implementation (Time spend is 2%)

There may be different ways in which these steps may be executed. For example in certain cases data collection may come before model formulation etc. Now in the coming section we are going to discuss all these five steps in detail.

Now consider a problem that comes into picture. In case of stock trading system the opportunity or problem is to create or maximize profit and minimize losses while trading. This the easiest part in this 5 step process. This is the most important part also. If we define the problem in a better way then we almost crossed the half way mark. If the problem definition is put in a wrong way then this results in wrong or vague solutions, which are not useful to us in any way. For this modeller should investigate the whole situation minutely. He should successfully found symptoms between symptoms and problems. Care must be taken such that in the beginning a different problem exists and in the end a different version of problem exists. Thus proper investigation will help modeller in avoidance of solving a wrong problem and saving time and energy.

2ns step is model formulation. Here we convert the problem into mathematical form or the problem is represented in a mathematical formula on a piece of paper. All the dependent and independent variables are pin pointed and relationship between these variables are established in form of equation. Various assumptions are also defined. Linear or non linear relationship, simplification and degree of reality have been fixed here. We should try to keep the model simpler and more representative of real world situation. So balance between these two factors should be done while constructing the model. This will require several fake iterations to be done, before coming to the final model formulation. Thus all the mathematical and soft computing based models should these three components in it i.e dependent variables, Independent variables and uncontrolled parameters. These three components are described earlier.

3rd step is data collection. Some times accusation of data is difficult and time consuming. In case of stock trading systems the data is radically available in the public domain of all stock exchanges. Here we are encountered with the problem of excessive data. With limited processing power and excess of data, our computer processing power and memory will be short in simulating the model. Here decision variables can be the amount which we want to get invested, dependent variables are previous day closing price, opening price etc. and uncontrolled variables are day high, day low, volume of shares traded, deliverability of shares etc.

4th and most important step is analysis of the model. Here we test how well our model work. The common questions are: Is the results given by the model are accurate? Does the model represent the real world behaviour? So to validate a model there are two steps: 1st step is to determine whether logic used in model is correct and right programming is done for it. 2nd step is to find that model represent the real world in a full view. After successful validation analysis of model is done by giving certain input values and obtaining results. Now compare this results with the actual the actual values of the past data. Traditionally to get best decision or output variables comprises of these five steps:

1. First generate a large number of alternatives.
2. Now find the fitness function value or outcome of each alternative.
3. Compare these result or outcome with the goal which we had previously decided or actual values.
4. Compare the outcome obtained from each alternative.
5. In the end select optimal value or the set of parameters which gives us the best possible solution.

By following this whole procedure we will be able to find magnitude of change in solution quality, if we make change in the independent variables. We will come to know which parameters are more sensitive and which are less. Robustness in the solution is obtained.

5th step is implementation. This step requires least thought process and time. Here model is implemented in any higher level language and run to test whether it is implemented correctly or not.

11.6.3 How to Apply Genetic Algorithms (GAs) in a Stock Trading System?

Genetic Algorithms (GAs) are generally powerful optimizers. We had a fair knowledge of Genetic Algorithms (GAs) working and about its operators as a whole. Here we will apply Genetic Algorithms (GAs) to optimise the parameters of a simple trading model. The trading model is explained below:

Here our trading system consists of four moving averages of varying lengths. First three moving averages are used to calculate Moving Average Convergence Divergence (MACD), a popular momentum oscillator explained before in the previous chapter. These three moving averages will be used to generate Moving Average Convergence Divergence (MACD) and a signal line. Fourth moving average will be used to compare with the current closing price. Our trading model will generate a buy signal if Moving Average Convergence Divergence (MACD) line is above the signal line and current closing price is above the fourth moving average line. Here in this system Moving Average Convergence Divergence (MACD) is slow and is used as trend filter and fourth moving average is used to generate or trigger buy or sell signals if there is a strong trend in stock price movement. A sell signal will be generated if Moving Average Convergence Divergence (MACD) line is below the signal line and current closing price is below the moving average line.

So to apply Genetic Algorithms (GAs) in order to optimize the moving averages length i.e there are four parameters values that re to be optimized. Thus we decide that all these four moving averages length will be of integer in nature. Thus the individual solution will consists of four integer values. To start with, a random population is generated in which each individual member consists of four integer values randomly generated. Artificial trading by taking these four integer values is done on past stock price data and profit obtained is the fitness function value for that population member. These fitness function values of each member of population are stored in the variable. During this process we will see that some population members generate profit, while other population members generate looses. Now we will apply selection operator on the population. The role of selection operator is to select the best individual member for mating, so that they can pass their values to the next generation. In the mating process we apply crossover and mutation operator on the members selected. In crossover there is a recombination of parameters in the two strings selected. Process is shown below:

```
Parent A:    A1 . A2 . A3 . A4
Parent B:    B1 . B2 . B3 . B4
```

After crossover at the mid point we may get two offspring such as

```
Offspring A:     A1 . A2 . B3 . B4
Offspring B:     B1 . B2 . A3 . A4
```

Considering our trading system suppose two strings that are produces are

```
String 1: 12    28    8    4
String 2: 4     11    7    12
```

It means in case of string 1 Moving Average Convergence Divergence (MACD) is calculated by taking difference of 12 and 28 day moving average and signal line of 9 day moving average of Moving Average Convergence Divergence (MACD) is generated. A 4 day moving average line is calculated, so that we can compare it with the closing price which in return will generate trading signal buy or sell. Crossover operator is applied and crossover takes place in the middle, then the two offspring generated are:

```
Offspring 1: 12    28    7    12
Offspring 2: 4     11    8    4
```

After mutation operator is applied. Here on every integer mutation is applied. It is a probabilistic operator. Here on integer mutation is applied, then that particular integer will be replaced by the any other integer generated randomly. For ex

```
Offspring 1: 12    28    7    12
```

Mutation Operator

```
Final Offspring 1: 12    28    3    12
```

So the main theory is that if both the strings give us good profit while trading, then various other combinations of their values will also give much better solution or profits. Mutation gives much needed diversity and prevents stagnation in the population, which may occur due to greedy selection operator. Thus randomization is crossover and mutation together with selection will lead us into the right direction and help us to find optimal solution.

11.7 CONCLUSION

Now a day's trading in the market is very difficult and is becoming competitive day by day with the increase in number of traders. Since market is a zero sum game which means that for every trader who loose there is every trader who wins and vice versa. So every decision is critical and it may lead you to a profit or loss. Those who are taking decision only on intuition and are not using some artificial intelligence based models are on receiving end. They are going to wind up soon in near future. In this chapter we have try to explain in brief the use of Genetic Algorithms (GAs) as a optimizer in order to find an optimal value for the trading model. So it is advisable if one wants to stay competitive in market, one should be familiar with the use of artificial intelligence.

REFERENCES

Bauer, J. (1994). *Genetic Algorithms and Investment Strategies.* John Wiley and Sons, Inc.

Deb. (2002). *Optimization for Engineering Design: Algorithm and Examples.* Prentice Hall of India Private Limited.

Goldberg. (2002). *Genetic Algorithms in Search, Optimization and Machine Learning.* Pearson Education.

Kapoor, V., Dey, S., & Khurana, A. P. (2011). Genetic algorithm: An application to technical trading system design. *International Journal of Computers and Applications, 36*(5), 44–50.

Letamendia, L. N. (2007). Fitting Control Parameters of a Genetic Algorithm: An Application to Technicl Trading Systems Design. *European Journal of Operational Research, 179*(3), 847–865. doi:10.1016/j.ejor.2005.03.067

Rajasekaran & Vijaylakshmi Pai. (2007). *Neural Networks, Fuzzy Logic, and Genetic algorithms, Synthesis and Applications.* Prentice- Hall of India Private Limited.

Chapter 12
Developing a Single Indicator or Multiple Indicator Market Timing System

ABSTRACT

In this chapter, the authors use genetic algorithms (GAs) to optimize the parameters of the trading system, which is made by various technical indicators. These trading systems or rules will give buy or sell signals when applied on past prices of a particular stock. Genetic algorithms (GAs) have an ability to find optimal trading indicators that will predict the market direction or trend with greater accuracy. Use of genetic algorithms (GAs) in conjunction to a trading rule refutes efficient market hypothesis (EMH) in a weak form.

12.1 INTRODUCTION

This chapter sets the stage on how we could interface Genetic Algorithms (GAs) or apply on a trading system in order to improve our accuracy and profits (Bauer, 1994). So the question here comes into our mind that why we use Genetic Algorithms (GAs). Before the answer to this question, I would like to ask one simpler question i.e why we are involving the use of computers to develop our trading system? Answer to this question is that human brain has limited processing power or cognitive ability. Though we imagine and do many things which are of superior in nature, but we have our limits. Our brain has limited intelligence. Human mind can imagine and find a small number of

DOI: 10.4018/978-1-7998-4105-0.ch012

combinations at a given time. If we imagine a certain thing, our imagination has limitation. Consider a game of chess; even best player will anticipate seven to ten moves in advance. Computers which have a huge processing power and large memory, can make a large numbers of combinations among different parameters which we haven't imagine and dreamt of. Consider a 7-bit binary string. Each position can have 0 or 1 value. Then total number of combination we can have is 27 i.e 128 total combinations. To find all 128 combinations will require a lot of imagination and thought process. But with the help of computers it will be a easy task and can be completed in a seconds time. Thus computers are helpful in solving complex problems such as stock trading indicator system.

Another advantage in using computers as a decision making is the consistency in its working, when in use. We humans are not always same as making good decision. It depends upon our mood. So the rules or parameters of the rules given by the computers are reliable and they are of great help as compared to the rule found by human intervention.

There are no less trading techniques which we can use. A lot of qualitative models are discovered by the researchers and are popular amongst the traders and stock market analysts. Genetic Algorithms (GAs) based models have an edge over other traditional models, as they are easy to use, less time consuming etc. We are going to discuss all these features in the coming section.

There is a lot of flexibility in the implementation of Genetic Algorithms (GAs) (Deb, 2002), (Rajasekaran et. Al, 2007). We can implement Genetic Algorithms (GAs) with different permutation and combinations, with different sets of operator's probabilities and so on. Since our imagination can go to the farthest end. Genetic Algorithms (GAs) can be applied until that end also. There is no limitation in applying Genetic Algorithms (GAs) as solution provider (Goldberg, 2002). Here in the coming section of this chapter we are going to explain in detail how Genetic Algorithms (GAs) is implemented to optimize the parameters of a stock trading system. The way by which we are applying Genetic Algorithms (GAs) to the technical trading system is going to be just one of the way. There are n number of ways by which Genetic Algorithms (GAs) can be applied. Genetic Algorithms (GAs) can be applied to optimized trading strategies based on fundamental analysis or technical indicators. Since technical indicators in use are simple mathematical calculation. Genetic Algorithms (GAs) in addition can be implemented as per user requirement and first choice. After the thought process to the implementation of Genetic Algorithms (GAs) i.e string mapping and representation, fitness function calculation is done. There are almost lot of ways in which Genetic Algorithms (GAs) can be implemented. The basic difference between the Genetic Algorithms (GAs) implemented for two different problems is string representation and mapping, fitness function formula. Basic working of Genetic Algorithms (GAs) is on strings and the internal procedure is a black box technique, as it does not care what these strings are mapped to or represent.

Let us consider that we are applying Genetic Algorithms (GAs) to optimize stock market trading system. Here our fitness formula is such that it should calculate annual rate of return on the invested amount. Since we had artificially applied Genetic Algorithms (GAs) on past year of stock closing price data, which is publically available. There are two choices, one if we take average of year wise returns. But it would be more advisable that recent year rate of return is more applicable. So instead of averaging, weighted average must be done i.e recent year return must be given more weights as compare to the distant year rate of return. So in case of Genetic Algorithms (GAs), we have to make changes in the fitness function formula, not on the whole Genetic Algorithms (GAs) procedure.

Thus the variation in the fitness function according to the user definition is one of the flexibility which is given by Genetic Algorithms (GAs). Considering this with a linear regression model. Here our fitness formula should be to minimize the sum of squared deviations. So if the similar previous case is to be applied i.e most recent deviation should be taken larger into consideration, then a large complication will be created in the calculation of the fitness function formula, which will not be as simple as in case of Genetic Algorithms (GAs). As we have seen in the past chapters that Genetic Algorithms (GAs) works swiftly. In case of combinatorial explosive problems or problems with a huge search space, where to apply brute force technique is time consuming and is not possible at all. Genetic Algorithms (GAs) will be able to find close to optimal solution with a few function evaluation.

It is seen from past researches (Mahfoud et. al, 1996), (Allen et. Al, 1998), (Letamendia, 2007), (Kapoor et, al, 2011) that the trading rule developed by Genetic Algorithms (GAs) or the parameters settings found out by Genetic Algorithms (GAs) are somewhat different and are of better values. These superior results are difficult to obtain while using traditional optimization techniques. Since Genetic Algorithms (GAs) works with a greater speed as compare to brute force technique, so they are more suitable for real time trading system. In comparison to the past data we can use more recently monthly data to find or correct our trading rules. Though the search space is large this correction can be done in hours, if not in minutes. A new trading rule will be available for the next day. Hence Genetic Algorithms (GAs) as an optimizer is very much suitable to all real time systems of any area. Other which adds to the popularity of Genetic Algorithms (GAs) is less or almost no knowledge about the system is required, whose parameters are being optimized. Only binary string mapping to the solution and fitness function formula is the required knowledge about the system domain. Genetic Algorithms (GAs) only works with the binary strings and try to find the optimal string just by having the string function evaluation value. All the user is to do is to correctly implement Genetic Algorithms (GAs) and it will actually find the optimal value and the parameter set. All though the user does not have any knowledge about the stock trading system. To implement Genetic Algorithms (GAs) we require knowledge of programming and its skills. Once the Genetic Algorithms (GAs) program is implemented, only thing we have to change in Genetic Algorithms (GAs), if we switch from one problem to other problem is the coding of fitness function formula. More user friendly interface can be given by the coder by which we could easily change our Genetic Algorithms (GAs) required code. In this way it is seen that Genetic Algorithms (GAs) are compared to other techniques.

12.2 FINANCIAL ANALYSIS AND INVESTMENT THEORY

There are two types of features which we should take into account, if we are entering in the stock market. On is market timing and other is portfolio management. In case of market timing, the analyst tries to enter the market in the lowest low and try to exit it at highest high. While in case of portfolio management the analyst choose only those stocks that are expected to give better returns. So Genetic Algorithms (GAs) can be used to optimize market timing rule parameters or they can be used for security selection also. Earlier before the use of Genetic Algorithms (GAs) or other technique it was done by intuition, convenience or by some interest. It is seen that Genetic Algorithms (GAs) when used to find optimal market timing have less computational complexity as compare to find optimal portfolio selection, which gives maximum profit.

There are two types of new or information that affect stock market as a particular stock is micro economic data or news and other is macro economic data or news. In fact it is seen that investor pay more attention towards macro economic data and news. As all of the stock values are effected largely to it. For the case of security selection macroeconomic news is an important factor.

As all companies work with in a legal frame or socio economic frame work. It is rational to take macroeconomic news or data to take into consideration, which will lead us to have profitable opportunities. Many investors take into account dividend given by the company as the major macroeconomic data to find the stock prospects in future. So to buy any stock we look for the dividend given by the company or it is going to give and what will be the future value of that stock would be. This is the same case when we sell the stock and some other person who buys that stock from us. The basic notion is always the same for all traders who buy stock from any one. Thus the value of a stock is strongly linked with the dividend given by the company. In a chain of linkages among the various parameters, stock price depends upon the earnings of the company. More earnings of the group, results in a more dividends pay outs per share. Earnings depends upon the sales of the product made by the company and last but not the least, that sales of a product depends upon the strength of the economy. Thus health of the economy is always shown in the macroeconomic data and news, which in turn affect the stock price and last will affect our investment decision.

There are a numbers of factors which tells about the strength of the economy. One of the factors is interest rate, inflation and risk. All these are interlinked with each other. Increase in one of them will lead to the down fall of others and so on. So a proper balance must be maintained between them. Inflation value also depends upon monetary growth, supply demand ratio etc. The security bonds given by the company has risk premium values attached to it. When a economy is at its brink, then risk values increases and vice versa.

If interest rate goes high then attractiveness of the stock market reduces. As the investor wants, higher rate of return from the stock market otherwise it will shift from market to fixed interest regime. As result valuation of the stocks will fall. Bond risks premiums are also negatively affected by the increase of interest rates. It will increase their risks premiums. Hence the effects on the stock price due to the changes in macroeconomic data are not very easy to predict. A very comprehensive study is needed to make this analysis fruitful.

In case of fundamental analysis we always start with certain assumptions. There is always a relationship between the economy, management decision and stock price movement. Thus the whole monetary policy such as interest rates, reverse repo rates etc. and other macroeconomic variables as decided by the central bank and fiscal policy, as decided by effects our stock prices.

In our country this all historic macro economic data is made publically available to all by ministry of commerce, both in hard copy and in electronic form. Monthly data on consumer index, inflation, industrial output, interest rates etc. all are made available by the concerned ministry of every developed and developing country. These all macroeconomic data in conjunction with historic return data of the stock price will help us to create a large number of trading rules, and on which Genetic Algorithms (GAs) can be applied to optimized these rules or the parameter lengths of the indicators in these rules for better profit or maximum return.

So in addition to this technical analysis, we can apply Genetic Algorithms (GAs) in fundamental analysis also. Here positive and negative relationships must be found macroeconomic data and stock price data to form a rule. This all thing cannot be generally done manually i.e we does not outlook connection between the parameters of fundamental analysis and technical analysis. We left this task to our computation machine to do this. One thing that is kept in mind in finding these relationships is they must be homogeneous not unfitting.

We do not recommend a analyst to apply computational power mindlessly or he should be explorative in nature. If some correction or relationship is explored in the two data series, then it must be judged with a high degree of rationale. For example if increase in inflation in some country and rate of return of the stock in some other country is matching. Then this relationship or connection we had found in the two time series we cannot rely on. As there is no rational theory to give, that tells us the connection between these two time series data. Hence we try to examine a large number of relationships between a lots of time series, we find that over fitting of relationship formula appears. Hence in this situation when there is an explosion of combinatorial possibilities among the variables, only few connections work consistently. Our comfort zone is also compromised when there is an explosion of possibility and over fitting of the variable data. So to prevent this we can buy robustness in our computation methodology. Genetic Algorithms (GAs) is one of the best soft computing techniques we can apply or we can use a large number of trading rule and not rely on one rule itself. This will reduce the impact of over fitting of rules.

12.3 TESTING OUR SYSTEM ON PAST HISTORIC DATA: CONCERNS AND ISSUES

Thus testing our notion and rule on past historic data is known as back testing. It gives us the performance of that particular rule in past. So our assumption that if this rule has worked in past, then it will work in future does not hold, that if a large number of analyst would have used that rule then the market would be different by now. But still we assume that this effect will be less and will affect the market movement in a large way. Stock market theory advocates that if we are investing billions of billions in the stock market, then even a small effect will give a large dent in the result. Though I believe these statements, but we have no choice to test our hypothesis but to back test it. So we feel that if our hypothesis works well in the past data, then it will work well in future also.

There are certain limitations of back testing the strategies made from macroeconomic data or fundamental analysis data. These limitations are data accuracy and easy and timely availability of data. In case of macroeconomic data there is a continuous or correctness in the data after a certain period of time. So the value we get today may have somewhat different in past dates. There is also time lag in the data we get. For example March month of fundamental data is available in May month. Another issue is the availability of data. Some of the high end data is generally available to financial institutions not to the general public. Many researchers divide the data into two set i.e testing set and training set. If we use 10 year data set then first seven years data set is used as training data set on which rule parameters set is optimized and next 3 years data set is considered to be testing data, on which optimized parameter set of the rule is applied and we see how they work or the results are excellent, good or bad. So our basic assumption is if the optimized rules or parameter set of rules hold good for the testing data set, then it will be good for future also. We may disagree with this assumption, but we have no choice. This is the risk we have to take conceptually. So we want that rule which out performs during testing phase must also work with the same efficiency in the future also. In the complex world of stock trading the actual truth and concept may be somewhat different or contrast. So in order to keep things simple what are the questions we should ask to ourselves to know weather or trading system is adequate in working or not. The main question is whether past better performance trading system will give same performance in future or not.

In case of using Genetic Algorithms (GAs), we assume that system evolved will work better in future also. We are not 100% sure about that. This our rationale guesses. Actually Genetic Algorithms (GAs) based trading systems are logically evolved, that may give better or positive results for a long period of time. So if we have Rs 100/- to invest, should we use one rule to make an investment or we should use 100 Genetic Algorithms (GAs) based trading system with Rs 1/- for each system to invest. Though Genetic Algorithms (GAs) is always used to evolve system in right direction, but there is always risk in it. Surety cannot be given for it. It has seen that trading system performance is not always consistent. Some systems that had worked well in past gives bad results in some other circumstances or time period. So it is advised to use variety of Genetic Algorithms (GAs) based optimal system and distribute our investment into them equally, rather rely on one highly successful system. It would be too risky to put all the eggs in the same basket.

12.4 GENETIC ALGORITHM VS GENETIC PROGRAMMING

Genetic Algorithms (GAs) belongs to machine learning algorithms, which are successful when applied to different branches of engineering and technology and other areas. Genetic Algorithms (GAs) researchers are growing their interest to implement them in financial or stock trading sector. Genetic Algorithms (GAs) are basically search and optimization procedures based on biological hypothesis of natural selection. They belong to a class of evolutionary strategies of which Genetic Programming is also a popular version of it. In evolutionary types of algorithm population, of various solutions is maintained. Each member of population is evaluated according to the fitness function formula defined. Next round of population is created by selecting better fit members and recombining them by use of a number of genetic operators as discussed in previous chapters. Various other evolutionary algorithms vary in solution representation, selection procedure and the use of various operators. In case of Genetic Algorithms (GAs) solution is represented as a binary string of fixed length. A mapping formula for binary string to the solution representation has to be made. A fitness formula has to be set which tells us about the solution quality obtained. In case of stock trading system fitness formula is pay off driven or profit generated. Genetic Algorithms (GAs) use random function in large way. Random walk in combination with appropriate selection process makes Genetic Algorithms (GAs)an efficient search and optimization process. Genetic Algorithms (GAs) always begin with a random set of solution i.e population generated. Next set of population is generated by the use selection operator which is design in such a way that it is biased to choose above average fitness function members for mating. Mating process includes the use of crossover and mutation operators. After this new set of solution members are generated. In this way one generation is completed. Generation after generation is passed, until we reach a particular stage or some other termination criteria which we had decided earlier is met. In last generations which is a set of optimal solutions, one or more of the solution to solve the problem statement.

Working through a set of population makes Genetic Algorithms (GAs) a parallel search process. Though this effective exploration takes place for large or ill defined search space. Thus using Genetic Algorithms (GAs) we came to know about the large number of schemata solution quality during the whole process. Thus there is exploitation in the search space where promising results are there and exploration of less visited search space takes place.

Main advantages of using evolutionary algorithms over other traditional technique is that they give better results for problems which have discontinuous objective function or multidimensional search space which cannot be drawn in 3-D Dimension. Some problems consist of large number of local optima, which may mislead traditional optimization algorithms such as Hill Climbing or Gauss Newton methods. Due to heuristic in nature and efficient use of probabilistic random number generation based operation such as crossover and mutation and selection operators, there is a very less chance that solution may converge to local optima. Evolutionary algorithms and its various types are useful to such problems where search space and uncertainty is large.

Some drawback of evolutionary algorithms are such that a execution time is more when compare with traditional search methods. A lot number of times fitness function is calculated repetitively generation after generations. Evolutionary algorithms use minimal information about the system or problem which is being solved. They are considering inferior to the problem specific, special purpose algorithms. If not implemented properly they may give poorer results or may face a problem of premature convergence. In this case they may be use in combination with other traditional algorithms. It means as soon as premature convergence is detected, traditional search technique comes into picture as Genetic Algorithms (GAs) makes no progress in solution quality. In many cases Genetic Algorithms (GAs) has completely replaced the traditional optimization algorithm. Though Genetic Algorithms (GAs) is not sure to give optimal solutions, but the solution quality given by them is universally acceptable. Evolutionary algorithms are applied to a large number of areas of engineering, economics, management decision science, cognitive science etc. Since its inception a large number of variants of evolutionary algorithms and their applications in various NP hard problems has comes into existence. A new branch of financial engineering known as econometric forecasting has come into picture.

In traditional Genetic Algorithms (GAs) the population members or solutions arte of fixed length strings. Though this is the most popular type of solution representation, but it may not be good for certain problems which are to be solved using Genetic Algorithms (GAs). This restriction is removed in Genetic programming which is a new type of evolutionary algorithms, developed by John Koza in 1992. It encompasses the strings of variable lengths in contrast to the fixed string in Genetic Algorithms (GAs). In case stock trading system we had an advantage of using Genetic Programming to optimized trading rule as trading rule formations could be of variable lengths.

Here the members of the population or solution are represented as function in various hierarchies. Here the solution is just like a decision tree type structure. Here each node has some sub functions as it successor. Nodes with no successor are called terminal nodes. Thus whole tree is a main function. Thus structure could be function of many types. There is no restriction in type of function used and length of structure. After selection and application of recombination operator, various s combination of sub tress, structure of variable lengths will be created. Genetic Programming consists of structures instead of strings as population. Thus here initial population is a set of random tress. Here the tree starts with a root node which is a sub function at its terminals. These proceeds downward until the function with no sub function i.e with no successors are reached. After the generation of random population, selection operator is applied, which choose better average fit individuals for crossover i.e recombined with other individuals. Here in this Genetic Programming case crossover operator exchange randomly selected sub tree from parent 1 to the randomly selected sub tree with parent 2. The node point is also chosen randomly. In case of mutation, a sub tree in the population is chosen randomly and replaced by a randomly generated another sub tree. Mutation is applied with a very small probability. Genetic programming has been applied by Koza to a variety of problems in a diversified field. An example of Genetic structure is given below:

Figure 1.
Rule 1 Explanation: Here moving average returns a buy signal if 30day moving average is smaller than the price otherwise sell
Rule 2 Explanation: Here buy signal is generated if 20 day maximum value is less than the price otherwise sell.

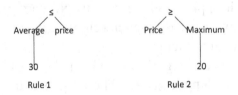

12.5 TO DEVELOP A TECHNICAL INDICATOR BASED RULE TO GENERATE BUY OR SELL SIGNAL

In this section we will work upon the creation of multi technical indicator stock trading system or rule, which will generate buy or signal on a daily basis. Though there are a large number of technical indicators present in the system. There is possibility that we can make infinite number of trading rules with varying length and efficiency. The lengths of technical indicators used in the trading rule was earlier taken heuristically or trial and error method. Our section will propose the use of Genetic Algorithms (GAs) too generate the length of these indicators, which in return will give us better profit or rate of return. Thus with the use of Genetic Algorithms (GAs), level of performance of prediction will be high. This is also seen in past researches though the optimal value is not obtained, but the length of parameters of technical indicators of technical trading rules is consistent in performance. This issue is however of technical in nature. For example one simple rule is using simple moving average. Here the length of two moving averages can be taken up heuristically or we can use Genetic Algorithms (GAs) to finf optimal trading lengths. In case of Moving Average Convergence Divergence (MACD), we take difference of two moving averages, a fast moving average and a slow moving average. If difference value is positive which means stock price is going up, if difference value is negative that means it is going down. Other type of indicator is stochastic oscillator (5K and %D), which is also popular. We can use all these three indicators in conjunction with each other to build a trading system. Then the length of the technical indicator of this trading system is mapped into binary strings and which are optimized using Genetic Algorithms (GAs). We are going to discuss them as a case study matter here.

12.5.1 Case Study 1

Moving Averages Crossovers

Moving averages (MAs) are the most popular and simple in concept in calculation and usage. Moving averages (MAs) is a trend following indicator. Its main function is to filter the noise and bring smoothness in the data. Moving averages (MAs) is also known as lagging indicators. It gives us the trend of the price movement, but with a time lag. It is advisable to use two

Moving averages (MAs). One will give us trend of price movement and other will be used to generate trading signals i.e buy or sell. Calculation of Moving averages (MAs) is the average price of the stock over a predefined period. Thus the Moving averages (MAs) moves with the movement of time duration. Here past data gets dropped and new data is made available. Moving averages (MAs) are generally calculated on the closing price of the stock. Formula for Moving averages (MAs) of 'n' days is given below:

$$MA\ (Close,\ n) = \frac{1}{n} \sum_{i=0}^{n} Pt - i \tag{1}$$

Here $P_{t\text{-}i}$ is the closing price of the t-I and n displays the number of past days taken to build Moving averages (MAs) (i.e length of Moving averages (MAs)).

If two Moving averages (MAs) are to be used then one will be longer and other will be shorter. Longer period of Moving averages (MAs) are slow and lethargic, while shorter Moving averages (MAs) are more sensitive to the price changes. For more effectiveness we use both shorter and longer Moving averages (MAs) in conjunction with each other. Popular Moving averages (MAs) rule is given below:

Crossing of Moving averages (MAs) rule is most popular and widely used by the stock market analyst. Since there are two Moving averages (MAs), one longer and other shorter, buy and sell signals are generated in the following way:

- A buy signal is triggered when shorter Moving averages (MAs) is above longer Moving averages (MAs):

$$\frac{1}{\theta_1} \sum_{i=0}^{\theta_1} P_{t-i} > \frac{1}{\theta_2} \sum_{i=0}^{\theta_2} P_{t-i} \tag{2}$$

Where $\theta_1 < \theta_2$

- A sell signal is triggered when shorter Moving averages (MAs) is below longer Moving averages (MAs):

$$\frac{1}{\theta_1} \sum_{i=0}^{\theta_1} P_{t-i} \leq \frac{1}{\theta_2} \sum_{i=0}^{\theta_2} P_{t-i} \tag{3}$$

Where $\theta_1 < \theta_2$

The parameters i.e lengths of two Moving averages (MAs) (Θ_1 and Θ_2) are generally chosen by trial and error methods or by any intuition by a stock trader or analyst. If we use two Moving averages (MAs) of length 500. Then there will be 500 * 500 = 2,50,000/- Moving averages (MAs) combinations. Our main aim in this model is to find the optimal value of Θ_1 and Θ_2 i.e Moving averages (MAs) lengths which gives buy and sell trading signal and best return. Thus to apply genetic Algorithms (GAs) to find the optimal value of Θ_1 and Θ_2 we first mapped parameter setting to a binary string. If shorter Moving averages (MAs) the string length is 9 bits and larger Moving averages (MAs) string length is 10 bits, then value of shorter Moving averages (MAs) ranges from 0 to 511 and values longer v ranges from 0 to 1023. Total concatenated string length here is 9 bits + 10 bits = 19 bits and total search space here is 2^{19} bits i.e 5,24,288 various combination of Moving averages (MAs). Thus 19 bits string will represents a chromosome.

Triple Moving averages (MAs) Rule: In earlier Moving averages (MAs) crossover rule, we have seen that if there is volatility in the market then there is a lot of whipsaws created by these Moving averages (MAs) crossovers which results in a lot of losses. Thus there is problem of false signal generation as confirmation of bullish and bearish trends has not been established by these two Moving averages (MAs) crossovers. So to tackle with this problem we develop a three Moving averages (MAs) concept. This will help us to get confirmation of bullish and bearish trends with less whipsaw and less losses. With the use of third Moving averages (MAs) we going to have an exit somewhat earlier. This will help us to reduce our losses or loss making trades during consolidation process. The whole procedure to use triple Moving averages (MAs) is given below:

Three Moving averages (MAs) that are being used are categorized as short term, medium term and long term Moving averages (MAs). A buy signal is generated or position is established when shorter term Moving averages (MAs) crosses longer term Moving averages (MAs) in the upward direction. An exit signal is generated when shorter term Moving averages (MAs) crosses medium term Moving averages (MAs) in down ward direction. Thus entry in the market is somewhat delayed by the combination of short term and long term Moving averages (MAs). This means if there is a confirmation of trend, then and then only we are going to have an entry into the market. In this way exit is not delayed. But it is done earlier, due to the combination of short term and medium term Moving averages (MAs). Here the crossover is far earlier then the crossover by longer term Moving averages (MAs). Here in the use of triple Moving averages (MAs) we are going to get zones or time period where no actions are being taken. This results in a reduction of loss making trades. It is seen in many stock movements that shorter Moving averages (MAs) crosses medium length Moving averages (MAs), but fails to cross longer length Moving averages (MAs) and then once again moves back. In this scenario no decision is to be taken. By seeing the pictorial representation we can be tempted that due to this feature of third Moving averages (MAs) many profitable trades are not executed, but the other fact is that many loss making trades are also prevented, So less risks, less gains and more risks and more gains.

Here the lengths of short term (Θ_1), medium term (Θ_2) and long term (Θ_3) Moving averages (MAs) have to be decided and optimal value is found out by using Genetic Algorithms (GAs). Encoding mechanism will consist of short term Moving averages (MAs) length (Θ_1) will have 4 bit i.e its values ranges from 0 to 15, medium term Moving averages (MAs) length will be encoded to 6 bit i.e its value ranges from 0 to 63 days and long term Moving averages (MAs) length (Θ_3) will be encoded to 9 bit i.e its value ranges from 0 to 512 days. Thus the chromosome length will be 4 bits + 6 bits + 9 bits = 19 bits, and total search space will be of 2^{19} i.e 5,24,288 number of solutions existed.

Four Moving Averages (MAs) Rule: This four Moving averages (MAs) rule is not common, though it is logically designed. Here we use two long term Moving averages (MAs) and two short terms Moving averages (MAs). Long term Moving averages (MAs) tells us about the trend and short term Moving averages (MAs) tells us about the trades to be taken. An old phrase is that "Trend is the trader friend". So if long term Moving averages (MAs) shows us bullish trend, then by using two short terms Moving averages (MAs), we will take only long position or buy trade generated by them. We will not exist until downward trend is given by longer term Moving averages (MAs) and sell or exit signal are generated by shorter term Moving averages (MAs). Thus here in some time zones no trades are being done and half of the positions are executed. Main drawback with this strategy is that longer term Moving averages (MAs) always act with a lag. So many profitable zones in some areas are not tapped. So we can apply Genetic Algorithms (GAs) to find the length of short term and long term Moving averages (MAs). So to start with the encoding mechanism two short term lengths of short term and long term length Θ_1 and Θ_2 will have 5 bit and 7 bit length. Θ_1 will have range from 0 to 128. Two long terms Moving averages (MAs) length Θ_3 and Θ_4 will have 9 bit and 11 bit length. Θ_3 will have range from 0 to 512 and Θ_4 will have range from 0 to 2047 days. Thus a total of 12 bits for shorter Moving averages (MAs) lengths and 20 bits for longer Moving averages (MAs) lengths and overall 32 bits chromosome length is there for the whole strategy. So the total search space for the strategy is 2^{32} i.e 4,29,49,67,296 solutions exist. To find an optimal one we can use Genetic Algorithms (GAs) to find it.

- A buy signal is generated

If (longer Moving averages (MAs) (Close, Θ_3) > longer Moving averages (MAs) (Close, Θ_4)) AND (shorter Moving averages (MAs) (close, Θ_1) > shorter Moving averages (MAs) (close, Θ_2)))

- A sell signal is generated

If (longer Moving averages (MAs) (Close, Θ_3) < longer Moving averages (MAs) (Close, Θ_4)) AND (shorter Moving averages (MAs) (close, Θ_1) < shorter Moving averages (MAs) (close, Θ_2)))
Θ_1 and Θ_2 are lengths of shorter Moving averages (MAs)
Θ_3 and Θ_4 are lengths of longer Moving averages (MAs)

12.5.2 Case Study 2

here we have used Moving averages (MAs) as a trend indicator. Further we have use Moving average of the Moving averages (MAs) as a buy or sell signal generated indicator. We have named this indicator as "Eureka". It calculates the deviation of current prises of Moving averages (MAs) of a pre defined length Θ_1. Our model is given below:
MA = Moving averages (MAs)

$$MA\ (close,\ \Theta_1) = 1/\theta1\sum_{i=0}^{\theta1}p\big(t-i\big)$$

$$Eureka\ (close_t,\ MA_{\ \theta1}) = (close - MA_t\ (close,\ \Theta_1))\ /\ (MA_t\ (close,\ \Theta_1))$$

Here close$_t$ is the closing price of the stock at time t, Moving averages (MAs) calculates closing price average values for time length Θ_1. Our system consists of "Eureka" and other is Moving averages (MAs) of Eureka. i.e

$$MA_t\ (Eureka, \Theta_2) = 1/\theta2 \sum_{i=0}^{\theta2} Eureka\left(t-i\right)$$

If MA_t (Eureka, Θ_2) crosses Eureka (close$_t$, MA $_{\Theta1}$) in upward direction or is of more value then buy signal is triggered.

If MA_t (Eureka, Θ_2) crosses Eureka (close$_t$, MA $_{\Theta1}$) in downward direction or is of more value then sell signal is triggered.

Genetic Algorithms (GAs) is used to find optimal value of Θ_1 and Θ_2. So Θ_1 and Θ_2 has to be represented in form of binary chromosomes to represent the solution. Then these two strings are concatenated to form a single string. If Θ_1 is taken as 10 bits i.e 2^{10} i,e 2024 values and Θ_2 is taken as 12 bits i.e 4096 values. So if the two strings are concatenated to form one string then the maximum string length is 22 bits and total search space is 222 i.e 41,94,304 total number of function evaluation or possible combinations of Θ_1 and Θ_2.

12.5.3 Case Study 3

We have seen various models which uses the concepts of Moving averages (MAs). Now we will formulate an investment strategy which will be a combination of buy and sell using various Moving averages (MAs) of different lengths. So these Moving averages (MAs) of different lengths can be used with different permutation and combination. Best possible permutation can be found out by Genetic Algorithms (GAs). Strategy is given below:

Sequence of Moving averages (MAs) we are using of various lengths are 1 day, 5 days, 15 days, 30 days, 60 days and 150 dys. Thus there are 6 Moving averages (MAs) in picture i.e MA_1, MA_5, MA_{15}, MA_{30}, MA_{60} and MA_{150}. Our original strategy will be:

```
IF (MA₁>MA₅>MA₁₅>MA₃₀> MA₆₀ >MA₁₅₀) Then Buy
Else {If (MA₁<MA₅<MA₁₅<MA₃₀< MA₆₀ <MA₁₅₀) Then Sell
Else Hold}
```

These sequences of Moving averages (MAs) of different lengths can be MA_1 and MA_5 is used as short term Moving averages (MAs), MA_{15} and MA_{30} as medium term Moving averages (MAs), MA_{60} and MA_{150} as long term Moving averages (MAs). So to map these Moving averages (MAs) to first six integer numbers is given below:

```
MA1     MA5     MA15     MA30     MA60     MA150
 ↓       ↓       ↓        ↓        ↓         ↓
 1       2       3        4        5         6
```

So these integers in various permutations give various investment strategies. If the permutations value is 3 5 1 6 4 2 for buy and 6 2 5 3 1 4 for sell then it is represented as:

```
IF (MA15>MA60>MA1>MA150> MA30 >MA5) Then Buy
Else {If (MA150<MA5<MA60<MA15< MA1 <MA30) Then Sell
Else Hold}
```

It means that if both buy and sell strategies is not satisfied then hold or do not invest or keep your money at yourself.

Here to start with encoding mechanism, the chromosome will be made up of integer numbers having range of value from 1 to 6. First 6 integer numbers represents buy strategies and next 6 integer numbers represents sell strategy. Here there are two set of 6 integers for buy and sell. Hence total search space here is $(6!)^2$ i.e 5,18,400. Genetic Algorithms (GAs) can be used to find optimal set of two set of 6 integer values.

12.5.4 Case Study 4

Until now we are focussed only on one technical indicators i.e Moving averages (MAs). In order to get more accurate results a trading system should be made by combination of various other technical indicators also. Moving averages (MAs) are trend giving indicators. Momentum indicators along with trend following indicators are popularly used to increase the accuracy and to confirm and falsify the signals of buy or sell generated. Our trading system developed and presented consists of three most popular indicators i.e Moving averages (MAs), Moving average Convergence Divergence (MACD) and Relative Strength Index (RSI)

MA = Moving Average.

EMA = Exponential Moving Average.

MACD = Moving Average Convergence Divergence.

RSI = Relative Strength Index.

- A buy signal is generated

```
If ((MA (close, Θ₁) < MAₜ (close, Θ₁))
AND
(MACD (close, Θ₃, Θ₄) < EMA (MACD, Θ₅))
AND
(RSI (Average gain, Average loss, close), Θ₆) < MA (RSI, Θ₇))
```

- A sell signal is generated

```
If ((MA (close, Θ₁) > MAₜ (close, Θ₁))
AND
(MACD (close, Θ₃, Θ₄) > EMA (MACD, Θ₅))
AND
(RSI (Average gain, Average loss, close), Θ₆) > MA (RSI, Θ₇))
```

Θ_1 and Θ_3 = short term MA and EMA.

Θ_2 and Θ_4 = long term MA and EMA.

Θ_5 = chosen number of periods for EMA of MACD.

Θ_6 = chosen number of periods for stochastic oscillator.

Θ_7 = chosen number of periods of MA for Stochastic oscillator

In encoding mechanism we have to represent various time lengths of the technical indicators Θ_1, Θ_2, Θ_3, Θ_4, Θ_5, Θ_6, Θ_7 in binary form. Short term moving average (θ_1) length is 8 bits i.e its range is $(1 - 256)$. Long term moving average (θ_2) length is 9 bits i.e its range is $(1 - 512)$. Short term exponential moving average (θ_3) length is 6 bits i.e its range is $(1 - 64)$. Long term exponential moving average (θ_4) length is 8 bits i.e its range is $(1 - 256)$. Length for exponential moving average of MACD(θ_5) is 4 bits i.e its range is $(1 - 16)$. Stochastic oscillator (θ_6) length is 5 bits i.e range is $(1 - 32)$ and length of moving average (θ_1) for stochastic oscillator is 4 bits i.e its range is $(1 - 16)$. All binary strings are concatenated to form a 44 bit chromosome.

Thus a total of 44 bits are used to represent a trading strategy. Thus total search space for genetic algorithms is 2^{44} i.e 1.7592E13 combinations or solutions exist. Here Genetic Algorithms (Gas) is used to find optimal values of various time lengths or optimal string.

12.5.5 Case Study 5

If we go for some other type of technical trading strategy. It will be first constructed by using various technical indicators. In a more advance form it will consists of entry rule, exit rule and a stop loss rule. Here we are going to use four popular technical indicators such as Rate of Change (ROC), Stochastic Oscillator (STO), On balance Volume (OBV) and PSY to make a trading strategy. Here the rule is for both long (buy and sell), short (sell and buy) positions. It consists of entry position, exit position and a stop rule. Trading strategy is given below:

Long entry rule

```
IF
Long not existing AND
Lag (ROC (n₁), l₁) op1 θ₁% AND
Lag (STO (n₂), l₂) op₂ θ₂% AND
Lag (OBV (n₃), l₃) op₃ θ₃% AND
Lag (PSY (n₄), l₄) op₄ θ₄%
THEN
Enter long at next opening price
Long exit rule
IF
Long not existing AND
Lag (ROC (n₅), l₅) op₅ θ₅% AND
Lag (STO (n₆), l₆) op₆ θ₆% AND
Lag (OBV (n₇), l₇) op₇ θ₇% AND
Lag (PSY (n₈), l₈) op₈ θ₈%
THEN
Enter long at next opening price
Long stop rule
IF
Long existing AND
Close < (1-r%) * highest high
```

Then stop long or exit at the next opening price.

Long entry rule states that if n_1 days ROC of l_1 days ago is greater or lesser than $\theta_{1\%}$ and n_2 days STO of l_2 days ago is greater or lesser then $\theta_{2\%}$ and n_3 days OBV of l_3 day ago is greater or lesser then $\theta_{3\%}$ and n_4 days PSY of l_4 day ago is greater or lesser then $\theta_{4\%}$ then enter market at next opening prices. All these indicators are generated using closing price of the stock. To start with the encoding mechanism i.e we need to specify the binary bits length of the parameters i.e n's, l's, op's, θ's and r.

Strategy of encoding is as follows:

Eight bits (0 to 255) for each i.e from n_1 to n_8 for each indicator
Three bits (0 to 7) for each i.e from l_1 to l_8 for each indicator
One bits (0 to 1) for each i.e from ops i.e 0 for < and 1 for > for each indicator
Seven bits (0 to 127) for each i.e from θ_1 to θ_8 for each indicator
And 5 bits for r for stop rule.

Thus a total 76 bits + 5 bits i.e 81 bits is used to represent parameters of long (buy and sell) trading strategy. So a total of another 81 bits will also be used to represent parameters of short (sell and buy) trading strategy also. So the chromosome length here will be of 81 bits + 81 bits i.e 162 bits. Thus the total search space here is of 2^{162} bits i.e 58460 E48. With the use of Genetic Algorithms (Gas) we will be able to get best parameter settings or optimal binary string which will give best rate of return.

After the encoding mechanism of the parameters of technical trading strategy is done we need fitness function formula to tell which parameter setting has performed well and which has not. The fitness function formula to find profit is given by:

$$TR_f = \prod_{i=1}^{f} \left(1 + DR_i\right)$$

$$DR_i = \left(P_i - P_{i-1}\right) \times \delta$$

TR_f is the total return for the sample period. DR_i is the daily return for the day i, P_i denotes the stock price for the day i. δ is the dummy variable which generates value *1* for buy (long) signals and *-1* for sale (short) signals. Trading system takes sell and buy positions, but no out-of-market-positions. Transaction costs are not included as our main aim in this paper is to find the possibility of solving an optimization problem by using genetic algorithm.

Here our main intention is to find these trading strategies or technical trading system and optimized their parameters by using Genetic Algorithms (GAs) is to generate profit or capital. It is impossible to construct a trading system which is 100% accurate. So our approach is to find a system with a reasonable high degree of accuracy. This can be find by applying these system on past data of a particular stock. Here or assumptions are that if it has worked well in past, then it will work well with same efficiency in future also. So the past data time frame we are considering is divided into two parts i.e testing set and training set. Training set is used to generate the trading strategies and testing set is used to test them. Thus to find over all best parameters of a technical trading system is converted to an optimization problem and can be solved using heuristic search methods such as Genetic Algorithms (GAs). From our past chapters in our book we have decided we will keep Genetic Algorithms (GAs) population size to 50, total number of generations will be 50. Thus total numbers of function evaluations are 50*50 i.e 2500. Roulette wheel selection is most popular selection operator and it will be made in use. Commonly used single point crossover with a probability of 75% will be use. Mutation rate is 0.01 i.e every 10 bits out of 1000 bits is mutated. Though these parameters setting for Genetic Algorithms (GAs) operators can be changed and use. It is seen from past researches that Genetic Algorithms (GAs) working is of robust in nature and it does not have much effect on the solution quality.

12.6 CONCLUSION

It is seen that technical analysis especially technical indicators are popularly used for making rational investment decisions by stock market traders or analysts. Here we have given insight to develop various investment strategies for buy or sell rule. These rules use various technical indicators connected to each other by various conditional statements. Sophisticated rules are made by using different versions of Moving averages (Simple, exponential etc.) and various types of technical indicators also. A better insight is given to optimize the parameters of the technical indicators of these rules by explaining the encoding mechanism and fitness function formula of all these rules. Genetic Algorithms (GAs) can be applied on them. Working and encoding is thoroughly explained in previous chapters. Thus decision on when to trade and when not to trade is taken by the rule which works on the parameters obtained from the use of Genetic Algorithms (GAs). This chapter overall explains the feasibility of the use of Genetic Algorithms (GAs) in trading strategy creation.

REFERENCES

Allen, F., & Karjalainen, R. (1998). Using genetic algorithms to find technical trading rules. *Journal of Financial Economics, 51*(2), 245–271. doi:10.1016/S0304-405X(98)00052-X

Bauer, R. J. Jr. (1994). *Genetic Algorithms and Investment Strategies*. John Wiley and Sons, Inc.

Deb, K. (2002). *Optimization for Engineering Design: Algorithm and Examples*. Prentice Hall of India Private Limited.

Goldberg, D. E. (2002). *Genetic Algorithms in Search*. Optimization and Machine Learning Pearson Education, Asia.

Kapoor, V., Dey, S., & Khurana, A. P. (2011). Genetic algorithm: An application to technical trading system design. *International Journal of Computers and Applications, 36*(5), 44–50.

Letamendia, L. N. (2007). Fitting Control Parameters of a Genetic Algorithm: An Application to Technicl Trading Systems Design. *European Journal of Operational Research, 179*(3), 847–865. doi:10.1016/j.ejor.2005.03.067

Mahfoud, S., & Mani, G. (1996). Financial Forecasting Using Genetic Algorithms. *Applied Artificial Intelligence, 10*(6), 543–566. doi:10.1080/088395196118425

Section 4
Genetic Algorithms in Other Areas

Chapter 13
Some Other Applications of Genetic Algorithms (GAs)

ABSTRACT

As we had already seen that genetic algorithms (GAs) are smart in their working. Here, the authors explore the rich working of genetic algorithms (GAs) in various diversified fields. Until now, they had discussed the historical nature of genetic algorithms (GAs). They have also discussed the programming code to run simple genetic algorithms (SGA). Lastly, they are going to take an overview of the application of genetic algorithms (GAs) in various fields (i.e., from business to non-business). Already, they have discussed the robust working of genetic algorithms (GAs) in various adverse conditions. Here, they discuss the application of genetic algorithms (GAs) in various other diversified fields.

13.1 INTRODUCTION

Genetic Algorithms (GAs) is a hot area of research (Goldberg, 2002), Rajsekaran et. Al, 2007). We came to know that a lot of work on Genetic Algorithms (GAs) is in under cover. It is done with a valid reason. The reason is to gain a better lead in competition of Genetic Algorithms (GAs) with other soft computing techniques. It is seen with the passage of time more and more researchers are coming with the application of Genetic Algorithms (GAs) in a large number of fields. A lot of publish work is available in it. In this chapter we are going to discuss the application of Genetic Algorithms

DOI: 10.4018/978-1-7998-4105-0.ch013

(GAs) in various commercial and non commercial areas. There is a thin difference between commercial and non commercial areas. Some of the workings or research in Genetic Algorithms (GAs) which seems to be pure research today may have a large commercial value in future. Since Genetic Algorithms (GAs) is a pure computational procedure, so its applications are in every field or areas.

It is difficult to start with the application of Genetic Algorithms (GAs) in various areas (Bauer, 1994). We had placed this chapter in the last section of this book and the knowledge about some advance features about Genetic Algorithms (GAs) will help us to apply Genetic Algorithms (GAs) in various areas. Until now readers of this book must be exhausted about the working of Genetic Algorithms (GAs) and eager to learn its application in various diversified fields.

13.2 FACE RECOGNITION

Manual face recognition requires a lot of creativeness. Genetic Algorithms (GAs) has also been used to recognize the faces. In Tv serials or a Hollywood or Hollywood movie, we have seen artists draws the sketch of criminal or of a witness to the crime. It is cumbersome, time consuming and complex process. Accuracy to this comes with experience. In the use of computers we had used various images stored in the libraries for various facial features. These libraries can be recalled with a high degree of accuracy. Human mind is very efficient or good in recognising a face by seeing it, but it is equally poor in recalling or describing it. So it is seen that a witness to the crime scene can efficiently pin point the criminal face by choosing from different photographs, but to recall the criminal facial features is very difficult for a person.

So our Genetic Algorithms (GAs) based system will work more on the recognition feature then on recalling it. First we will create a library of various facial features. Here the building block will contains the images of foreheads, ears, nose, chins, eyes, lips etc. A large number of binary strings combination of various permutations and combinations can be made. Here the bibary string will be decoded to give us a face with certain eyes, nose, ears, fore head etc. features. The Genetic Algorithms (GAs) will start with the random generation of strings population, which will be decoded into various types of faces. The witness to the criminal in crime scene will take a look about all the images and recognize the image and gives it a rating from 1 to 10. Thus after the fitness function is assigned by the witness, various operators such as selection, crossover and mutation are applied to produce population for next generation. This will go into a loop form until convergence or desired result is not obtained. Here in order to increase the efficiency of Genetic Algorithms (GAs), if forehead features in some picture in a generation population member exactly matches with the criminal forehead, then we will freeze that feature and will look or concentrate on other features. Past researches has shown that here convergence took place after a lot of generations.

13.3 MUSIC COMPETITION

With the advancement of technology, field of music is getting intervolving with the field of technology. Computers have been a major instrument now a day's used by the music composers to produce newer music. Genetic Algorithms (GAs) also comes to aid musician with the passage of time. David E. Goldberg (1989) in his work has applied Genetic Algorithms (GAs) in a particular relevance called thematic bridging. Here we got some input pattern of music transformed into some other pattern which is desired. In a given example if sequences of four nodes are there and sequence of three nodes is desired. This can be done in a simple manner i.e deletion of last node and rearrange the rest of nodes manually in a hit and trial manner. In this way best sequence is obtained.

In Goldberg Genetic Algorithms (GAs) based approach population of binary strings called chromosomes with the length equal to three nodes, each string will be mapped to any of the music notes. Here our fitness function will be the degree of correlation between the string match with the desired notes. Based on the fitness score of the strings, selection operator selects string for crossover and mutation operations. Goldberg in his experiment get better results and success. He has been able to find attractive newer vantage points or solutions with success in a small level, larger music with n number of notes can be composed by the composer.

13.4 SCHEDULING

Genetic Algorithms (GAs) has been successfully applied for scheduling for any type of transportation i.e to explore routes with cost effectiveness. Here the model when develop manually can be of complex in nature. Use of Genetic Algorithms (GAs) reduces the complexity of these models.

Moving of automobiles i.e cars, jeeps, SUV etc. around various destination places through various routes is very cost intensive. Any error in scheduling of it will result in an exponential increase of cost. Generally we group cars into various blocks. So train which takes them to the destination consists of locomotive and blocks. A group of cars is called blocks which has same origination and destination. Route is number of nodes between origination and destination. So the route must be such that it has lower costs. Use of Genetic Algorithms (GAs) must have a string which is mapped to a route. The fitness function is the cost of route which is given in the master index. Here our objective is function minimization i.e lowering of costs. Major usefulness of using Genetic Algorithms (GAs) is in its easy simulation. The complex interaction of parameters whose optimized values is to find using Genetic Algorithms (GAs) is difficult to find using traditional techniques if search process is high. In case of scheduling problem, they are generally complex if number of routes or nodes is large. Brute force search process generally tries to test all the routes by testing a large number of combinations. It is not advisable as it is time consuming. Genetic Algorithms (GAs) being a heuristic based search process tries to find close to optimal solution with only trying few iterations. It is seen that problem representation in form of strings and fitness function formula is important part of Genetic Algorithms (GAs). The main aim of Genetic Algorithms (GAs) is to find best schedule. Past results by researchers show that Genetic Algorithms (GAs) has been able to search from a large number of orderings. It is the perspective of Genetic Algorithms (GAs) researcher to use basic crossover, mutation and selection operator. He can make intelligent changes in the operators working depending upon the problem to problem. In case of mutation he can randomly change the string that is being mutated or we can interchange the position of the string. Thus from the whole study we had come to make an beautiful inference that application of Genetic Algorithms (GAs) is half engineering and half art.

13.5 RUGBY BETTING

Genetic Algorithms (GAs) can also be use to find which horse will win in the race. Here various rules are made, using horse edge, last race performance etc. Genetic Algorithms (GAs) form various rule by the use of these parameters. Fitness function formula is find by using the winner data for previous race. Genetic Algorithms (GAs) was successful in finding rule that has an accuracy of 80%. This outperforms the manual system of picking a horse and placing bet on it.

13.6 CHEMO METRIC ANALYSIS

Chemo metric is a branch in chemistry. Changes in chemical composition are generally captured by various devices. Time series models can be used to find the inside trend of change in chemical composition. Chemo metry consists of various sample of strategy, calibration of various instruments, optimization and pattern recognition. So to find the best parameters for a best fit curve is a complex process and is also time consuming in nature. So for every such problem, Genetic Algorithms (GAs) is best suited to apply on it. In case of noisy time series also Genetic Algorithms (GAs) can be used effectively for curve fitting.

13.7 DATA BASE OPTIMIZATION

It is seen that with the use of computers in every part of life, data bases and there are increasing with an exponential speed. With this data base management system (DBMS) are becoming complex day by day with newer foreign keys and primary keys to connect them. So the system analyst has to make tedious queries in Data Base Management System (DBMS). These complex queries are combination of algebra and logical operators with in the various entries in the data base.

As more and more tables are added in the data base the possibility of queries that can be formed is increased exponentially. In this way query search space is more. We develop query and query optimization is the need of the hour. Genetic Algorithms (GAs) is finally used to optimized the query. Here chromosomes are represented as a binary tree and on it crossover and mutation can be applied with newer variations. Thus Genetic Algorithms (GAs) based optimization gives us better results in comparison to the traditional optimization procedures.

13.8 AIRCRAFT DESIGN

Aircraft design is a very complex procedure. It consists of different steps. Starting with macro design which tells us where the wings, and where the engine should be. Once this is fixed, we go for micro parameters for design. There is a long list for these parameters which include height, width, height to width ratio, weight to thrust ratio, nozzle diameter etc. Considering these parameters values ranges, aircraft design becomes an combinatorial explosive problem. A designer task is to find best parameter values for the aircraft. These type of situation is perfect breeding ground for Genetic Algorithms (GAs) to be applied on it. Here if problem search space is almost infinite and objective function has multiple local peaks, then we can use Genetic Algorithms (GAs) singly or in combination with other optimization procedures such as hill climbing algorithm or simulated annealing procedure. Best features can be thus found out from it.

13.9 CONCLUSION

In this chapter we had discussed rich usage of Genetic Algorithms (GAs) in a number of diversified fields. Earlier chapters we had simply simulated a simple Genetic Algorithms (GAs) for function optimization. It is just a simulation of natural genetics. This gives us insight about the practical application of Genetic Algorithms (GAs) in a variety of areas as discussed above. Careful experimental set up for Genetic Algorithms (GAs) implementation should be done. Past published researches has shown that Genetic Algorithms (GAs) has its application in the field of medicine, engineering, sociology, computational science etc. i.e almost in all areas where we could think of. It means that the problem which faces combinatorial explosion, large search spaces etc. are to be solved with the use of Genetic Algorithms (GAs). There is still a lot of research that has to undergo. Hence effectiveness of the algorithm in various diversified areas is the main cause of its popularity. Hence Genetic Algorithms (GAs) is a genetic based machine learning process.

REFERENCES

Bauer, R. J. Jr. (1994). *Genetic Algorithms and Investment Strategies*. John Wiley and Sons, Inc.

Goldberg, D. E. (2002). *Genetic Algorithms in Search, Optimization and Machine Learning*. Pearson Education.

Rajasekaran & Vijaylakshmi Pai. (2007). *Neural Networks, Fuzzy Logic, and Genetic algorithms, Synthesis and Applications*. Prentice-Hall of India Private Limited.

Chapter 14
Introduction to Some Other Nature-Inspired Algorithms

ABSTRACT

In order to solve any problem through the use of computation, algorithms are required. These days, algorithms are inspired from the working of nature. These algorithms are becoming popular among researchers. Many real-world solutions are being obtained from them. Nature-inspired algorithms are powerful, flexible, find better results within a small period of time, and can be used to search optimal values for the problems. This chapter introduces some of the popular nature-inspired algorithms other than genetic algorithms (GAs), which were studied earlier.

14.1 INTRODUCTION

A lot of problems in the field of science and engineering are optimization problems (Goldberg, 2002). They are of intricate and non linear in nature. The solution of these non linear problems requires some sophisticated procedures. Traditional problem solving procedures or algorithms are not well equipped to solve them. When applied they struggle a lot to find universally acceptable solutions. In current practice various advance nature inspired algorithms has come into picture. They are flexible and effective in their working. This recent field of nature inspired algorithms is of very importance in the area of soft computing techniques. They possess a very high degree of computation

DOI: 10.4018/978-1-7998-4105-0.ch014

intelligence for optimization in them. Due to these features interest of lot of researchers and academicians from every field is growing day by day.

Researches in the public domain shows that these nature inspired algorithms are being applied in almost every field i.e from basic research to almost all real world application i.e in the areas of engineering, science, economics, business and industry etc. These nature inspired algorithms exploit the working of nature i.e their physical laws, movements to found better solutions. It is due to these features research in this area is rich in nature. The working of the nature inspired algorithms is effective. They consist of powerful operators in them, which make them ideal to solve real world complex problems. Since this real world complex problems are not fully solvable by the use of traditional algorithms or standard mathematical procedures. These nature inspired algorithms are of different in working and they does not require any mathematical conditions to be proven or falsify. Classification of nature inspired algorithms is of two types: 1. Evolutionary Algorithms 2. Swarm Intelligence. The publish research of most recent years shows that these nature inspired algorithms is increasing in popularity in recent years. Our book in earlier chapters has summarized the working and implementation of evolutionary algorithms such as Genetic algorithms (GAs) in a elaborative way. In this chapter we have introduce some popular nature inspired algorithms (Yang, 2014). We will try to explain their basic concepts, their key features and how to implement them. Here we are going to explain them in an introductory way and their implementation is not discussed here. Here the working of the algorithm with the help of programming languages is not explained as we had explained Genetic Algorithms (GAs) in the past chapters.

It is seen that all problems from simple to complex requires attention. Upon implementing them to find a solution, a small amount of gap or lag always remain between theory and its practice. Nature inspired algorithms are efficient, powerful, flexible and they obtained optimal solution in a practically affordable time. These algorithms can be mathematically represented. They lack in pre mature convergence, solution accuracy is always high and less computational power is require running them. We can fine tune their control operators to get better results. Since from the beginning of the earth existence, nature has evolve itself i.e for past trillion of years. This has provided inspiration to the researchers to mimic the nature into an algorithm and use them for problem solving. Researchers in past has done so with a varying degree of achievement. Our aim in this chapter is not to instigate researchers to develop new algorithms only for the sake of newer procedures or to get them publishes. These all type of algorithm may increase confusion and distraction to the readers and researchers. Newer nature inspired algorithms may only be developed or comes into picture, only when our present problem is not solved by the existing nature inspired algorithms or there is a altogether new idea which may be really efficient and powerful in their working. Our aim in this chapter is to get valuable insight about the working of some popular nature inspired algorithms, so that they can take up the challenge to solve newer types of problems or existing problem in a newer way. To give a solution to the real life problem or Non Deterministic Polynomial (NP) hard problem is more important now a day's then in past. These nature inspired algorithms consists of features such as efficiency, intelligent in their working, self adaptive and self evolving in nature. In this way many business problems such as stock trading, travelling salesman problem etc. can be solved by using them. A brief insight given in this chapter will have a huge impact on how researchers solve certain tough problems in different areas.

It is seen in many problems to be solved in many areas of engineering, science, business designs that optimization is an essential activity. In optimization the end results should be the best parameter settings which maximizes or minimizes fitness function. The need of optimization is due to the fact that we have limited resources available such as time, processing power, capital etc. So our solution should use these resources optimally under various constraints. Real world problems are of non linear in nature. They require out of thought and more sophisticated algorithms to solve them. Use of traditional mathematical procedures and algorithms do not give satisfactorily results for them. These nature inspired algorithms are simulated on computers are of indispensible in nature and are of efficient in working. There computational simulation process follows certain procedures or rules. Here basic components of these algorithms interact with each other to get better or optimal results. Now coming to the essence that what is an algorithm? An algorithm is a set of instructions or calculation which is to be done step by step. In our book we are mainly concerned about Genetic Algorithms (GAs) and in past chapters our main emphasis were to get better understanding of various iterative steps of Genetic Algorithms (GAs), rather than constructing a new algorithm itself.

In real world optimization problem, after we have defined the problem in a right manner. Our main aim is to find some procedure that will give us best possible solution found so far. Actually in real sense finding the best possible solution is just like finding a treasure or needle in a hay stack. Consider a uneven, hilly or rugged terrain. We have to find treasure within a specified time frame. One extreme case is that we are without any clue of guidance.

Thus if we want to search a treasure or a solution, it will be a random attempt. This process is purely not efficient. Other side of extremeness is that if we know that if treasure is at the hill top. In this case we will try to to climb the hill and reach its peak. This is a hill climbing type of algorithm which is popularly used for these types of problems. Not all but for many cases real world problems lie in between these two extremes. First we have some clue, but we do not know the exact region. Second we cannot go for brute force type of search technique i.e to search every single space in the search space.

So in a move we can find some clue or hint for the solution and act randomly. Then find a clue and act randomly and so on. In this way we are going to reach our destination. This randomness is the main feature of any sophisticated optimization or search algorithm. Second method is trajectory based. Simulated Annealing is such type of search technique. Another type of search technique is that we try finding some search space or solution and share this information and go for search hunting. This we will do this for many iterations, till better solutions are found. Another scenario is that if solution to be found is extremely important and search area is very vast and there is no limitation of time. Then we are bound to find the global optimal values or set of parameters.

If we go for more sophistication in search and optimization process. Then we generate random set of solutions. We will select better solutions for next iterations and found newer solutions. This type of search procedure is Genetic Algorithms (GAs) or evolutionary algorithms type. Here after every set of iterations we move to a new search area. Thus in all heuristic based algorithms we choose best solutions and replace them with lesser best solution found so far after evaluating their fitness and search for newer spaces. With this we get better or optimized set of values or parameters.

Search and optimization algorithms are classified popularly into two parts: Deterministic and Stochastic algorithms. In case of deterministic way we always will start with a same point, and some values will be given by the algorithm when ever to apply it to a particular problem. Degree of randomness is very low. Popular example is hill climbing technique. In contrast to deterministic algorithm, stochastic process has a high degree of randomness in their working. Genetic Algorithms (GAs) is the best example for it. Here the set of solutions found every iteration will be different, each time we run the algorithm on a particular problem. Though every time we reach the best solution but the path that is followed is different each time algorithm is run on the machine.

Another most popular type of algorithms is a combination of both deterministic and stochastic process. For example hill climbing is a deterministic algorithm i.e in combination in combination with some randomness i.e stochastic is one of the way by which we can use hybrid technique. So here a number of hill climbing algorithm will work together parallel with different points. This may delay the chances of any hill climbing algorithm to get stuck at a local peak. Any degree of randomness in an algorithm weather deterministic or non deterministic will come under stochastic category.

Now two types of question arises i.e 1st for a problem which algorithm will be use to solve them. 2nd for a algorithm which is the best problem it can solve. The answer for these two questions is not easy to find and they are typical. Since a large number of search and optimization algorithms exists, so find algorithm for a particular problem is difficult to find. Some algorithms are in its infancy and a lot of work is to be done to develop them in a full flesh manner. The choice to choose a particular algorithm to solve a particular problem depends upon the researcher and the expertise he have and knowledge depth he possess. My advice is to see the resources we have and constraints we face in solving a problem. Resources are the computational power, software language available, time, memory etc. Constraints are time, problem complexity etc. Thus the decision to choose an algorithm is based upon the experience of a researcher also. In order to find answer, we can also choose a particular algorithm by applying various other similar types of algorithm to similar types of smaller problems and find their ranking by comparing the results obtained by them. By this process advantages and disadvantages of the particular algorithm will be judged and we can intelligently and we can pick a particular algorithm to be applied on our problem.

Next by studying the various published literature on the various algorithms, we can make an judgement on which algorithm we can use. For newer nature inspired algorithms more extensive study is to be done in order to choose one from them. Subject knowledge about the area of which problem is to be solved is an added advantage along with the expertise in the particular algorithm. In all algorithms from recent to past, development and design changes are continuously ongoing. This is however more challenging then applying that algorithm on to a particular problem. It is found that all of the traditional algorithms are of deterministic in nature. These algorithms works well for simple unimodal and multi modal functions. They are of gradient based or non gradient based. Stochastic based algorithms are classified into two types: Heuristic and Meta heuristic. Though there is a very small line between heuristic and Meta heuristic algorithms. Till date there is no fixed definition available to explain the difference between heuristic and Meta heuristic algorithms. Heuristic means to explore or find by trial and error. Here acceptable solution for a tough or NP hard problems can be explored within specified time limits. It is of no guarantee that best solution will be found. They may find best or close to best solution. These stochastic processes are better in working when we do not want best solution, but a universally accepted solution. Furthermore invention in heuristic algorithms leads us to a higher level called Meta heuristic. The performance parameters of these Meta heuristic algorithms are higher than these heuristic algorithms. Still there is a very thin line between heuristic and Meta heuristic classification of algorithms. These both terms heuristic and Meta heuristic can be used interchangeably. These all stochastic heuristic and Meta heuristic algorithms uses randomization in combination with local search. More is the randomization more is the chances to obtain a global solution. It helps us to move from local search to global search. In this way randomness feature in these stochastic algorithms are better way to search for global optimized values.

Heuristic means trial and error by nature. With this we produce solution for computationally complex problems in reasonable time period. Some problems have so large search spaces such that it is practically not feasible to test each and every combination of the parameter of the solution. With the use of heuristic based algorithms, we are able to find real world acceptable or feasible solutions in a limited time frame. These algorithms do not guarantee best solution but globally accepted solution. Solution found by them must be close to optimal. Major constituents in heuristic and Meta heuristic algorithms are exploration and exploitation. In exploration we made an attempt to search the space in a global level. Exploitation means, once local region is pin pointed, then to find the best solution in that region. Hence best solution from each region is selected and then we move forward. Thus selection of best combination of parameters in conjunction with exploitation will ensure the convergence of solution towards the global optimality space. Some degree of randomness in the algorithms ensures that solution in the successive iterations does not get stuck up in local optima. Thus combination of exploration with selection and randomness leads us to a global optimal solution, which is achievable in a limited time frame.

These heuristic and Meta heuristic algorithms can also be classified into two types. One is population based, for example Genetic Algorithms (GAs), and other is trajectory based i.e simulated annealing. In population based Meta heuristic algorithms, we use multiple agents while trajectory based there is a single agent which search throughout the search space or follows a certain trajectory. There is always some probability that will reach global optimum, no matter what the trajectory we follow. Here is the list of some nature inspired algorithms that are heuristic and Meta heuristic algorithms in their working:

14.1.1 Swarm Intelligence (SI)-Based Algorithms

Ant Colony Optimization, Ant Lion Optimization, Artificial Bee Colony, Bacterial foraging, Bacterial-GA Foraging, Bat Algorithm, BeeHive, Bumblebees, Cat swarm, Consultant-guided search, Cuckoo Search, Krill Herd, Monkey search, Particle Swarm Optimisation, Weightless Swarm Algorithm.

14.1.2 Bio-Inspired (not SI-Based) Algorithms

Atmosphere clouds model, Biogeography based Optimization, Brain Storm Optimization, Differential Evolution, Dolphin echolocation, Japanese tree frogs calling, Eco-inspired evolutionary algorithm, Egyptian Vulture, Fish-school Search, Flower pollination Algorithm, Firefly Algorithms, Gene expression.

14.1.3 Physics and Chemistry Based Algorithms

Big bang-big Crunch, Black hole, Central force optimization, Charged system search, Electro-magnetism optimization, Galaxy-based search algorithm, Gravitational search, Harmony Search, Intelligent water drop, River formation dynamics, Self-propelled particles, Simulated Annealing, Stochastic diffusion search, Spiral optimization, Water cycle algorithm.

14.2 ARTIFICIAL INTELLIGENCE

Definition: Artificial Intelligence (AI) is a branch of computer science in which we are concerned with the intelligent behaviour of the program. Artificial Intelligence (AI) is based on firm theoretical and practical principles of computer science. For Artificial Intelligence (AI) to be in working, we should be well versed in the field of data structure, analysis of algorithms, programming paradigms and at least in simple high level programming language. These all things are needed in their implementation. To till data

Artificial Intelligence (AI) is clearly defined and understood. It is a fact that we should see intelligent behaviour when we run it. The implementation depends upon person to person. Some a implement with a high degree of intelligence some with a less degree of intelligence. This depends upon the IQ level of the Artificial Intelligence (AI) researcher.

So to define Artificial Intelligence (AI) one should be intelligent enough. Artificial Intelligence (AI) is a collection discrete and related and unrelated quality that your algorithm or problem solving method should posses. It includes the learning process, creativity, intuition, observation of behaviour, self awareness. These all features play a vital role in developing an Artificial Intelligence (AI) based system. Basically we want to develop a computer program that posses almost all the feature of human intelligence. Thus we want to display that intelligent property is not the inheritance of a biological system, but it can be embedded in a human made computer program with a higher degree.

These all answers we will get in the field of Artificial Intelligence (AI). It helps us to find better solution to the problems and is the basic core of Artificial Intelligence (AI). Still there is a lot research is to be done and definition of Artificial Intelligence (AI) is changing day by day. We always fell short of defining the Artificial Intelligence (AI) system. Every time we try to find answer to this question, more questions arises as we to explore more and more in this field. This is a never ending process. It is almost impossible to give exact definition of Artificial Intelligence (AI). Artificial Intelligence (AI) is still in its naive state and its working, definition, concerns, process are not clearly explained in comparison to more mature field such as physics, chemistry, life science etc.

In the use of Artificial Intelligence (AI) we are ever expanding our capability in the field of computer science rather than limiting it. Artificial Intelligence (AI) has no boundaries and has no limits. Artificial Intelligence (AI) features should have strong theoretical principles, then and then only they are going to give better results when implemented practically. Thus Artificial Intelligence (AI) like any other science is exploring new height due to human endeavour and intervention. We first identify certain area of problems and try to solve them with Artificial Intelligence (AI) techniques. Among Artificial Intelligence (AI) selected nature inspired algorithms are Neural Network, Genetic Algorithms (GAs), Simulated Annealing, Particle Swarm Optimization, ant colony algorithms etc. We are going to discuss some of them in the coming section of this chapter.

14.2.1 Neural Networks (NN)

Neural Networks (NN) has been used promisingly by the researchers as a tool to solve many real world problems. A lot of internal design changes in Neural Networks (NN) implementation can be done. This affects the accuracy also. These design factors consists of input data, architecture, number of nodes, number of layers etc. Neural Networks (NN) has been efficient to search and map non linear system in between output and input. They are well suited for problem that exhibit chaos for example stock market prediction. Stock market is a random walk and it cannot be easily expressed with the help of traditional mathematical models. The ability of Neural Networks (NN) is to find solution in these non linear deterministic, chaotic process. We keep Neural Networks (NN) in a different set when we compared with traditional system to solve the real world problem. Neural Networks (NN) inside procedure is somewhat of black box in nature. Here we identify the input variables and results are obtained by not much knowing the system. Processing of Neural Networks (NN) is parallel in nature, less time consuming and fault resistant. Here we don't have to formalize rules while implementing it. As many of the complex real world problems are very less or partially understood. It is not necessary in Neural Networks (NN) to formulate rules in it as compared in the expert system. In stock market environment there is a high degree of dynamic data, which can be handled efficiently by Neural Networks (NN).

As in real world hard problem consists of non linear liaison among the input data. Neural Networks (NN) is judged in three areas:

1. Its environment and training data.
2. Network organization.
3. Network Performance.

Training of Neural Networks (NN) should be done on some input data. Second most important feature is to find that what a network will learn. So there is a challenge to collect enough input training data, so that a network can learn from it. Input training data or variables must be less so that recalling and training time required is less. There must be certain pruning process which can be used to discard useless variables or inputs. Thus a number of proper input variables is important to train the network and for its efficiency. Second step is that architecture or training should be such that it should give better results with a least error and better performance. So the training algorithm is just the Neural Networks (NN) architecture. A lot of Neural

Networks (NN) architecture exists, among them the most popular in the past researches is back propagation network. Here we back propagate the errors in the system during the training process. As hidden layers have not been the training objective, so they can be trained by the process of back propagation. This helps the output layer which only has the training target. Due to back propagation the connection weight values can be changed. This goes on and on as error generated is squeezed down, so that they can be accepted universally. Thus question which comes into existence is when to decide that we stop training. In past researchers has reported that over training can be a serious problem, since it helps to memorize the system and generalization ability of the system is weakened. A lot of input variables and hidden variables results in an over training of data. This problem of over training can be covered by training network on a lot of data and testing it on remaining pattern. So if the performance is very less. Then network architecture and input data variables are to be changed. In this way retraining of the network is being done and more satisfactory performance is obtained. So we are able to squeeze the error and optimal network architecture is obtained. Training the network on a very large old data set is time consuming, as network will learn about pattern which is no longer viable.

In case of back propagation network there is always a supplementary learning, as weights are depending upon the errors. If the error generated exceeds in its tolerance then they have to be back propagated. Due to this it is faster and we can experiment on large volume of data. Thus the weights are also change randomly in order to squeeze the error in the data that has been back propagated. So in order to avoid the problem of over training, system must be cross validated from time to time. Now it is clear that neural network is just a complicated form of multiple regressions. Here network can be of varying sizes i.e small number of input variables to a thousand of them, from two to three layers to a dozen of layers. These parameters are chosen by seeing the complexity of the real world problem, which we are addressing. It is still debatable which neural network architecture is optimal or best. In present scenario neural network is applied to almost all the complicated real world problems. In neural network research pruning and to find optimized neural network architecture is hot area of research. This will help end user to remove redundant layers and speed up the delivery of result. A lot of research work is being done to find the better practices to use neural network in a optimal and less time consuming way. Neural network is a complete black box technique with least human involvement is required to run them. Hence in future the focus of researchers is to improve Neural network performance and through it get more insights in the chaotic real world system that we are trying to tap it. Though Neural network is not the best procedure to solve a real world problem, but it is one of the desirable system to get a better understanding of the chaotic and complex system which has not been understood for a long time.

14.2.2 Simulated Annealing

This process to find global minimum resembles the molten metal cooling by using annealing process. At higher temperature atoms in the molten metal has a large degree of freedom in comparison to one another. As molten metal moves towards the room temperature the degree of freedom of atoms or their movement gets restricted. Thus here in a natural system of molten metal when metal cools then it forms a crystalline state with a lesser energy state. If metal is cooled in a faster rate then, instead of crystalline state polycrystalline state is achieved. It has a higher energy state as compared to crystalline state. So to obtain lesser energy level or crystalline state the molten metal should be cooled at a slower rate. This whole procedure of slow and controlled cooling is called annealing. Thus Simulated Annealing simulates or mimics the process of slowness of cooling molten metal in order to get global minimization values. Here cooling of something is controlled by introducing a parameter called temperature encapsulated by the concept of Bolzman probability distribution. It says that any system in thermal equilibrium at temperature T has its energy distributed probabilistically in accordance to the formula P (E) = exp (-E/kT), where k is the Bolzman constant. At higher temperature there is a larger probability of a system to be at higher energy state as compare to the system at a lower temperature. Thus by controlling temperature T and search process follows Bolzman probability curve the converging property of the algorithm is controlled.

Simulated Annealing searches by point to point. So start with the algorithm we start with some initial point at higher temperature. A second point is generated randomly in closeness to the initial point generated and distinction in objective function standards of these two points is calculated. If second point ha small function value then it is accepted, if not then it is rejected or accepted with a probability exp(-A E/T). This is the one iteration of the whole process. In next step another point is selected randomly in vicinity to that current point. Thus based on its objective function value this point is accepted or rejected. Thus at a particular temperature a large number of points are generated randomly and tested. After this, temperature is reduced and this procedure goes on for a number of iterations. When we test for a less temperature then negligible changes in function values are obtained. Thus introduction of the term temperature have effects on the learning rate. We start with a very high temperature, and moves over the error space. As the training process continues, the temperature decreases and thus the learning also slow down and get converge to a near optimal solution. Thus search in the solution space reduces the process of oscillation in order to reach minimal point on the search or error space.

14.2.3 Particle Swarm Optimisation

Particle Swarm Optimisation (PSO) is also a popular and established Meta heuristic based algorithm. We encounter a lot of literature based on this algorithm. In past successful attempt has been made by the researchers to efficiently solve real life complex problems. Particle Swarm Optimisation (PSO) is somewhat similar to Genetic Algorithms (GAs) as discussed in detail in previous chapters. They are also population generated optimization process. Initially Particle Swarm Optimisation (PSO) was inspired by Bird flocks and schooling fish algorithms. In comparison with genetic Algorithms (GAs) they also start with random generated population. All the member of the population represents a solution. These solution search for the optimal value parallel in the large search area and a new updated set of solutions are obtained generation after generations.

In Particle Swarm Optimisation (PSO) there are no operators such as crossover or mutation, as in the case of Genetic Algorithms (GAs). Here random solution first generated is called particles. They keep moving in the search space finding better solutions. In comparison to Genetic Algorithms (GAs) Particle Swarm Optimisation (PSO) is very fast and requires less memory. The negative features are that they are practically obsolete and less accurate when compare with Genetic algorithms (GAs). Due to this, in order to get best of both the worlds features Particle Swarm Optimisation (PSO) is used in combination with Genetic algorithms (GAs) to get better and more accurate results.

Particle Swarm Optimisation (PSO) are a computational process in which various solutions initially generated are improved with view to solution quality as decided by the practitioner. Here population solution is considered as particles. These particles move in search space in accordance to some mathematical formula, with a particular position and velocity. The movement of the particle is dependent on its position it is holding. With regard to this original position a relative better position is obtained which is guided by the zeal to search best position in the search space. Thus solution set is flooded with the newer solutions or particles. Thus in this way generation after generation we move towards better solution.

Particle Swarm Optimisation (PSO) is a Meta heuristic algorithm. No problem information is needed that is being optimized. They can search very large search spaces, generally that cannot be searched using brute force techniques. Here the drawback is that they guarantee better worldly acceptable solutions instead of the best solution. Since their working is of black box in nature, gradient information is not required about the problem being solved in comparison to gradient decent based or Newton Raphson process.

In Particle Swarm Optimisation (PSO) the working is a balance between exploratory and exploitative behaviour. In explorative behaviour we search in a vast region of search space and in exploitation we search in the local region and try to achieve local optimal value. So in order to get efficiency in the algorithm a proper balance between exploration feature and exploitation feature is to be made. This will result in effective searching of the solution space. Hence the control parameter in the Particle Swarm Optimisation (PSO) must be chosen in such a way, so that they avoid early convergence of the solution set to the local optima or converge on to a global solution space. It is seen that working and choice of control parameters of Particle Swarm Optimisation (PSO) is different for various high dimensional search spaces and for problems that are noisy and random walk in nature. More work in studying the working of Particle Swarm Optimisation (PSO) has to be done by researchers as it will lead to better implementation and it's working.

14.2.4 Ant Colony Optimization Algorithm

Ant Colony Optimization Algorithm is a computational method based on probabilistic technique. Here we found better paths. This algorithm is inspired by the working of ants in the nature and is one of the popular nature inspired algorithms. It is a total mimic of the action of ants in their colony. Artificial ants are popularly known as simulation agents; try to locate various solutions by moving through the search space which represents a number of solutions. In real biological environment, these ants put a trail of pheromones in their path. This directs other ants to the resource which is found by its member or real ants. These simulated ants will take a stock of their position and quality of solution they had found so far. Thus in the coming simulation or iteration they will try to locate other better solution in the search space. This Ant Colony Optimization Algorithm is similar to bees algorithm, an another type of social insect.

Ant Colony Optimization Algorithm was initially discussed by Marco Dorigo in 1992 in his Ph D dissertation work. In biological environment, ant used to search randomly for food. Once they find food they return to their colony or home by laying down pheromones trails. Other ants when found this pheromones trails will abandon their random path and will follow that trail and will find food. As time passes, or there is large path between food and colony then this pheromones trail will get evaporated. Thus in shorter paths pheromones density is more. There is an advantage in evaporation of pheromones, such that in real world it will not allow algorithm to converge at the local optimal point or solution. This will results in better exploration of solution space. This evaporation of pheromones in real world is copied in the artificial working of the algorithm. Thus simulated ant search the global search space and are of explorative in nature, while real ants search for local search spaces and are of exploitative in nature.

This chapter in a whole has made its focus on the use of nature inspired intelligent computational methods. These nature inspired algorithms enhanced, adaptive and improved in their working as compared to traditional algorithms in terms of efficiency and efficacy. We have discussed their theory and brief methodology, so that they can work in complex and challenging scenarios. There are being now a day's applied in diversified engineering application problems.

14.3 CONCLUSION

Most of the researchers, engineers and analyst in solving real world problem come to know the importance of optimization and their role in to make our life easier. Initially optimization was a mathematical or operation research related procedure. With the introduction to the computer, they are being seen as a computational process. The aim of optimization is not to find some parameters, but to find the best parameters found until so far. In optimization a lot of iteration is being done to find best solution. Here newer parameters are being tested to find best solution find so far. Nature inspired algorithms mimic the working of nature or living being or certain natural phenomenon. They had more potential as they are parallel in their working and has a population based approach. The feature of stochastic also adds efficiency in their working. The main objective of this chapter is to get feel about the other nature inspired based optimization process already used by researchers.

REFERENCES

Goldberg, D. E. (2002). *Genetic Algorithms in Search. Optimization and Machine Learning*. Pearson Education.

Yang, X.-S. (2014). *Nature-Inspired Optimization Algorithms*. Elsevier.

About the Authors

Vivek Kapoor is working as Assistant Professor in Information Technology Department at Institute of Engineering and Technology, Devi Ahilya University, Indore, India. He Received Bachelor of Engineering (B.E.) in 1996 from Pt. Ravishankar Shukla University, Raipur (Chattisgarh), Master of Technology (M. Tech) in 2003 and Ph. D degree in 2013 in Computer Science from Devi Ahilya University, Indore. He has around 20 years of experience in teaching various courses like B.E., M.E., MBA and MCA. He has been teaching various subjects like Data Structures, Database Management System, Computer Networks, Information Security and Programming Languages. His research interests include Computational Finance, Genetic Algorithms and Data Mining and Information Security. He has got more than Forty research papers to his credit in International journals and in International conferences of repute on the above topics.

Shubhamoy Dey is a faculty in the area of Information Systems at IIM Indore since 2002. He has obtained his Ph.D in Data Mining and Knowledge Discovery in Databases from the School of computing, University of Leeds, U.K (2002). He also holds B.E. (1985) and M.Tech (1988) degrees from Jadavpur University and IIT Kharagpur respectively. Dr. Dey`s research interests are Data mining and knowledge discovery in databases, Spatial databases, Data warehousing, Database systems, Empirical modeling, and Computational finance. He has published papers in national and international forums on Data Mining, Spatial Data Mining, Text Mining and Computational Finance. His teaching interests are Management Information Systems, Decision Support Systems, Database Systems, Enterprise Systems, Data Warehousing, Business Intelligence, Data Mining and Text & Blog Mining.

Index

Publisher of Peer-Reviewed, Timely, and
Innovative Academic Research Since 1988

www.igi-global.com

IGI Global's Transformative Open Access (OA) Model:
How to Turn Your University Library's Database Acquisitions Into a Source of OA Funding

Well in advance of Plan S, IGI Global unveiled their OA Fee Waiver (Read & Publish) Initiative. Under this initiative, librarians who invest in IGI Global's InfoSci-Books and/or InfoSci-Journals databases will be able to subsidize their patrons' OA article processing charges (APCs) when their work is submitted and accepted (after the peer review process) into an IGI Global journal.

How Does it Work?

Step 1: **Library Invests in the InfoSci-Databases:** A library perpetually purchases or subscribes to the InfoSci-Books, InfoSci-Journals, or discipline/subject databases.

Step 2: **IGI Global Matches the Library Investment with OA Subsidies Fund:** IGI Global provides a fund to go towards subsidizing the OA APCs for the library's patrons.

Step 3: **Patron of the Library is Accepted into IGI Global Journal (After Peer Review):** When a patron's paper is accepted into an IGI Global journal, they option to have their paper published under a traditional publishing model or as OA.

Step 4: **IGI Global Will Deduct APC Cost from OA Subsidies Fund:** If the author decides to publish under OA, the OA APC fee will be deducted from the OA subsidies fund.

Step 5: **Author's Work Becomes Freely Available:** The patron's work will be freely available under CC BY copyright license, enabling them to share it freely with the academic community.

Note: This fund will be offered on an annual basis and will renew as the subscription is renewed for each year thereafter. IGI Global will manage the fund and award the APC waivers unless the librarian has a preference as to how the funds should be managed.

Hear From the Experts on This Initiative:

"I'm very happy to have been able to make one of my recent research contributions *freely available* along with having access to the *valuable resources* found within IGI Global's InfoSci-Journals database."

— **Prof. Stuart Palmer**,
Deakin University, Australia

"Receiving the support from IGI Global's OA Fee Waiver Initiative *encourages me to continue my research work without any hesitation*."

— **Prof. Wenlong Liu**, College of Economics and Management at Nanjing University of Aeronautics & Astronautics, China

For More Information, Scan the QR Code or Contact:
IGI Global's Digital Resources Team at eresources@igi-global.com.

Printed in the United States
by Baker & Taylor Publisher Services

Printed in the United States
by Baker & Taylor Publisher Services